OXFORD

Edited and Produced by Brian Bell

A P A
PUBLICATIONS

First Edition

ABOUT THIS BOOK

When **Brian Bell**, Apa Publications' London-based editorial director, began to research this book, he was not surprised to find that Oxford, like most of the world's significant cities, has been written off time and time again. In 1929, for instance, the *Architectural Review* wrote: "The awful villa residences, the ramshackle modern street rows, petrol stations, and shops with their large commercial signs have all but obliterated the peculiar atmosphere of one of the unique towns of the world."

Fortunately, Bell was in a position to know that there is another side to the story. Whenever he can, he escapes from London's hubbub to the tranquillity of a cottage in the middle of Oxfordshire's green countryside, just 20 miles (32 km) from Oxford itself. The drive into Oxford, he admits, does expose him to some cheerless suburban housing and almost inevitable traffic snarl-ups, but it is worth the effort to savour a city whose history has not been embalmed and whose atmosphere remains seductively relaxed. He agrees with John Betjeman's description of Oxford as "an unplanned muddle", but believes that this "hopeless disorder" (another Betjeman phrase) adds immeasurably to its attractions for the inquisitive traveller.

Uninhibited Abandon

Bell's first task as editor was to find someone to write the "Places" chapters, the heart of any *Insight Cityguide*. He turned to **Christopher Catling**, who has edited Apa guides to Florence, Amsterdam and The Netherlands. Catling's knowledge of the city was long-standing: he grew up in the Cotswolds

and was taken to Oxford for birthday treats and Christmas shopping expeditions. By the end of his rebellious teenage years, he wanted to get as far away from home as possible and chose to study English at "the other place" (Cambridge). He did not regret this decision, but still admits to liking Oxford better, especially in the heady weeks of late May and June when students celebrate the end of exams with uninhibited abandon. He would like to live the life of an Oxford don, surrounded by magnificent architecture and fine gardens, but doubts whether there will ever be a vacancy for a tutor in guidebook authorship.

For the vital history chapters, Bell approached **Roland Collins**, another Apa stalwart. After a career in advertising, he now devotes himself to researching social history and to his painting (which has been exhibited by London's Royal Academy and by the Royal Watercolour Society). Bearing in mind Oxford's proverbial traffic problems, he has always preferred approaching by river in a cabin cruiser—a pleasurable though not always practical option. What saddens him most about recent developments in the city is the erection of some "very unattractive buildings, such as Pembroke College's student accommodation."

The same concern is shared by **Helen Turner**, who brought history up to date with her chapter on "Tradition versus Progress" and provided invaluable help with picture research. She is a former features editor of the *Oxford Times* and the author of several books on consumer topics. An Oxford University graduate herself (St Anne's College), she became increasingly interested in planning and environmental issues, and took over as administrator of the Oxford Preservation Trust, which was founded in 1927 to protect

Bell

Catling

Collins

Turner

the city's ever-threatened heritage. "Local history is now a passion," she says, "and a particular delight is finding ways around Oxford that avoid using the main shopping streets, for Oxford is a pedestrian's city."

Several of the informative one-page panels in the book were written by **Yvonne Newman**, who also undertook to compile the fact-packed Travel Tips section. Having worked abroad with the British foreign office, she now lives in Headington, on the outskirts of Oxford, and devotes herself to lecturing and freelance writing.

Simon Veksner, who writes about "Academic Life" and who compiled the listing of colleges ("The Good, the Bad and the Ugly"), edited the University newspaper *Cherwell* before graduating in 1990. "What surprised me most about coming to Oxford," he remembers, "is that the different colleges were so, well, *different* from each other. But the unique aspect of Oxford for me was its intensity. There is incredible academic pressure, and yet most students also have a dauntingly heavy social life and keep up a variety of non-academic activities and sports."

The equality of women at the University has long been a subject of fierce debate. **Elisabeth Dunn**, a freelance journalist who writes widely for Britain's national newspapers, brings the subject into the 1990s with a witty and informed assessment.

David Leake writes about Oxford's "secret gardens" from a true insider's viewpoint: he's a gardener at Corpus Christi College, of which he says: "It's a very feudal society, but if you're a peasant within it, they look after you well."

There's more to Oxford than the University, of course: for a time it was Britain's top car-making centre. This aspect of the city's history is recounted by **Ray Hutton**, for nine years editor of *Autocar* magazine and now a freelance writer specialising in the motor industry. He shares residents' frustrations with the city's traffic. "Oxford was one of the first British towns to offer park-and-ride bus schemes from the outskirts," he says. "But it remains one of the most difficult places in which to use a car. This is ironic because Oxford's Morris was, with Birmingham's Austin, responsible for encouraging motoring for the masses in Britain."

The Fleeting Moment

As ever, Apa's approach to photography promotes this book into a different league from most conventional guidebooks. Fortunately, many first-rate photographers choose to live and work in Oxford and several of them—**Chris Andrews**, **Chris Donaghue**, **Jon Davison** and **Norman McBeath**—are strongly represented, along with Apa regulars such as **Lyle Lawson** and **Alain Le Garsmeur**. "What appeals to me about Oxford visually," says Chris Andrews, "is the soft light hitting the stone of these lovely old buildings." Representing the era before the camera took precedence is a selection of elegant illustrations by the renowned **Rudolph Ackermann**, first issued by subscription in 1814 as the two-volume *History of the University of Oxford*.

Special thanks for assistance go to **Dr Malcolm Graham**, local history librarian at the city's Central Library, and to the library staff of **Oxford & County Newspapers**. The maps were produced by **Berndtson & Berndtson** and proof-reading and indexing were capably handled by **Kate Owen**.

Newman *Veksner* *Hutton*

CONTENTS

PLACES
—by Christopher Catling

TRAVEL TIPS

COMMISSIONED BY CROWN HOUSE PROPERTIES · PAINTED BY INSIDE ART '89

DREAMS AND DISILLUSION

It is small wonder that Oxford is one of the world's most anthologised cities. Many famous writers, having attended its University, have tried to recapture on paper an experience which profoundly affected their lives. Often, their feelings recall the relationship between child and parent: a complex cocktail of love and resentment, admiration and disdain.

Matthew Arnold, whose poetry immortalised Oxford as "that sweet City with her dreaming spires", captured this ambivalence in a letter to his mother in 1861: "I always like this place, and the intellectual life here is certainly much more intense than it used to be; but this has its disadvantages too, in the envies, hatreds, and jealousies that come with the activity of mind of most men."

In *Wealth of Nations* (1776), Adam Smith was less equivocal, dismissing Oxford as "a sanctuary in which exploded systems and obsolete prejudices find shelter and protection after they have been hunted out of every corner of the world." A century later, George Bernard Shaw was just as beastly: "It is characteristic of the authorities that they should consider a month too little for the preparation of a boat-race, and grudge three weeks to the rehearsals of one of Shakespeare's plays."

Those writers, of course, are equating Oxford with the University, and it is certainly the aura of learning that draws most visitors to the city. But there are many other sides to Oxford: it is a thriving market town, for example, and it manufactures motor cars. John Betjeman, an influential architectural critic as well as a poet, once lamented that the car factories "could have been a model for the rest of England, so that visitors to the University, instead of trying to pretend no industrialism was near and bathing themselves in a false twilight of grey Gothic things, would have naturally hurried to see the living beauty of industrial Oxford after the dead glory of University architecture." The failure of such hopes led another poet, W.H. Auden, to moan: "Oxford city is sheer hell. Compared with New York, it's five times as crowded and the noise of the traffic is six times louder."

Yet even the complainers keep coming back, forgiving the city its foibles as they would forgive a venerable but wayward parent. Its allure is elusive but its myths are powerful, offering to visitors what the writer Peter Ackroyd called "a clutter of broken images" that demand to be seen again and again.

Preceding pages: the University crest (frontispiece); having a hearty time at the boat race; mural; gargoyle on the Church of St Mary the Virgin; Magdalen College spires; a tired bicycle. **Left**, a meeting of minds.

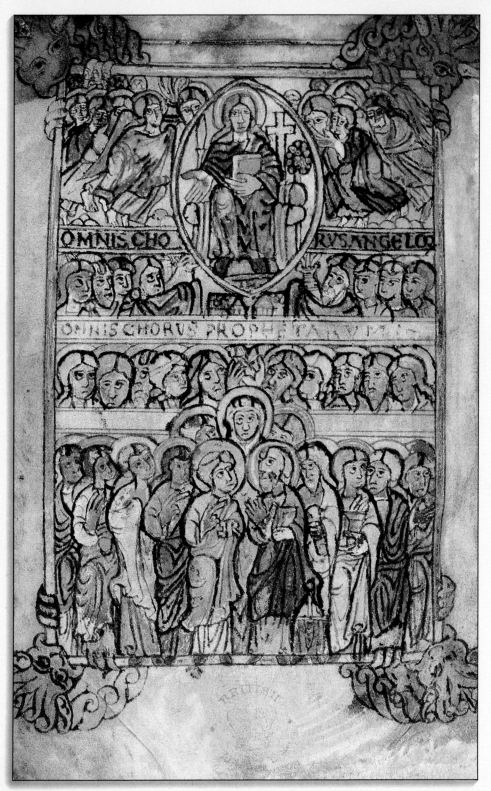

OMNIS CHO   RVS ANGELO

OMNIS CHORVS PROPHETARVM

Oxford was a late starter. Shunned by Stone-Age man, avoided by the Romans, it had to wait on the Saxons, who always lived and moved by water, to launch it in importance as one of England's great defensive and cultural centres. If that is a simplistic view of local history, then the evidence to the contrary is thin on the ground—and, indeed, in the museums. A few axe-heads, some bronze tools and perhaps the burial mounds of farmers and cattle herders in Port Meadow by the river and in the University Parks are all that remain to span thousands of years.

It is not difficult to see why the site of Oxford was an unattractive one to early settlers. It was low-lying and traversed by the unfordable streams of Thames and Cherwell. The Icknield Way, high road to the west, kept well away south to the hills.

The Romans, who hated clay soil for their roads and never settled at fords, by-passed the site to the east and north, building their villas away from the rivers. West of Oxford, they established a pottery industry that became one of five principal centres of Roman Britain, one kiln at Cowley anticipating a different artefact in our time: the motor-car.

There may be an earlier Oxford down there, under the modern city, buried by the rubble of a thousand years of rebuilding. Ironically, demolition and excavation for yet another massive redevelopment in the centre may just provide the missing links the archaeologists are looking for that will give Oxford history an earlier start. The rest is myth or guesswork.

Memphric and miracles: In the Middle Ages assorted worthies were credited with founding Oxford—a legendary King Memphric in 1,000 BC, or Brutus bringing Greek scholars after the fall of Troy, and, more credibly, Alfred the Great. University College went so far as to forge deeds to prove its foundation by Alfred, and relinquished its claim only in

Queen Victoria's time, with red faces all round. Even the origins of the name Oxford have been open to interpretation, but its most likely derivation is the obvious one. Why there was a need for oxen to cross the river is another question.

That river crossing, embanked and stone-lined, may have been where the first settlement grew up. Was it at St Aldate's, the causeway to the river? Recent excavations point to its construction by Offa, King of

Mercia from 757 to 796.

Those dates are narrowly beaten for the founder's stakes by the persistent legend of St Frideswide. Daughter of a Mercian king, virginal Frideswide seems to have resisted the unwelcome attentions of a princely suitor by blinding him with the aid of a well-aimed thunderbolt. Relenting, she restored his sight with water from her own private holy well by the river. At Binsey, just beyond Oxford's western fringe, that well still exists in the churchyard, and is credited by a notice on the church door with being "the very beginning of anything at Oxford".

Left, one of many 10th-century illustrated manuscripts kept in the Bodleian Library. **Right**, King Alfred, posthumous victim of a forgery.

Frideswide, vowed to celibacy, went on to found a priory on a site near the present cathedral. Rather surprisingly, it may have been for monks as well as nuns. The time: the early 8th century. The place: a gravel spit near where Thames and Cherwell meet. Nothing is recorded of the 400 years of the priory's existence, and then it was in the nature of an obituary. It was burnt down during a massacre of the Danes in 1002.

In the cathedral that replaced the priory, between the choir and the north aisle, is the shrine of St Frideswide. Stand near it and you are at Oxford's heart and Oxford's beginning. From the fragmented canopy of stone,

faces peer through sculptured leaves of ivy and sycamore, oak and vine, a medieval mason's interpretation of the virgin princess's escape from her tormenter to the safety of the forest.

Fact or fiction, St Frideswide is remembered every year on 19 October in a service at the cathedral attended by both Town and University. The body of the saint is no longer there; it disappeared during the upheavals of the Reformation in the 16th century.

Alfred and the Danes: If King Alfred did not found the University, he at least played a prominent part in the development of Oxford

as a strategic frontier town in his defences against attacks by the Danes. The natural barriers of Thames and Cherwell, an already established nucleus in the settlement at the gate of the priory, a central position in the kingdom, and access to the important West Saxon port of Southampton combined to make it an obvious choice and one which was to be of tremendous importance to the growth of civilisation in England.

Alfred's experience in re-using Roman defences at Winchester probably persuaded his son Edward, who succeeded him in 901, to lay out his streets to a similar pattern within rectangular walls, a pattern that is reflected in the city's modern streets. Certainly, by 912, when Oxford is mentioned in the *Anglo-Saxon Chronicle*, the town was already head of a district. London and Oxford, "Ludenburg and Oxnaford", were held by Edward the Elder, "and all the land pertaining thereto".

Carfax was central to the small, compact town, its walls supported by bank and ditch on the western, northern and eastern sides, with the Trill stream a natural barrier to the south. At first gravel ramparts supported timber walls, but these were later rebuilt in stone. Roads had a surface of pebbles or cobbles and drained into a channel down the middle.

Oxford has come up in the world since those days and the Saxon roads are in places more than 12 ft (4 metres) below the modern pavement. One, and only one, building survives from that period: the tower of St Michael's Church, Cornmarket Street. Built against the town wall by the north gate, it served the garrison as a look-out against marauding Danes.

The town, now the sixth largest in England, developed as a sort of Saxon conference centre, but the lives and habits of its ordinary townsfolk can only be deduced from pots unearthed, rubbish holes and cesspits. There seems to have been division of bigger properties to form smaller "hall" houses with first-floor all-purpose rooms over ground-floor stores, and the width of the main streets, wider even than now, indicates their use as markets for the produce of agriculture and husbandry.

There was an uneasy integration with the Danes, brought to bloody conclusion in 1002 by the king's ordered massacre of all those living in Oxford. Seven years later the Danish army sacked the town as a reprisal, which may account for the derelict condition of much of the town and its suburbs outside the walls.

The Norman Conquest in 1066 ushered in an even bigger physical change. Robert d'Oilly, the governor, set about the upgrading of the defensive works by building a castle which destroyed an entire western suburb and involved the diversion of the road to the west. Keep and mound were raised and

ing of the Secular Canons of St George we can anticipate the beginnings of the University itself.

English power politics were played out here in the castle. When Henry I died in 1135 the throne was disputed between his daughter, Empress Matilda of Germany, and Stephen Blois. In the fighting that followed, Matilda was besieged in the castle for three winter months. Then, taking advantage of the ice-covered river, she escaped. No-one saw her go: she was camouflaged in a white sheet!

Oxford was becoming attractive to royals in spite of St Frideswide's curse on royalty

a moat fed from the Thames. Walls were extended to include the castle and the eastern suburb near the Cherwell.

It is also more than probable that d'Oilly was responsible for building Grandpont, the first stone bridge, where Folly Bridge is now, and the stone causeway to it that crossed the marsh for a considerable distance. Within the castle walls d'Oilly erected a chapel to St George, one of the first known dedications to the patron saint of England, and in the found-

Left, the Battle of Hastings, which decided England's fate. Above, 11th-century haymaker.

after her misfortune. At Henry I's great palace of Beaumont, just beyond where the Ashmolean is now, Richard the Lion-Heart was born and, probably, King John. Henry had also built a palace, or, more likely, a hunting lodge at Woodstock, 8 miles (13 km) from Oxford in the forest of Wychwood.

Following its 11th-century decline, the fortunes of the town were rescued by the growth of the trade in wool and cloth. This brought the formation of trade guilds, of which the weavers and corvesers (shoemakers) were the earliest, and provided the embryo of civic rule. The right to produce, sell and buy goods was strictly controlled. No-one could set up a loom within 15 miles (24 km) of Oxford or sell leather without the guild's consent. The weekly market was held under a similarly strict protectionism.

Prosperity was reflected in the establishment of a number of religious houses. St Frideswide's Priory was re-founded in 1122 on the site of the Saxon church, and was joined seven years later by Osney, which seems to have been founded on superstition and magpies. Edith, Robert d'Oilly's wife, was drawn to the noise of "pyes" from a tree by the river. Told by her confessor that "these are not pyes" but souls in torment, she

product of spontaneous combustion, the pursuit of knowledge fusing with the convenience of physical and spiritual community that Oxford provided. From the early 12th century, English scholars, all of them clerks in holy orders, customarily went to the University of Paris to complete their education, but, following an unresolved quarrel with the King of France in 1167, Henry II ordered them home.

Oxford was a natural place for them to settle. There were already centres of learning in the Augustinian monasteries of St Frideswide's Priory and Osney Abbey, and there were already "Masters" lecturing on the

persuaded Robert to bring them relief in the form of a monastery.

Nearly 30 years later Osney was raised to an abbey, the third largest in the country. The magpies are still there in the cemetery by the railway, but the abbey has gone, leaving "Great Tom", the abbey's bell, to speak from its own tower at Christ Church. There followed the foundation of Godstow nunnery in 1133, and the Duke of Cornwall's Rewley Abbey near Osney, where the Cistercian monks played an important part within the University.

The scholars arrive: The University was the

scriptures and Roman Law. There were mutual advantages, too, for Henry in his palace at Beaumont and for the students gathering at his gates. From this pool of talent the king could readily recruit the civil servants who would implement the power of royal government.

Life for the early students at Oxford was organised along the lines of the tradesmen's guilds. Like apprentices, they lived and studied for seven years with their Masters in "Halls". After four years they took their Bachelor of Arts degree, and at the end of the course their Master's degree, which entitled them in turn to lecture. Those who chose to do so hired houses, boarding and teaching their students under one roof. Today, Beam Hall in Merton Street is one of these halls. Most disappeared as colleges gradually took their place.

Town versus Gown: There were obvious ways in which unscrupulous property owners, traders and Masters could abuse their position, and they did, sowing the seeds of conflict between "Town" and "Gown" that was to polarise their interests for hundreds of years. Murder brought things to a head. In 1209 a woman was killed by scholars and two were hanged in revenge, the towns-

Controls were introduced on the price of food and other necessities to scholars, and on their house and room rents. Any scholar arrested had to be passed over to the ecclesiastical authority. The University was to have a charter of privileges and Robert Grosseteste, the future Bishop of Lincoln, was appointed at its head as Chancellor.

As the University had no buildings, Congregation, the governing body, met in the church of St Mary the Virgin. There were no students either. The first colleges were founded by bishops, catered only for graduates and were exclusively for the wealthy. They were organised like monasteries, with

people claiming the right to do so because the country was under an Interdict as the result of a quarrel between the Pope and King John. Fear scattered the students; some went to Cambridge where they founded Oxford's "sister" university.

The quarrel having been patched up, stringent penalties were imposed on the town in the form of fines—which were, incidentally, to provide the first university endowment.

hall, chapel, lodgings, kitchen and quarters for the Master; the pattern is the same today.

The atmosphere of a medieval college is most nearly captured in Merton. Founded in 1264 by Walter de Merton, it shares the "oldest" title with University and Balliol, both of which look to the Bishop of Durham for their inception. University College earned its name from being administered by the University from 1249 to independence in 1280. John de Balliol was nudged rather forcibly by the Bishop into endowing his college in 1260 to square his arguments with the Church.

Left, the Quadrangle at Balliol. **Above,** a Vice-chancellor, Esquire and Beagle. Both paintings are by the celebrated Rudolph Ackermann.

F

Engraved by J. Sk

Founders & Benefactors of St John's

Pl. 37.

nal by G. Vertue.

'ege with a view of the inner quadrangle.

From the 13th century, Oxford's 6,000 people became increasingly dependent on the growing university. The most important trades—weavers and cloth merchants, shoemakers, masons, workers in metal, artists in stained glass, manuscript painters and scribes—demonstrate this all too obviously.

As the University's star moved into the ascendant, so that of the town waned. Relegated to the status of a country and market town, it became more and more subservient to the University's needs. As a cuckoo in the town's nest, puffed up with self-importance and royal patronage, the University forced trades and residents out as more and more sites in the central area were acquired for colleges, and wholesale demolition of houses took place.

The plight of the Oxford townsfolk is illustrated only too vividly in the fortunes of the weavers, whose guild was one of the earliest in England. In the 12th century there were 60; by 1270 only 15 remained; 50 years later there was none.

Poverty and poor living conditions bred disease; in 1348 a quarter of the town's people succumbed to the plague. Labour became scarce and an attempt was made by both Chancellor and Mayor to control wages. Widespread dissatisfaction led to popular demonstrations against authority.

Poor priests: A religious movement that is credited with being partly responsible for the Peasants' Revolt had its origins in Oxford. John Wyclif, Master of Balliol in 1361, spoke against corruption and worldliness in the established Church, sending his disciples into the country to preach to the people in a language they could understand: English. The Lollards, as his "poor priests" came to be called, used a Bible that Wyclif had translated into common English. Support inside the University brought a swift reaction from Pope Gregory and the Archbishop of Canterbury. Excommunications followed and some of Wyclif's supporters recanted. By the middle of the next century the movement had withered away.

In the years following the Black Death, relations between Town and Gown deteriorated to the point where a tavern brawl unleashed pent-up hatred in an explosion of mob violence. It began in the Swindlestock Tavern, since then a victim of road widening at Carfax, on the Feast of St Scholastica in 1355. Fighting started after some scholars threw wine in the landlord's face and followed it with a quart pot. By pre-arranged signal, the bells of Carfax tower were rung to

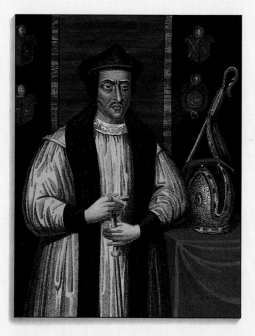

summon the townsmen and the students rang the bell of St Mary's. In the bloody battle that ensued in the streets and in and out of the colleges and hostels, 60 scholars were massacred. The rest fled.

The townsfolk won the battle but lost the war, because the help of the king and the Bishop of Lincoln was invoked. Penance was to be done for 500 years. On each anniversary of St Scholastica's Day until 1825, 63 reluctant burghers went in procession to St Mary's to pay a fine to the Vice-Chancellor for those souls lost in the riot.

The University was given control of the

market, the price and quality of goods sold, and weights and measures. For the first time "privileged persons" appeared. These were mostly craftsmen, but included people like barbers, becoming "servants" of scholars and thereby enjoying special privileges. By the 17th century this hierarchy was to form an eighth of the townspeople.

Building the colleges: For 200 years, from 1350, the history of Oxford is the history of the University. New colleges were founded

serves this valuable link with the city's past.

A clutch of colleges followed: Lincoln in 1427, founded by the Bishop of Lincoln; All Souls, by the Archbishop of Canterbury with Henry VI as co-founder in 1438; Magdalen in 1458 by another Bishop of Winchester, on land outside the city walls. The aims were always the same: to sustain the material superiority of the aristocracy. Brasenose, was founded by another Bishop of Lincoln in 1517, and Corpus Christi by the Bishop of

by bishops investing in learning as an insurance for the future power and influence of the Church, king and realm. "Men of learning, fruitful to the Church" was the prescription of William of Wykcham, Bishop of Winchester, for his students when founding New College in 1379. With the land went part of the 12th-century city wall and an obligation to keep it in repair that still con-

Winchester in 1525. Trinity was set up by a civil servant in 1555, and St John's, also in 1555, by a Lord Mayor of London.

Because colleges were by now accepting undergraduates as well as graduates, rich men could buy their sons a university education, and clever scholars could get assisted places. Colleges replaced halls, and by 1543 only 12 halls remained. Two related events were to have far-reaching importance for the growing University. Until the late 15th century, books were scarce and teaching and examinations were oral. In 1478 Theodoric Rood gave teaching and learning a new

dimension with the production of his first book on his press in the High Street, a best seller then as now: the Bible.

The other event was the generous gift of books by Duke Humphrey of Gloucester, brother of Henry V, which formed the nucleus of the later Bodleian Library. They were housed over the Divinity School until borrowed, if that is how their removal can be described, by Edward VI. Not until 1602 was a new library formed by Thomas Bodley, the Ambassador to the Netherlands. The lesson had been learned. Then, as now, no book may be taken away. Even Charles I and Oliver Cromwell had their requests refused.

buildings quarried for their stone for new buildings elsewhere and the sites were greedily developed.

The pressure on Henry grew as his advisers urged that the University should follow the same fate as the monasteries, but Henry was a scholar and had a personal reason for wishing to see it survive. In 1532 Wolsey, his Chancellor, had founded Cardinal College on the site of St Frideswide's Priory. After Wolsey's dismissal Henry refounded it as Henry VIII College. After the suppression the college re-emerged as Christ Church. The remnant of the priory church became Oxford Cathedral and went on to enjoy a

The severing of the link between the established Church and the Pope in Rome by Henry VIII's assumption of leadership of the Church of England brought the University itself to the brink of destruction. The wealth of the colleges and their essentially ecclesiastical nature made them a prime target when Parliament authorised the dissolution of the monasteries in 1536, and their property and revenues were made over to the Crown.

As Franciscans and Carmelites, Cistercians and Benedictines were expelled, the door closed on medieval Oxford. Their property was dispersed among the colleges, the

double life as the College chapel. Henry's epitaph on the outcome was: "No land in England is better bestowed, than that which is given to our Universities."

The Oxford Martyrs: The spread of the New Learning and the Protestant Reformation continued under Henry's son, Edward VI. Translations of the Bible into English began to appear in churches so that everyone who could read could do so in their own language, and the services themselves were conducted wholly in English. In 1549 the first Book of Common Prayer was issued and the laws against heresy were repealed. Protestants could now worship in their own faith. It was a short honeymoon. When the boy king died, that freedom was to be cruelly denied them.

Queen Mary brought what can accurately be described as a burning zeal to the re-introduction of Roman Catholicism. Following the repeal of anti-papal legislation by a compliant Parliament, 300 people met their deaths by burning at the stake for heresy in the three years from 1555 to 1558.

Just why the Queen chose the streets of Oxford for the public humiliation of the three most influential and resistant of the Protestant leaders—Bishops Ridley and Latimer and Archbishop Cranmer—is not at all clear.

he thrust into the flames the hand that had signed the recantation.

Oxford's memorial to the martyrs faces the threat of traffic in St Giles in a Victorian Eleanor Cross that has Cranmer in a niche holding his Bible with "Maye 1541" on the cover, the first year of its circulation. A cross in the road marks the scene of the burnings, and in Balliol College nearby is preserved a door blackened by the fire that consumed the flesh of three brave men.

Another death, that of Mary herself, brought the burnings to an end in the cooling-off period of Elizabeth I's reign. Another Act of Uniformity made the Church

Perhaps it is of some significance that all three were educated in Cambridge. At first held in the Golden Cross Inn, then in the Bocardo prison by Northgate, Latimer and Ridley went to the stake in Broad Street. Cranmer, it is said, was forced to watch from his cell as attempts were made to get him to recant. This he did, but when fastened to the stake his courage and his faith returned, and

Left, Sir Thomas Bodley, founder of the Bodleian, and John Balliol, co-founder with his wife of Balliol College. **Above**, Ackermann's *Kitchen at Christ Church*.

Protestant again, this time permanently. Use of Edward VI's second prayer book was made compulsory, and outward recognition, at least, of the new state religion was secured by fines for non-attendance at church.

In this climate of comparative tolerance, learning flourished and the city's population and prosperity increased. While theology was still predominant, other subjects were becoming popular as careers in public life and the professions influenced well-off and well-placed parents to choose the University for their son's education. The age of privilege had arrived.

Elizabeth I smiled on "dear Oxford", visiting several times and being welcomed with fulsome expressions of loyalty. To her hosts' orations in Greek and Latin she gave as good as she received—in Greek and Latin!

Oxford will remember the Queen for something which touched the heart and imagination of her people. One in particular, Sir Walter Scott, used the story in *Kenilworth*. Amy Robsart, wife of Robert Dudley, Earl of Leicester, was staying at Cumnor House, a few miles from the city. Her husband and Elizabeth were having an affair and Amy was an obvious obstruction to Dudley's marrying Elizabeth when she came to the throne. Servants returning from a fair found Amy dead at the foot of a staircase. At first buried at Cumnor, her remains were later, on Dudley's orders, removed to an unmarked grave in St Mary's. His chaplain, who conducted the service, made what we would call today a Freudian slip in referring to the lady as "so pitifully *murdered*" when he meant to say "so pitifully *slain*". Public opinion had already made up its mind.

Elizabeth and the Bard: Oxford has a rather slender claim to association with Shakespeare, but John Aubrey, the historian, recorded that Elizabeth's favourite actor/playwright broke his journey every year on his way from London's Globe Theatre to Stratford-upon-Avon to stay at the Crown Tavern in Cornmarket. Such was his friendship with the innkeeper that he was godfather to his son, and the probability is that Shakespeare was at William Davenant's baptism in St Martin's across the way. With such a start in life, it comes as no surprise that William went on to become a playwright himself, and, in 1638, Poet Laureate.

The other connection with Shakespeare lies through the First Folio which the Bodleian had acquired. Later it was sold and replaced with a third edition. Not until 1905,

when a First Folio was sent to the Bodleian for repair was it recognised as the original and acquired by subscription.

Town and Gown took their differences into the 17th century, spilling less blood but spending more money on legal arguments over an ever-increasing number of issues. In 1609 the city complained of proctors' high-handed treatment of citizens, the excessive number of alehouses licensed by the University and the drunkenness and bad manners of

its members. Little was resolved, but legal fees accounted for half the city's income.

Fresh disputes: Thirty years later came the last of the great charters reinforcing the University's powers and incidentally breeding fresh disputes. The University gained the right to appoint its own coroners and the Chancellor was given the right to veto new building in the town. Dunghills and poor paving would attract fines, and the right to police the streets was bandied about between Mayor and Chancellor.

Behind the walls of their colleges, gardeners were drawing their battle lines with spade

Left, Ackermann's *Magpie Lane*. **Above**, Queen Elizabeth I, who gave as good as she got.

and fork, and under the command of Lord Danby made a sortie to the banks of the Cherwell. Here, opposite Magdalen tower they created, in 1621, Britain's oldest Botanic Garden; "Physick" Garden at first, since it produced herbs and plants for medicine and was linked with the scientific studies of the Faculty of Medicine. Danby's bust over the entrance gate nods gratefully to his royal patrons Charles I and Charles II in their niches on either side, where both are shown by the sculptor as Romans.

Civil War capital: In the struggle ahead Oxford was to be the stage, and King and Parliament merely players. Charles I's con-

nection with Oxford thrust it into the forefront of the conflict between Crown and State that erupted in civil war in 1642. The miracle is that the city emerged virtually unscathed from the extensive works undertaken to put its defences in readiness for assault, and from the siege that subsequently took place but which was abandoned, without the expected battle.

The King already had strong support in the University. His Archbishop of Canterbury and chief adviser, William Laud, had been a student at St John's and was Chancellor for a time. He and Charles shared a common dislike for Puritans. On the occasion when the King brought his Queen, Henrietta Maria, and his nephew, Prince Rupert, to open Laud's new Canterbury Quad, the entertainment was so lavish that it cost half what had been spent on the building.

Nearly all the dons and scholars were sympathetic to the Royalist cause. But the townspeople disliked Laud, whom they suspected of being a Papist. Also, they resented the University's control over their affairs and so supported Parliament.

A surprise visit in 1642 from a troop of Royalist cavalry under Sir John Byron brought the citizens out on the streets and a half-hearted attempt was made to close the gates. After some confusion the Royalists were welcomed in by the scholars. Eleven days later the cavalry went, leaving a divided city to receive a Parliamentary force with Lord Saye at the head. The University was disarmed, the townspeople armed, the head was shot off the Virgin on the porch of St Mary's, and the troop left for what was to be the first great battle of the Civil War.

The Battle of Edgehill made Charles look for a new headquarters, now that London was in the hands of Parliament. Oxford's central position, natural defences and accessibility to areas of support in the west and north made it an obvious choice.

An accommodating Christ Church provided a good substitute palace for Charles, Prince Rupert, his brother Maurice, the young Prince Charles and his brother the Duke of York. Not for some months were they joined by the Queen, who was then billeted in nearby Merton College, a gate being made in a garden wall so that she and Charles could meet easily. Although the citizens presented the King with money, the Mayor was under pressure to replace aldermen unsympathetic to the Royalist cause. Their Member of Parliament was arrested for subversive activity, and the city was forced to give up its arms.

After an abortive attempt to capture London, in which his army got no further than Turnham Green, Charles returned to Oxford and set about improving the out-dated defences. With the help of a Dutch engineer, ditches were dug and ramparts raised by the reluctant citizens and enthusiastic students. Halls and colleges became warehouses for food and supplies, factories for the manufacture of gunpowder and uniforms, and foundries for cannon. Townspeople looked on aghast as Magdalen Bridge was demolished and a drawbridge erected in its place, and watched with disbelief as cannon so heavy that they needed teams of 15 horses and 26 men to pull them were brought to the parks near Magdalen.

All this and the maintenance of the garrison required a lot of money. The King's answer was to make it. The Royal Mint was brought here from Shrewsbury, to New Inn

with their wives and camp followers can be imagined. There were in addition visiting courtiers, Members of Parliament sympathetic to the Royalists, their servants and entourage, all to be fed and boarded, prisoners of war to be secured, and hospitals found for the wounded from battles elsewhere.

It was inevitable that disease should breed in the filthy conditions of streets and sewers, and there were outbreaks of camp fever and plague. Just as inevitable was the danger of fire. In 1644 the centre of the city was devastated by a blaze that began in a kitchen and destroyed hundreds of houses.

The Parliamentarians seem to have made

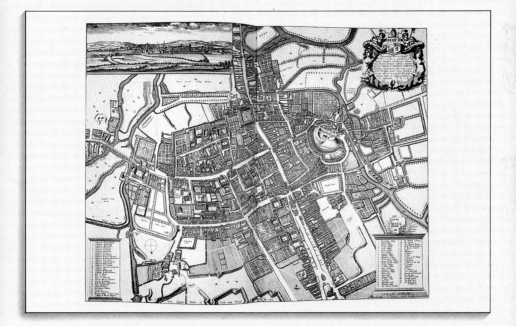

Hall Street, and college plate was pillaged for silver and gold to turn into coin. Unfortunately it did not make enough. City and University were asked for cash "contributions", and to keep the army happy and fed through the winter, sheep, cattle and horses were "removed" from the countryside around.

The burden put on accommodation in the city by the influx of more than 5,000 soldiers

rather ineffectual attempts to contain Charles in Oxford. Prince Rupert was able to make excursions as far north as Yorkshire, winning Newark and losing Marston Moor, a battle in which his poodle, Boy, was killed. With 5,000 men the King slipped away through Port Meadow to Worcester, went on to trounce the Earl of Essex in Cornwall, and was back over the drawbridge five months later to turn down peace overtures from Parliament.

The reaction from Parliament's commander-in-chief, Sir Thomas Fairfax, who had just joined forces with Cromwell outside

Left, Oliver Cromwell, educated at Cambridge, fought at Oxford. **Above**, the city in 1676 as mapped in *Oxonia Illustrata*.

Oxford, was to lay siege to the city. Fortunately for Oxford, but unfortunately for the attackers, Charles had left again and the futility of pursuing the siege was recognised. The elusive King was able to escape again after the decisive battle of the war at Naseby, returning to Oxford and a renewed siege. Looking for guidance in his predicament, he decided to borrow a book on other civil wars from the Bodleian Library, sending a peremptory note. His request was refused: the Library *never* lends books, not even to kings.

The last Oxford saw of Charles, who had decided on escape and surrender to the Scots, was as a humble servant with short hair on

Bodleian and had the city policed by his soldiers. For the citizens there were old scores to settle. Council members sacked by the King at the beginning of the war were reinstated and their leader John Nixon was elected Mayor.

Farmers and landowners in the immediate vicinity of Oxford complained of damage by Royalist troops to their houses, woods and cattle, and of the loss of income from not being able to grow crops. They found the University inflexible, as did those in the city who had suffered by the occupation, and negotiations were abandoned.

The business of Oxford settled down

horseback riding out over Magdalen Bridge in the middle of the night. For the garrison, surrender was near. Fairfax sent a message to the Governor with the words: "I very much desire the preservation of that place (so famous for learning) from ruin." With the King's assent, conditions were agreed and the soldiers marched out on 25 June 1646. The war was over and Oxford was saved.

War wounds: Picking up the pieces was not easy for the University. There were few scholars, but the college buildings and the churches were undamaged. Such was the concern of Fairfax that he set a guard on the

slowly to its only real trade: selling to the University. With this obvious limitation, small shopkeepers were kept small and the only growth was in poverty. The city persisted in its attempts to win better conditions from its "employers", and in 1684 sought a new charter with the object of extending boundaries, increasing the markets, gaining more control over policing and licensing, and increasing power for the Mayor with the support of additional aldermen. None of these aims was achieved.

After the monarchy was restored, the Puritan influence soon evaporated from

Oxford and serious scholars, as so often subsequently, bemoaned the attitude of their students. Anthony Wood, in *Life and Times, 1631–95*, wrote: "Why doth solid and serious learning decline, and few or none follow it now in the university? Answer: because of coffee-houses, where they spend all their time; and in entertainments at their chambers, where their studies are become places for victualers, also great drinking at taverns and ale-houses (Dr Lampshire told me there were 370 in Oxford), spending their time in common chambers whole afternoons, and thence to the coffee-house."

But the University also began devoting its

unique evocation of the Tower of the Winds in the Radcliffe Observatory. Hawksmoor contributed the twin towers of All Souls, Gothic without and classical within. Palladian architecture jostled medieval, and stone replaced brick.

The glory of Oxford in our time was assured; the University's academic achievement anything but. Student sons of the wealthy and well-born drank much and learned little. Examinations became a farce. The seeds of 19th-century reform and revival were sown in this climate of stagnation.

Delivering the goods: Oxford's self-interested clergy sponsored Oxford's canal. Col-

attentions and money to building. A place for grand ceremonial was provided in Wren's Sheldonian Theatre, and a place for the bell from Osney Abbey in Tom Tower. The Clarendon Building of 1715 found a new home for the Oxford University Press, and the fantastic curiosities collected by Elias Ashmole joined experimental science in the Old Ashmolean Museum. There followed Gibbs' masterpiece, the Radcliffe Camera, the world's first library in the round, and the

Above, an Oxford book auction in 1747, painted by William Green Jnr.

lege heads invested in a proposal which put cheap coal from the Midlands in their hearths instead of sea-coal brought from northeast England and up the Thames. Opened in 1790, the canal survived competition from the Grand Junction Canal and only succumbed with the coming of the railway, suffering a final indignity when its terminal was filled in for Nuffield College in 1937.

The city and University were less inviting to the railway pioneers. A proposed terminus for the Great Western Railway at Magdalen Bridge in 1837 was opposed and abandoned. Successive Bills before Parliament failed in the face of considerations like the morals of the students and the fear of what might happen if the lower classes could move about more freely. Concessions were made, however, and the railway finally steamed into Oxford in 1844.

The workshops for the whole of the Great Western could have followed. Town now accused Gown of holding back progress when the University resisted the scheme, but with hindsight it looks as if it was right for once. The works went to Swindon instead.

Housing boom: New enterprises brought workers to the area and a consequent demand for new housing. When the Oxford Univer-

Bench by Carfax for another seven years.

The new market, open every day, was extended and roofed over in the Victorian "iron" age, then as now the preponderance of butchers a barometer of prosperity. It was also an indication that Oxford's population was increasing rapidly. In the first 40 years of the 19th century it doubled to 24,000.

The character of shopping was changing. Earlier restrictions on the sale of goods other than those produced locally were abandoned. Factory-made goods were being brought in from London and the Midlands by railway and canal, ousting the work of all save the specialised craftsmen. Choice be-

sity Press moved to Walton Street in 1830 it became the principal single employer, its employees finding homes nearby in the new suburb of Jericho.

Towards the end of the 18th century the main streets around Carfax were still cluttered with market stalls just as they had been in medieval times, impeding the free movement of traffic, unhygienic and untidy. Both city and University agreed that a market building was the answer, and in 1774 meat, fish and vegetables were moved to an area behind High Street. Butter had a special dispensation, lingering on at the Butter

came wider, credit was no longer given, and price fixing and price tickets replaced bargaining.

Unfortunately for the growing number of retailers, the student population halved in the first half of the 19th century and many shopkeepers found themselves in difficulties. The shops, too, were changing, and the shopkeeper no longer lived upstairs. The plate-glass window and the department store were not far away.

Above, agriculture and academia meet on the outskirts of 19th-century Oxford.

WHAT'S BREWING

Oxford had a head start when it came to brewing: it was in the middle of malting barley country. Farm and cottage, mansion and abbey, college and castle practised do-it-yourself beer-making—and, after 700 years, that is what is happening again with the arrival of the beer-kit and the revival of innkeeper brewing. Now, at the Red Lion in Gloucester Green, beers are once more being brewed in the old way.

A glass of beer added drama to much of the city's history. Shed a tear for the garrison at Oxford castle, who, it seems, must have gone thirsty from 1255, when their brewhouse collapsed, until 1267 when it was rebuilt. Spare your sympathy for the Chancellor who had to take on responsibility for the brewing trade after the St Scholastica's Day riots. Reserve your praise for the President of Trinity College in 1600, who observed: "The Houses that had the smaller (*i.e. weaker*) beer had the most drunkards, for it forced them to go into the town to comfort their stomachs." Trinity's beer was best, and they had the fewest drunkards.

Roundly condemn the beer at All Souls in 1609 which was so good but so strong that it was held responsible for the college's "decriments", whatever those may have been. Weep, too, for the Keeper of the Ashmolean in 1729, who died at Christ Church from "a pretty deal of bad small beer".

From the Middle Ages onwards, most of the monasteries and some of the colleges brewed their own beer; some colleges without brewhouses obtained permission to use the facilities of those that had. One of these, Queen's, was founded with a brewer among the servants, and brewing was carried on for 600 years until 1939 in a building which still exists in the Fellows' Garden. Changes in taste and a new building accounted for the end of college-produced beer and left a clear field to the professional brewer.

There were professional brewers in Oxford from the 13th century and the Poll Tax of 1381 identified as many as 32 in the city. Taxes and tolls, price, quality and measures of pollution

prevention (yes, in the 13th century!) imposed severe restrictions. Although there were frequent breaches of the regulations, which brought tighter controls by the University, brewers became men of wealth and standing in the community.

Between 1350 and 1500 no fewer than 10 became Mayor, and one was Mayor three times in succession. Among those who took office, John Sprunt, who died in 1419, is commemorated by an engraved brass in St Peter's College Chapel. Unfortunately, for a brewer, it has no head on it.

Brewers came and went, but by the 18th century the leading brewing families of Oxford had begun to emerge. The old-established Swan's Nest Brewery—it was by the river—was bought by William Hall in 1795, and, after a partnership with the Tawney family, became Hall's Oxford Brewery Ltd in 1896. Take-overs followed. They quickly acquired the St Clement's Brewery, the Eagle Steam and Hanley's City Breweries.

Distant deliveries went by rail and river, but locally more than 60 horse-drawn drays were used, and on May Day mornings before World War I they paraded through the city. Hall's themselves were taken over, first by Allsop's in 1926, then Ind Coope. Hall's is now brewed at Burton and their brewery is now the Oxford Museum of Modern Art.

Morrell's had a brewing relationship with Hall's through the Tawneys, who were partners to both, and a personal one by marriage. Brewing had already been going on for 200 years on the site in St Thomas Street chosen by Mark Morrell and his son James in 1782 for their new brewery. More than 200 years later it is still there and is controlled by the same family. A pair of rampant lions, each holding aloft a spray of hops like a lover's bouquet, flank the gates to the brewery, a graphic insistence that Morrell's beer remains, as ever, a wedding of malt and hops.

Another branch of the family was active in legal, local and national affairs. Best remembered is not Philip Morrell, the Member of Parliament, but his wife Lady Ottoline, of whom Virginia Woolf wrote: "It must be fairly crushing to live in the shade." Garsington Manor, their house near Oxford, sheltered assorted members of the Bloomsbury literary set during World War I.

Between 1830 and 1850 one question engaged members of the University to the exclusion of everything else. In the words of a contemporary scholar, Mark Pattison, it "entirely diverted our thoughts from the true business of the place". Such was the Oxford Movement, which began with a sermon and left Oxford, with its protagonists, to be debated elsewhere.

It all began on 14 July 1833 when John Keble, Fellow of Oriel and Professor of

with gold. The poor humble Roman Church hard by is quite plain, simple and Low Church in its ritual."

Of the leading churchmen associated with the Movement, John Newman, vicar of St Mary's at the time, addressed his readers of the first Tract as "Fellow-Labourers". After the last Tract appeared he left Oxford, embraced the Roman Catholic Church, and was made a Cardinal in 1879.

John Keble's posthumous contribution to

Poetry, preached the Assize Sermon in the University Church. It stimulated the publication of the controversial *Tracts for the Times*, which gave the Movement the alternative title of "Tractarian". The main thrust of the arguments put forward was in support of a "Catholic" church, but not Roman Catholic, and the most tangible outcome was the revival of ceremonial in Anglican churches.

One in particular, St Barnabas, built to serve the growing working-class suburb of Jericho, was visited by the Rev. Francis Kilvert in 1876. He noted in his *Diary* that the priest wore "a biretta and a chasuble stiff

Oxford was the college named after him in 1870. The intention was to provide people with small means with an academic education based on the principles of the Church of England. The chosen architect was William Butterfield, a follower of the Movement, who produced a building in Gothic Revival style. When the sun fell on its patterned brick, John Betjeman thought it appeared at its worst. Norman Shaw saw Butterfield as "paddling in a boat of his own". His building is certainly unique and striking.

At the beginning of Queen Victoria's reign the collection of rarities of the rather dubiously acquired inheritance of Elias Ashmole was still installed, neglected and deteriorating, in the Old Ashmolean building in Broad Street. What was needed was a suitable home for the display of these and the University's treasures and works of art, which two timely bequests made splendidly possible. In 1841 Charles Robert Cockerell produced his design for a neo-classical Ashmolean that so magnificently today introduces the wonderful diversity of its con-

Tram to North Oxford: There is a romantic idea that the development of the area north of the Martyrs' Memorial that is North Oxford came about when the University allowed dons to marry. The need for large family housing, however, was earlier felt by the city's wealthy merchants and traders.

No doubt St John's College, which had acquired the land as long ago as the 16th century, was alive to its development potential as well. Gothic was the flavour of univer-

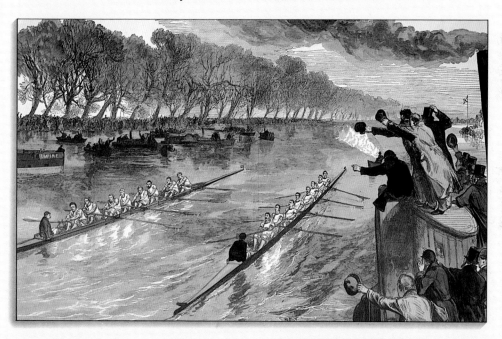

tents. Somehow the most significant and compelling of the exhibits is the Alfred Jewel—the Alfred who could have been the founder of the University.

Diversity is the essential element of the growth of Oxford in the 60 years of Victoria's reign, a diversity of demand from an expanding city that ranged from books to breweries, marmalade to melodrama and town houses to trams.

Left, Ackermann's *Bachelor of Arts* and *The Astronomical Observatory*. **Above**, dead-heat in the 1877 Oxford–Cambridge Boat Race.

sity architecture; red and yellow brick its chosen medium; gables and gardens characterised the style. Keble and the Parks' Museum welcomed the villas like hens with chickens. By 1880 most of the houses had been built, and dons, after 1877, were moving in with their families.

Five years later North Oxford's first trams followed them up the Banbury Road all the way from Carfax for a penny. The horse-drawn single deckers on 4-ft gauge rails also ran from east to west over a specially widened Magdalen Bridge, up the High Street and out to Jericho via Walton Street. Speed was limited to eight miles an hour and further restricted if confronted with a herd of cattle. Worse, a flock of sheep called for a dead stop. Passengers were not allowed to smoke or travel in dirty work clothes.

It was the turn of the century before an electric tramway was mooted, and 1913 before the idea was effectively scotched by the motorbus. William Morris, later Lord Nuffield, was refused a licence by the city to run these, but tickets to ride could be bought in shops. The Tramway Company followed suit, but with buses instead of trams, and eventually won exclusive rights to run Oxford's first official bus service.

they began the steamer trips that have opened Oxford's fluid asset to millions.

Rights for women: The seeds of the slow and grudging acceptance of the equal right of women to higher education were sown not by the University authorities but by central government through the Parliamentary Commissions of 1850 and 1874. Oxford, however, came a conspicuous second to Cambridge in relaxing rules on the admission of women. As early as 1863 examinations had been open to girls at Cambridge, and Girton became the first residential college for women in 1869.

It was nine years before Oxford followed

Blackwell's bookshop is so much one of Oxford's important institutions that you expect it to go back further than 1879, yet it was only then that Benjamin Henry Blackwell started his business at his house in Holywell Street. Demands on space soon forced expansion into other premises.

Down on the river at Folly Bridge, Salter Bros had been quietly contributing to Oxford's sporting prowess and public pleasure since they established the firm in 1858. Boats and college barges were built here, including the eights which took the University to victory over Cambridge, and in 1886

suit with Lady Margaret Hall, for Church of England girls, and Somerville College, the first to place no religious requirements on its entrants. St Hugh's joined them in 1886 and St Hilda's Hall in 1893, founded by the Principal of Cheltenham Ladies' College for women from that college. Further concessions were wrung from the University. Examinations were opened to women in 1894, but degrees and equal status for women's colleges had to wait until the 20th century.

Above, Henry Taunt's 1907 photograph of St Aldgate's, looking towards Carfax.

THE PIED PIPER OF CHRIST CHURCH

Alice in Wonderland is a love story. It expresses indirectly Lewis Carroll's feelings for the young daughter of the Dean of Christ Church and reveals his thinly disguised passion for Oxford itself. Growing up brought the first affair quickly to a close—"No thought of me shall find a place/ In thy young life's hereafter," he wrote in dedicating *Alice Through the Looking Glass* to her. The other relationship ended only with his death. In all that time he was scarcely ever away from his beloved Oxford.

Carroll was born Charles Ludwidge Dodgson in Christ Church rectory, Lincolnshire, and joined Oxford's Christ Church College at the age of 18 in 1850 from public school at Rugby. He became a lecturer in mathematics and was ordained Deacon. Outside his academic studies he was a keen photographer, developing his own plates in a darkroom he was given permission to build on the roof of his rooms overlooking Tom Quad.

Extremely shy, he was most at ease with children and they became his favourite subjects. He had left seven sisters behind at the rectory, so perhaps the young daughters of the Dean made him feel at home. Charles Dodgson's first meeting with them was in the Deanery garden where his intention of photographing the Cathedral was diverted by their insisting on getting in the picture.

The friendship with the Liddell girls grew, and soon they were posing for his camera in his rooms. Dressed in Chinese costumes or the rags of beggar waifs from the cupboards in his dressing-room, the children began their games of "Let's pretend", and Alice's adventures were about to begin.

During the summer Dodgson took the children on the river, making up stories that lived and died "like summer midges" to keep them amused and interested. They rowed to Iffley and beyond, and if time allowed went ashore at Nuneham to picnic in the park of their friends, the Harcourts.

One of these expeditions, on 4 July 1862, took them upstream to Godstow. The children, as always, pressed their friend for more stories and, when they returned to the Deanery, Alice implored him to write down her adventures. Ever willing to please her, Dodgson began the carefully hand-written book with his own illustrations and gave it to her as a Christmas present.

Alice's Adventures were so well thought of that Dodgson agreed to their professional publication, and on the advice of John Ruskin, the artist and social reformer, to have them illustrated by a professional artist. John Tenniel was chosen, and the author's name changed to one of four suggested pseudonyms, Lewis Carroll (Lewis from Ludwidge, Carroll from Charles).

A second book, *Through the Looking-glass and What Alice Found There*, was not published until 1871. The relationship had ended with the end of her childhood, and Alice was now 19. She married a Christ Church man and went to live at Lyndhurst. The Rev. Charles Dodgson died in 1898, still a bachelor.

From the moment Alice clutches the jar of "orange Marmalade" from the cupboard in the well, Lewis Carroll provides us with an intriguing guessing game in identifying Oxford references and characters. Dodgson was currently advertising for sale his brother's orange marmalade. The Cheshire cat is Dinah, Alice's tabby, sitting on a tree bough in the Deanery garden. Lorina and Edith, Alice's sisters, become the Lory and Eaglet. Her governess, Miss Prickett—"Pricks" to the children—is the Red Queen, "one of the thorny kind". The Rev. Robinson Duckworth, friend of Lewis Carroll's, who often went on the picnics, becomes, affectionately, the Duck.

The Dodo derived from visits to the new University Museum. The extinct bird, whose unfailing logic in organising the Caucus-race "to get us dry", is the author himself, and recalls picnics in the rain at Nuneham. The Dormouse's story of three children living at the bottom of a treacle-well leads us to the healing well at Binsey. Deer from Magdalen Park and eels from the wicker traps at Godstow mix fact and fantasy, and in St Aldate's, opposite the college, is the shop where Alice bought her favourite barley-sugar from the old sheep.

You've only to push open the door...

Vera Brittain, author of *Testament of Youth*, went up to Somerville College in 1914, an innocent ex-deb who had been born into "that unparalleled age of rich materialism and tranquil comfort", as she describes the Edwardian age. The Oxford she discovered in the first year of World War I still basked in that mellow security even a decade into the new century.

This was the Oxford of Zuleika Dobson, the eponymous heroine of Max Beerbohm's novel who caused titled undergraduates, besotted with her, to drown themselves in the Isis. Colleges dominated the University, and the University controlled the city that existed to service it. Around the stately quadrangles narrow, medieval streets contained small businesses and close-knit communities. Public transport was still by horse-drawn trams that were advertised as meeting every train at the sleepy, non-mainline station. In the North Oxford suburb, built to house the large Victorian families of the dons, croquet was played on the lawns, and afternoon tea was served with ceremony.

In 1915, Vera Brittain left Oxford to train as a nurse. In 1919 she returned to Somerville. "It seemed unbearable that everything should be exactly the same when all my life was so much changed." She had lost her brother, her lover, many friends; 2,700 Oxford men had died in the trenches.

It is invidious to select one name from these thousands, but H.G.J. (Harry) Moseley, who was killed at Gallipoli in 1915, and had graduated from Trinity College, was the most promising of all the physicists of his generation. His work on atomic structure using the relatively new X-rays was in four short years already enough for a Nobel prize to be confidently predicted. His classic equipment has an honoured place in the Museum of the History of Science at Oxford.

In every college the memorial slabs went up, and the ancient buildings were haunted for those who survived. The great eccentric, William Spooner, Warden of New College, had a plaque erected in the chapel to record the names of college members who had died fighting on the enemy side: "In memory of the men of this college who coming from a foreign land entered into the inheritance of this place and returning fought and died for their country in the war 1914–1919".

But life, of course, went on, and for many

the top priority was to live it as on a roller coaster, for excitement and risk. Between the wars, Oxford University, so often an exaggeration of the contemporary mood, experienced the excesses of hearties and aesthetes.

Evelyn Waugh's novel *Brideshead Revisited* presented the fictional version of this life style, and Vera Brittain wrote of her contemporaries: "One and all combined to create that 'eat-drink-and-be-merry-for-tomorrow-we-die' atmosphere which seemed to have drifted from the trenches via the Paris hotels and London night clubs into Oxford colleges."

Preceding pages: 1908 picture of St Giles' Fair. Left and above, women at work in World War I, as ticket collectors and unpaid social workers.

A woman's place: Under this hectic surface, a fundamental change had been taking place. Women, admitted to lectures of the University in 1880, and permitted to take examinations in 1884, were first given degrees—the ultimate equality—in 1920. Four women's colleges had been founded between 1878 and 1893, so the academic groundwork was well established. It was the post-war emancipation which gradually freed the female undergraduates to take a more active part in University life.

Christopher Hobhouse, a traditionalist, did not welcome the invasion, and wrote caustically: "They are perpetually awheel.

Week still brought throngs of families and girl-friends to cheer on the boat races and socialise on the picturesque college barges lining the river bank below Christ Church Meadow, now replaced by brick boathouses.

Many of the clubs remained exclusively male, notably the Oxford Union debating society that was founded in 1823, and by mid-century occupied its own premises between Cornmarket and New Inn Hall Street. Its debates were the nursery of a glittering succession of politicians, lawyers and clerics, the most famous of whom were always ready to return in later life as guest speakers. The Union resisted admitting women as

They bicycle in droves from lecture to lecture, capped and gowned, handlebars laden with notebooks and notebooks crammed with notes." That the women worked hard was hardly surprising, since, under the Intercollegiate Rules for Women of 1924, they could only have social dealings with men with their Principal's permission, within limited hours, and accompanied by another female.

Yet the circumspect invasion of Oxford by women made little impact on male undergraduate life in the inter-war years. The traditional sports and clubs continued. Eights

members until after World War II. The myriad other clubs were gradually opened to women, but the majority of male undergraduates had little contact with their female counterparts.

Equally far-reaching changes had been happening to the city of Oxford. By the 1920s, it was no longer a sleepy market town, but an important industrial centre. As early as 1898, William Morris had opened his garage, and the first Morris car came off the line in 1913. By 1923, the Cowley factory's production was over 20,000 vehicles a year. The area east of Magdalen

Bridge had become a town in its own right, owing no allegiance to the University.

Between 1911 and 1951, the population of Oxford grew from 62,000 to 97,000, much of the growth due to the immigration of industrial workers. Many of these came from the valleys of Wales, creating a strong and obstinately self-contained Welsh community in Cowley, that made its own social life, complete with choirs. The villages close to Oxford—Headington, Marston, Iffley, Wolvercote—experienced the same fate as Cowley and became suburbs of the city.

The industrial expansion of Oxford caused dismay to many for whom Oxford to preserve Oxford's Green Belt, so that the historic city in its ring of hills may retain its special setting, free of urban sprawl.

A new look: The architectural face of Oxford changed greatly between the wars. There were some undoubted improvements in the city centre. The elegant new Elliston & Cavell store was built in Magdalen Street, and the corner of Broad Street and Cornmarket was dignified by the pillared curve of William Baker's furniture shop. Beaumont Street, with its fine 18th-century facades, suffered little from the inclusion of the Playhouse, a piece of infill in the very best of taste.

was Matthew Arnold's "sweet city with her dreaming spires". In 1928, Dr H.A.L. Fisher, Warden of New College, was the prime mover in establishing the Oxford Preservation Trust, whose first act was to raise the money to buy land on Boars Hill and at Marston, in the Cherwell valley, to safeguard it from development. The Trust, still active today, owns 300 acres (120 hectares) of land in and around Oxford, and campaigns

Left, Godley's Own Oxford Volunteers march past the Emperors' Heads in World War I. Above, dinner in hall in the 1920s.

The New Theatre in George Street, spacious inside and simple outside, was welcome, but the Ritz cinema further west (now the ABC), presents disconcertingly blank walls both to George Street and to Gloucester Green. The junction of Park End Street and Hythe Bridge Street, facing the railway station, was appropriately filled by the Royal Oxford Hotel.

For the University, there was much new building in the Parks Road area. The Radcliffe Science Library filled with dignity the northern corner of South Parks Road. Opposite, an eccentricity was designed by Sir

Herbert Baker: Rhodes House, headquarters of the Rhodes Trust and its scholars. This was aptly described by the writer Christopher Hobhouse as "a Cotswold manor house with a circular temple of heroic scale deposited in its forecourt." Where Parks Road joins Broad Street, another corner site accommodated the New Bodleian Library, a curiously uninteresting building above ground, but fascinating below, where the vast book stacks are linked by conveyor belt under the street to the subterranean reaches of the Bodleian proper.

The commercial building of the 1930s reveals how prosperous a city Oxford had

become, even during the Depression, thanks to the motor industry. The University, too, was expanding with the coming of science and medicine, much of the expansion due to the generous patronage of Lord Nuffield. He endowed poorer colleges, acquired the site round the Radcliffe Infirmary and Observatory to create a medical institute, and in 1936 gave the University £1.25 million for medical research. More funding was poured into the physical sciences, and social science came to Oxford for the first time with the foundation in 1937 of Nuffield College "to encourage research especially… in the field of social studies, and especially by making easier the co-operation of academic and non-academic persons."

The new boys: The University was gradually changing its character in the 1930s as an increasing number of undergraduates entered with the aid of scholarships. By the end of the decade, about half the student population was grant-aided, leading to a profound change of attitude to the three years spent at Oxford. For the scholarship boy, the University was a place achieved through luck and hard work, carrying the obligation to strive for the best degree possible.

It was also a totally unfamiliar environment for some. A Yorkshire miner who won a scholarship to Oxford described the contrast in *A Pitman Looks at Oxford*, written in 1933 under the pseudonym of Roger Dataller: "Goodbye, University!… Big Tom Tower bell groaning out its plaint… gang of roaring hearties on the tavern doorstep—handkerchief of blackberries on the slope of Cumnor… old port, biscuits, waiters, butlers—white stone, grey stone, greenstone, cloisters—black and white of proctors—sober gait of 'bulldogs'… Now headstocks, coal ranged in many waggons, flicker of pulleys, ochre of fumes, the clatter of clogs."

Yet, despite these changes, the public schools were still the market from which the colleges took the majority of their intake. The criterion of selection was by no means only intellectual ability. It was considered essential for a college to have its quota of sportsmen and gentlemen, irrespective of their academic quality. As Ronald Knox put it: "They don't do much harm, and when they've finished playing here, they can go out like good little boys and govern the Empire."

But in 1939, Oxford again sent out its young men to fight in another war, at the end of which running the Empire was no longer to be an option. The Oxford University Air Squadron contributed its quota to the Few who fought the Battle of Britain, among whom was Richard Hilary, author of that great war book *The Last Enemy*.

World War II had a far less profound effect on University life than the Great War. In 1914, the University simply emptied as the undergraduates rushed to enlist. In 1939, the government actively discouraged this, and residence of one year was expected for those who had won places. So college life, though muted and restricted, continued, and the historic city escaped bombing.

Medical breakthrough: Oxford made many contributions to the war effort, of which the most dramatic was the discovery of penicillin, which founded the science of antibiotics. Penicillin was described and named in 1929 by Alexander Fleming, but he was not able to make it chemically stable. This was the achievement of Howard Florey and his team, who first used penicillin on a patient in the

home in Oxford, and laid a significant part of the foundations of modern physics at the Clarendon Laboratory.

Then, as Oxford entered another post-war period, the same uneasy mixture of ex-service men and women and youngsters straight from school was being shaped through three years in the University's old, inimitable way. It was at this time that the city, having grown to an unwieldy size, began to realise that traffic was becoming a major problem. A planning consultant, Thomas Sharp, was engaged for three years by the City Council to produce a detailed study, which was published in 1948 under the title *Oxford Replan-*

Radcliffe Infirmary in 1941, the start of a breakthrough in healing of the greatest magnitude. The discovery is commemorated in a formal rose garden between Oxford's Botanic Garden and the High Street, the gift of the American Lasker Foundation in 1953.

Another remarkable Oxford contribution to the war was the work of Professor F.A. Lindemann, later Lord Cherwell, who was Churchill's controversial scientific adviser. Lindemann, a wealthy German, made his

Left, the High Street in 1939. **Above**, a stall in the Covered Market in the early 1950s.

ned. More than 40 years on, one marvels at its confident comprehensiveness, and thinks, if only it were as simple as that to manage the growth of a city.

Sharp's study has deservedly become a classic, but its fame rests largely on one of its proposals, the Meadow Road. Sharp wrote: "In the case of Oxford one piece of surgery is required to release the city from a pressure on its spinal column which will otherwise eventually paralyse it." The spinal column is the admired High Street, ruined by motor traffic; the surgery was to create a new east/west relief road, running through Christ

Church Meadow to cross the river by a new bridge south of Magdalen Bridge. The patient being a city of such fame, the storm that greeted Sharp's proposal was of international proportions, and rumbled on for the next 25 years.

After a period of shock, the battle lines were drawn. Christ Church, and behind it the University, refused to consider a Meadow Road. But the idea of a relief road, once mooted, continued to occupy the planners' minds, and bore fruit in another route further south, proposed in the 1960s, and called the Eastwyke Farm Road. This was part of a complex of urban motorways that would

icy, using reduced car-parking, improved public transport, and a park-and-ride scheme to contain city centre traffic.

The wreckers move in: Though urban motorways did not bring about the wholesale destruction of housing, the new-buildings-for-old enthusiasm of the 1960s produced what we now see as the tragic destruction of the old Oxford. The late Victorian terraces of St Ebbe's, between the city centre and the Thames, were completely pulled down, and in the resulting wasteland a huge shopping centre and multi-storey car park were built. The Oxford Preservation Trust succeeded in saving a small group of 17th-century cot-

have carved up the inner residential areas of the city, and for which approval was actually given in 1969.

At this point it was the turn of Oxford's citizens to protest. A Civic Society was formed, a best-selling booklet called *Let's Live in Oxford* was published, and vigorous opposition mounted to the motorway scheme at a Public Inquiry. A combination of political factors, lack of money and public protest caused the Eastwyke Farm scheme to be abandoned. A couple of years later, a Labour City Council adopted what was known as the Balanced Transport Pol-

tages at the eleventh hour, and these now huddle incongruously beside the towering Westgate Centre.

The modernisation of the Cornmarket began with the demolition of the Clarendon Hotel in 1957, to be replaced by a Woolworth store. Though discreetly designed by Sir William Holford in stone, this building brought the multiples into the centre of Oxford, and was followed by the loss of the fine old grocers, Grimbly Hughes, Webbers in the High Street, and Capes of St Ebbe's.

In the 1980s, another shopping centre has been built to link Cornmarket with Queen

Street, a sensible idea marred by crude and inappropriate execution, with the main entrance through the former Woolworth building marked by much criticised blue-painted metal hoops. But conservation policies have been gaining credence, and more sites have been treated with sensitivity. On the corner of Ship Street, for example, a medieval building has been restored by Jesus College, and is a superb shop for Laura Ashley.

Changes in the University after World War II were no less significant and controversial. With its usual capacity for pulling a rabbit out of the hat, Oxford suddenly produced a sporting star of international magni-

Franks, whose Report led to far-reaching changes in the University's structure. The achievements of the 1960s were extraordinary in financial and practical terms. The Historic Buildings Appeal raised over £2 million, making it possible for the grime of centuries to be removed from Oxford's stone, and restoration work on a huge scale to be done.

The College Contributions scheme, which required the richer colleges to provide funds for the poorer, as well as generous outside funding, enabled new building work to the value of £11 million to be carried out. Six new colleges were established: St Cath-

tude in Dr Roger Bannister (now Sir Roger, and the Master of Pembroke College), who used his knowledge of physiology to run the first four-minute mile on the Iffley Road track in June 1954.

There was a strong feeling that the University must modernise its administration itself or find itself forced to do so by outside forces. The result was the establishment of a committee under the chairmanship of Lord

Left, in 1954 Roger Bannister was first to achieve a four-minute mile. **Above**, in 1978 Richard Nixon was guest at an Oxford Union debate.

erine's for undergraduates on the pattern of the older colleges, but the other five for graduates only. The science area burgeoned, with 4,000 undergraduates and graduate students working there.

Oxford suffered less than many of the newer universities from the student unrest that was a feature of the 1960s. But it did not escape entirely, and its reaction was predictable: a committee on relations with junior members, the Hart Committee, was set up, leading to the creation of a Student Representative Council. Pressure for mixed colleges built up all through that radical decade, and this change—perhaps the most revolutionary to hit Oxford University in its long history—was implemented from 1970. Today, all the former men's colleges take male and female undergraduates, and only two of the women's colleges, Somerville and St Hilda's, are single-sex. It is interesting to note that the ratio today of men to women in the University is 3:2 and that of arts students to scientists the same.

Political snub: The 1980s saw none of the spectacular spending of the previous two decades. All academic spending was restricted by the Conservative government, and Oxford found itself at odds with Margaret Thatcher, despite the fact that the Prime Minister was an Oxford graduate. An attempt to award her an honorary degree was actually voted down.

early donation came from the publisher Rupert Murdoch: on the day his best-selling *Sun* was censured by Britain's Press Council for describing homosexuals as "poofters", he announced a £3 million donation to the University to set up a professorship to improve the use of English.

And what of the city? Oxford will soon be close to one of the new motorways, the M40, linking London and Birmingham. Its completion will—maybe—reduce some of Oxford's now legendary traffic congestion. But the battle is still on between the conservationists who want at least something of the old city to remain intact, and the pressure for

The result of government cuts in finance, and the University's wish to expand into new fields of study, was the launch in 1988 of the Campaign for Oxford, a massive fund-raising effort with a target of £220 million. It is planned to spend the money on securing academic posts and the University's infrastructure of libraries and museums, and on a wide range of projects, such as computing, business and environmental studies. One

more jobs and more housing. The latest development gimmick is for science parks, to house high-tech industry. Cambridge has a thriving science park, so Oxford must have one too.

At Oxford, the tension between tradition and progress is always there. Will the call to move with the times prove strong enough to persuade University and city to jettison the stored riches of the past? The question seems more urgent today than ever before.

<u>Above</u>, Oxford's paradoxical fate as a car-making town: interminable traffic jams.

INSIDE THE OXFORD UNIVERSITY PRESS

Oxford University Press, known to the trade as OUP and to its staff as "the Press", publishes more than 1,000 new titles a year in Britain alone, 70 percent of them relating to academic disciplines. It employs 2,000 people worldwide and began the 1990s with a turnover of £100 million.

Among its most influential publications is the *Oxford English Dictionary*, first published in 12 volumes and dedicated to Queen Victoria. Today it has four supplements and has been republished in combined form in 20 volumes, costing £1,500.

As many of its catalogues remind us, the OUP "exists to serve the purpose of the University by furthering the advancement and spread of learning in the humanities, the arts, the sciences, and social sciences, through the publication of books, scholarly journals, Bibles, and music". Sir Roger Elliott, its chief executive, says: "It supports research projects on a breadth and scale unequalled by other university presses, with the possible exception of Cambridge University Press." (There has always been a healthy rivalry between the two.)

OUP has no board of directors but is controlled by a body of senior Oxford scholars who are the Delegates of the Press and a finance committee that includes various distinguished people.

Although it may appear to resemble any large commercial publisher, it differs greatly because of its objectives. Like any university press, it is dedicated to serving education and research but it differs from most other such presses (except for Cambridge) in having to pay its own way. It is also the largest and very international in its outlook: OUP has branches and promotion offices in more than 50 countries, and many branches have their own substantial publishing programmes. It also publishes in many languages, chiefly in the Indian subcontinent and in Africa.

It is more than 500 years since the first book was printed in Oxford, though the date in Roman numerals on the title page actually reads 1468 instead of 1478—an unfortunate beginning for a press renowned for its high standards of accuracy. The guardians of OUP were often highly eccentric characters, from Archbishop Laud and Dr Fell in the 17th century to Henry Frowde, the first to bear the title "Publisher to the University", in the late 18th and early 19th centuries. His successor, Humphrey Milford, had notoriously unpredictable instincts but seemed invariably to be right, leading to considerable expansion of OUP's operations both at home and overseas.

The OUP has had a succession of Oxford homes, including the Sheldonian Theatre and the Clarendon Building, partly financed by the profits from the first edition of Lord Clarendon's *History of the Great Rebellion*, which also gave the coveted Clarendon Press imprint its name. In 1830 it moved to its present home in Walton Street, a series of elegant buildings grouped, in true Oxford college fashion, round a quadrangle complete with ornamental pond, lawn and copper beech. It has frequently had a London presence, too: a Bible warehouse in Paternoster Row, and later offices in nearby Amen House. From 1965 its London home was Ely House, once the town house of the bishops of Ely, where it still keeps a small base, but all publishing is now based in Oxford. For nearly 50 years the Press also had a warehouse in the northwest suburbs of London until a vast new distribution centre was opened in Northamptonshire.

Since World War II, OUP has been through various phases of development. There was little planning then, with the Press concentrating on English literature and scholarly titles. Other academic firms such as Macmillan became prominent and Cambridge shot ahead in disciplines such as archaeology and philosophy. In the late 1970s and early 1980s, OUP launched a catching-up operation to broaden its range and become a major publisher in the main academic disciplines.

The recession of the early 1980s hit British publishing hard and in the financial year 1980–81, despite a turnover of £49 million, OUP's British printing and publishing operations lost £2.5 million. The Press recovered more rapidly than other academic publishers, however, and by the end of the 1980s, despite heavy investment in electronic publishing, its annual profit (or "surplus") was touching £12 million.

The career of William Richard Morris, Viscount Nuffield, has been described by British industrial historians as "the biggest success story of the century". His success had a profound effect on Oxford and the surrounding area, for it was through Morris's efforts that a major industry—motor manufacturing—was added to what had been a predominantly academic city. He was also one of the great benefactors of his time, distributing some £30 million to various charitable causes before he died in 1963 at the age of 85.

Morris cars were made in the district from 1912 and today the sprawling Cowley factory complex, on the ring road to the southeast of the city, is part of the Rover Group, producing the Rover 800, Maestro, and Montego cars as well as bodyshells for Rolls-Royces. A little further out, some of Britain's most famous sports cars were made in the MG factory at Abingdon until it closed in 1981.

Two wheels: William Morris was born in Worcester in 1877, but his parents were from Oxford and the family moved back to the city when he was a young child. He attended the Church School in Cowley, leaving at the age of 14 to become apprenticed to a bicycle repairer. Within months, and with just £4 of capital, he had established his own cycle repair business in a shed behind his parents' house in James Street, Cowley St John.

Rebuilding old bicycles soon led to building new ones, the first order being for an abnormally large frame to suit the towering rector of nearby St Clement's Church. The young Morris became the local cycling champion and by 1901 his exploits and machines were so well known that he was encouraged to open a sales shop at 48 High Street, Oxford, with more extensive workshops round the corner in Queen's Lane.

Next came Morris motorcycles, or what

Preceding pages: Morris manager Cecil Kimber with a 1923 MG. **Left,** original MGs are now collector's items. **Right,** Lord Nuffield.

would today be called mopeds, being bicycles with a small De Dion engine added. Bigger premises, in disused stables at the junction of Longwall and Holywell Street, backing on to the gardens of New College, were also used for garaging some of the city's increasing number of motor cars, particularly those belonging to rich undergraduates. With his mechanical skill and eye for a business opportunity, it was not long before the Longwall signboard read: "Morris Cycle

Works—cycles and motors repaired".

Morris became an agent for a number of British car and motorcycle manufacturers. By 1910 he had given up making two-wheelers and built a new garage on the Longwall site. He began to consider producing a car of his own. It would be a small car of high quality, made in large numbers and sold at a low price. The way to achieve that, he concluded, was to reduce the cost of design, tooling and manufacture by purchasing all the major components from outside companies and simply assembling the cars in Oxford. Longwall was not big enough, so

Morris moved out to the suburb of Cowley, to buildings that had once been Hurst's Grammar School (which his father had attended) and become the Temple Cowley military training college.

Appropriately, this first car, delivered in 1913, was called the Morris Oxford. It was priced at £175 and became famous as the first of the "Bullnose" Morrises, so-called because of the rounded shape of their brass radiators. The engines and gearboxes were supplied by White & Poppe of Coventry, the chassis frames imported from Belgium, and the bodies made by Charles Raworth & Sons of Oxford. A bigger, second model with four

by as much as £200 a car—a lot of money in those days. While others scoffed, he predicted that sales would double—and he was right. By 1923 Morris was selling 20,000 cars a year; in 1925 demand reached 55,000.

New blood: Initially, the cars were manufactured by WRM Motors, which became Morris Motors in 1919. Morris Garages continued as a separate enterprise in Oxford city centre and by the early 1920s William Morris was too busy with manufacturing to have much to do with the garages and was happy to leave them in the hands of a manager called Cecil Kimber.

Kimber also had ambitions as a car maker

seats instead of two and a more powerful engine supplied by the US firm Continental, was called the Cowley.

Morris sold 393 Oxfords in the first year and more than 900 in 1914; the numbers seem small today but 75 years ago this represented the beginning of mass production in Britain. After World War I, Morris production increased sharply but so did costs and therefore prices. Then came the slump. By 1921, 60 cars a week were coming out of Cowley—but sales had reduced to a trickle. Faced with a stockpile of cars, William Morris took the bold step of slashing prices

and designed special, more rakish, bodies for the Morris Oxford and Cowley which were then sold as MG (for "Morris Garages") and carried the distinctive octagonal badge. The MG Super Sports models were so successful that by 1929 a separate MG factory was set up, first in Cowley and then at Abingdon, from whence the best-selling Midget sports cars emerged. It was the T-series successors to these that, 20 years later, converted a generation of young Americans to lightweight British sports cars.

By the end of the 1920s, Morris was Britain's most successful car maker, producing more than 100,000 cars a year, and responsible for one third of all the cars sold in the UK. As it grew, the original idea of assembling from mostly bought-in components became less attractive and Morris started to make more of the vehicles themselves. The Cowley factory kept on expanding. It even had its own railway halt.

William Morris had been knighted in 1928, became a baron in 1934 and Viscount Nuffield in 1938, the last honour being awarded as much for his generosity to charities as for his success as an industrialist. He chose the name Nuffield after the manor house in a small Oxfordshire village near Henley-on-

future use—both habits inherited from his father and his own poorer days as a child. He insisted that an Ericsson telephone, installed in 1913, be retained until it could no longer be repaired, just a year before he died.

Asked to comment on his wealth, Lord Nuffield once said: "You can only wear one suit at a time." His own luxuries were a continuous supply of specially made (but apparently, to others, notably unpleasant) cigarettes and long sea voyages to distant lands—travel for which he acquired a taste when he visited America to study the production methods of Henry Ford and others.

Money for medicine: Lord Nuffield and his

Thames which he had made his home.

Though he became rich beyond dreams, Lord Nuffield was a man of simple tastes. He used the same small and modestly furnished office upstairs in the old school building at Cowley for 50 years; it is now part of the Nuffield Press printing company, a subsidiary of Maxwell Communications.

His desk always had a pile of neatly sliced used envelopes to use as notepaper and he carefully unknotted string from parcels for

Left, old horsepower outside Morris's original shop. **Above**, new horsepower in the 1933 works.

wife Elizabeth (who died in 1959) had no children and he was determined not to leave his fortune to be decimated by death duties. Medicine was a lifelong interest and in the 1920s he donated sums of money to hospitals in Birmingham, Coventry and London. In 1930 he supported the care of crippled children at the Wingfield Orthopaedic Hospital in Headington and later paid for the hospital to be rebuilt. He funded a new maternity wing at Oxford's Radcliffe Infirmary, and many other medical projects and new hospitals around the country. In 1937, he put up £900,000 to establish a new university establishment, Nuffield College, to the west of the city; World War II intervened and the foundation stone was not laid until 1949.

Although he loved Oxford, William Morris had not, in his earlier years, enjoyed very friendly relations with either the city authorities or the University. He was suspicious of graduates in business and for a long time would not employ anyone who had been through the University. Disagreement with the city council went back to 1913, when he had proposed motor buses as an alternative to the electric trams which were to replace Oxford's horse-drawn trams. The council rejected the idea, so Morris bought a fleet of

The man to do the job was Leonard Lord, a forceful character who, to the surprise of many, was appointed managing director of Morris Motors in 1933.

The ruthless Mr Lord succeeded in restoring the company's fortunes but left in 1936 when Nuffield refused him a share of the increased profits he had generated. Lord swore revenge—and not long after joined Morris's arch-rival, Austin, in Birmingham.

Growing concern: Morris continued to absorb weaker rivals; in 1938, they took over Riley. In 1939, just before the conversion of all their factories to aid the war effort, Morris, MG, Riley and Wolseley were consoli-

six buses and put them into operation illegally. His audacity paid off, for the bus service was popular, the city was spared ugly and disruptive trams, and he eventually sold the vehicles to the council.

Nuffield's relationships with his employees were sometimes less benevolent. He was generally regarded as a fair, if tough, employer but was notorious for his autocratic style, unwilling to heed advice even from his senior colleagues. By the early 1930s, after the acquisition of many of Morris's suppliers as well as the rival firm Wolseley, the Morris empire was badly in need of reorganisation.

dated into the Nuffield Organisation.

During World War II, the Cowley plant produced battle tanks, repaired aeroplanes, and made Tiger Moth trainers, as well as engines for military aircraft. An airstrip was built on the factory site.

When peace returned and car production re-commenced, the question of a merger arose once again. Sir Herbert, later Lord Austin, had died during the war. Leonard Lord was in charge at Austin, which had more modern designs and had overtaken Morris's sales. He approached his old boss Nuffield and clearly took delight in becoming the dominant partner in a deal which created the British Motor Corporation in 1952. Lord Nuffield, by then 75 years old, was appointed chairman of BMC but retired after just six months.

BMC was Britain's biggest motor manufacturer, and the fourth biggest in the world. There was a fusion between Nuffield and Austin products from an early stage, perhaps best exemplified by the most important British small car of the immediate post-war era, the Morris Minor, which quickly adopted an engine that originated at Austin.

Lord Nuffield did not like the post-war Minor, which he said looked "like a poached

models were virtually the same as counterparts from Austin, Wolseley, Riley and even MG; this became known, disparagingly, as "badge engineering". In 1968, after further mergers, BMC became British Leyland.

The Morris Marina, an unremarkable design, was introduced in 1971 as a belated successor to the Minor and it was this car, restyled and renamed Ital, which was the last to carry the Morris name. Eventually, after a troubled period of heavy losses which led to government control, British Leyland became the Rover Group and, in 1988, a division of British Aerospace. In the future, the new owners intend to concentrate Rover ex-

egg", but it was to become the first British car to sell a million. It was designed by Alec Issigonis, the brilliant engineer who went on to develop the 1959 Mini. That was sold originally as both a Morris and an Austin, and built at both Cowley and the Austin plant at Longbridge, Birmingham.

From then on, the future of Morris and the activity of the Cowley plant became enmeshed in the BMC grand plan. The Minor remained the Morris mainstay but other

Left, the popular Morris Minor (in the foreground). **Above**, the even more popular Mini.

ecutive car production in the 90-acre (36-hectare) Cowley body plant—the former Pressed Steel works—and shut down Cowley North and South, which include Morris's original buildings.

Oxford's days as a site for high-volume car manufacturing may be numbered; but, because of the engineering facilities available in the area, it has a new role as a centre of the racing car industry—in which Britain leads the world. Indianapolis 500 winners March, for example, are in nearby Bicester, as are Reynard, currently the country's largest racing car maker.

The image of Oxford conveyed in countless films and books has given rise to two great myths. The first is the so-called "Brideshead" image, after Evelyn Waugh's *Brideshead Revisited*, which shows beautiful young aristocrats living a life of eternal summer and champagne in ancient ivy-clad colleges. Max Beerbohm's 1911 novel *Zuleika Dobson* paints a similar picture. The second myth is that of pale intellectuals and palaeolithic dons festering in crumbling cathedral-like libraries, their lives devoted to the study of Homer or Hegel. Both myths are out-dated; but try as it might, the University cannot completely break free from its past.

Oxford is very different from any other university in the world, except perhaps Cambridge—often referred to in Oxford as "the other place". To differentiate itself, Oxford has its dons, scouts, tutorial system, Union, Boat Race and balls. But the people who inhabit the place are not, in reality, all that different from students elsewhere.

A recent survey showed that, politically, only one in four Oxford students supports the Conservative party. The most-read national newspapers are *The Independent*, a middle-of-the-road quality paper, and *The Sun*, Rupert Murdoch's down-market tabloid. More than a quarter of students admit to being virgins and about three-quarters describe themselves as "very or fairly ambitious". So far, so normal.

However, there is a very high proportion of public school-educated students (48 percent, compared with a figure of 20 percent in higher education nationally), and a low percentage of women, 41 percent. Mixed colleges were not introduced until the 1970s, and Oxford is still very much a male-dominated institution, with especially few women dons (only 12 percent).

The myth of Oxford as a book-lined ivory

tower is not entirely without foundation either. Academic concerns are still very much a priority; and, although Oxford no longer enjoys the pre-eminent status it once did, university departments find it relatively easy to attract funding from industry, especially in the sciences. One University fund-raising group, the Campaign for Oxford, trades on Oxford's elitist image and confidently set a target of £220 million. So the University must be held partly responsible

for propagating its own myth.

Student life: The student's way of life has remained essentially unchanged for hundreds of years. Training for the ministry as an undergraduate's principal objective began to decline in the 19th century, and over the years new subjects have been added so that there are now 18 separate faculties. But all students' lives are still shaped by the fact that they are members of a college—and that is how they think of themselves, rather than as members of a faculty.

The college has always been much more than just a place of residence; lectures and

Preceding pages: punting on the Cherwell; the Sheldonian Theatre; graduation ceremony. **Left**, the formal party scene. **Right**, the less formal party scene.

exams are organised by the University, but the colleges are responsible for a student's weekly tutorials and classes. In addition, the college is the centre of the student's social life. Every college has sports facilities and organised teams in most sports, plus a bar and a Junior Common Room. JCRs, which were first formed in the 1890s, usually provide newspapers and a TV set for the use of students. All the colleges have numerous clubs, some of which are hundreds of years old; these can be musical, cultural and academic in orientation or purely social dining and drinking societies.

Most colleges provide their students with

they reach their third year at the university.

Concerns about the welfare of Oxford students are nothing new. The suicide rate has always been very high, and 43 percent of students claimed to have suffered from bouts of depression or anxiety. There is a 12-month waiting-list for psychotherapy.

However, all is not doom and gloom. The city's bars, pubs, clubs and cinemas do a brisk trade during term-time, and some are almost deserted during the vacations. If anything, Oxford students are notorious for "japes"—many see alcohol as the easiest antidote to essays. Complaints about student indiscipline are as old as the University it-

accommodation for at least two years, some of it in modern buildings but much of it in the college itself. Living in an ancient college room is a unique experience—romantic, stimulating and extremely draughty. Most students have to "live out" at some stage or another, usually sharing a house with other students. The average rent in Oxford is high (almost £40 a week) and the introduction in 1990 of the Community Charge, popularly known as the "poll tax", looked certain to increase student debt; the poll tax was set at £94 a year for students. Currently, 64 percent of students have an overdraft by the time

self: Proctors were appointed to enforce discipline as early as 1248.

The don's life: All teaching at Oxford was originally conducted by clergymen, but this practice ended a long time ago. However, Oxford academics are still known as "dons", from the Latin *dominus* (master). Famous dons have included Lewis Carroll, A.J. Ayer, J.R.R. Tolkien, C.S. Lewis, Iris Murdoch and Mary Warnock. Not all dons actually do any teaching. Many students are taught by post-graduate students, or Junior Research Fellows, who are normally appointed for a three-year period. The next step up is a Lectureship, a permanent teaching post attached to a particular college.

A Lecturer can then become a Reader, with fewer teaching duties and more opportunity to concentrate on his or her own research. Readers may become Professors, who are responsible for overseeing a particular subject area, in which they are said to hold a "Chair".

Oxford dons live a fairly comfortable life. Their accommodation is provided by their college, they have the right to dine on High Table, and of course they have long holidays. There are as many different types of don as there are of student. Some never leave the

phy—have lain vacant through lack of funds. Fewer graduates are seeking to become dons and, of those who do, many decide to leave for the private sector before they are 30, owing to poor prospects and salaries.

College figures: Aside from the don, the scout is probably the best-known Oxford figure. Scouts date back to the early 18th century and have traditionally been attached to a particular staircase of a particular college. As late as the 1950s they performed the role of a manservant, waking up their students in the morning, cleaning their rooms, preparing light meals and running errands.

library (the "old fogey"). Others appear regularly on television (the "trendy young don"). Then there is the "young fogey", who is too untrendy to appear on TV but too youthful to be accepted as an academic. The "Great and Good don" who has the ear of the Prime Minister is dying out. Many feel the prestige of being a don is beginning to wáne.

The University currently has 159 Professors, 111 Readers and 181 Lecturers, but many Chairs—including those of French Literature, Greek and the History of Philoso-

Left and right, academia spills into the open air.

Nowadays nearly all scouts are women and act simply as cleaning ladies or waitresses in hall. The close bond that used to exist between a student and his scout has all but disappeared, though some of today's scouts have their favourites among their students and may perform little extra services for them.

The other familiar college figure is the porter, who fills the duties of receptionist and security guard at the entrance to every college. They are involved in college discipline, and a minority are notorious for their obstinacy and rudeness. Each college is headed by what is variously titled the Rector, Master, Principal, President, Warden or Provost, who is the supreme authority within the college as well as the face the college presents to the outside world.

The academic life: Oxford's academic reputation is second to none, though its teaching is sometimes criticised for being too intense and too traditional. The intensity springs from the fact that terms are only eight weeks long (compared to at least 10 at most other British universities) and students are required to complete a minimum of one essay or problem-sheet a week, and sometimes as many as two or three. And the

tutorial—an ancient book-lined study, an even more ancient don sipping sherry, a timorous student stumbling through his Aristotle—still holds true. But "new-fangled" seminars are becoming increasingly popular.

Lectures are still solemn occasions. The students rise as the gown-clad don enters the lecture hall. The don then, all too often, mumbles semi-coherently for an hour. Exams are even more solemn. All students taking exams must wear "sub-fusc", a mode of dress descended from 13th-century ecclesiastical costume. It consists of dark suit, gown, white tie and mortar-board for men;

rigidly traditional nature of many of the courses is quite exceptional—for example, law students are required to study Roman Law, and English students have to study Anglo-Saxon.

However, the University's famous tutorial system means most courses are quite unstructured. Science students may have compulsory lectures and practicals, but for Arts students there is little formal teaching apart from the one hour a week spent with a tutor. The system works brilliantly if the student and tutor are "compatible", but it can backfire badly. The traditional picture of the

gown, white blouse and black tie, skirt and stockings for women.

Students sit a preliminary exam, called Mods or Prelims, in their first year. Finals, which were first set in 1807, are taken in the summer of the third year. Students are awarded a degree, or "Final Honour School", of either a First, 2:1, 2:2 or Third. Roughly 12 percent get a First, and 8 percent a Third. About 50 percent are awarded a 2:1, which in practice is what most students hope for. When Finals end in mid-June there is

Above, A don in his den.

"WOMEN: WHO LET THEM IN?"

Never let it be said that the colleges of Oxford University do not adapt to changing social conditions while keeping alive the traditional ceremonies which have enriched life through the centuries. One of these is the Christ Church Rain Dance, an elaborate ritual in which a dozen young men gather in an inner quadrangle of the college and sing, at some volume, incantations to their gods. These anthems are accompanied by the symbolic removal of each of the young men's garments until, clad only in socks and shoes, they dance around the quad directing their penises towards the upper windows of the main accommodation block.

This rich and colourful display, threatened with extinction thanks to disciplinary measures, is part of a tradition stretching right back to 1981, when women were first admitted to the college.

Oxford's cautious approach to accepting women in men's colleges means that fewer than one-third of its undergraduates are women and, as one pointed out, most men are from boys' schools where women tend to be motherly bodies who count socks. Its attempts to broaden its intake and strengthen its appeal to state school students have, up to now, had the unfortunate effect of *reducing* the number of women, because girls in comprehensive sixth forms are rarely encouraged to fix their sights on the dreaming spires. Balliol, where the Junior Common Room voted to make a special play for state-school applicants, has five first-year men to each woman.

The numerical imbalance of students and tutors means that women are likely to be isolated in tutorials. "The whole of Oxford education, especially in arts subjects, rests on your relationship with your tutor," observed Claire Athis Edwards, a student at Christ Church. "Tutorials are taken in pairs and you hear of women who say that they are completely dominated by their male tutorial partner. The tutor asks *his* opinion all the time. Even if your tutor is not overtly sexist, your male colleagues will have a relationship where they're on first-name terms, they'll go out for lunch together, whereas my relationship with my tutor is very much a teacher-pupil thing."

Individual colleges have evolved their own response to their female undergraduates. Brasenose saw the emergence of The Moosehunters, a group of young warriors who strapped antlers to their heads and crashed around in pursuit of first-year maidens. One Junior Common Room debated a motion that: "Women should be hired out on the same basis as college punts."

One by one, the colleges (of which only two remain single sex, both women's) are formulating codes designed to enable women to put their case to various levels of authority. In real life, the procedures are not widely used and the women seem well able to fend for themselves.

Some colleges will provide security locks for girls living in. Wadham, for example, will supply rape alarms free to its female students. The Students' Union circulated a questionnaire on personal safety (in language designed to make a woman feel very unsafe), the upshot of which was a night-bus service. Run by the Students' Union in conjunction with the city council, a 12-seater minibus will collect a woman at her door and deliver her to her destination. Another telephone number connects the late-night lone woman to a walk-you-home service.

What disturbs some students far more deeply is the record of women's examination results over the period since Oxford went more or less co-educational. The figures show that in 1958, 8.1 percent of men and 7.9 percent of women got first-class degrees. Throughout the 1960s and early 1970s, the numbers climbed: in 1973, for example, 12 percent of men and 12.1 percent of women got firsts. The shock came in the mid-1980s when integration was established—if unequally—and it was found that 16.1 percent of men got firsts but only 8.9 percent of women did.

Some would argue that there just aren't enough intelligent women at Oxford to keep the figures up; others believe that Oxford is male-dominated in an all-pervading way. There are, for example, only four women on the senior governing bodies of colleges. Statistics, as always, provide the basis for dispute; the argument, one suspects, may be eternal.

quite a spectacle on the streets of Oxford as the finalists are doused with shaving foam, confetti and champagne.

First impressions: The chaotic first week of their first term is an experience no-one forgets. First-year students, known as "Freshers", go through a hectic schedule, dominated by two events: Matriculation and Freshers' Fair.

The Matriculation ceremony is a ritual by which students are officially admitted as members of the University, and is conducted by the Vice-Chancellor in the Sheldonian Theatre. Students dress up in sub-fusc and listen to various Latin formulae. Other im-

The end of the week is marked by a series of college "subject parties", at which the second and third-year students in each subject ply their Fresher counterparts with large quantities of alcohol. If a student can survive First Week, he can survive anything Oxford is likely to throw at him.

Acting, journalism, politics: Talented and/or ambitious students will seek to climb to the top of the organisations which control acting, journalism and politics in Oxford—a traditional preparation for assuming real power in later life.

The clique-filled world of Oxford drama is presided over by OUDS, the Oxford Univer-

portant first-week ceremonies include registering at the Bodleian Library, at which students have to swear, among other things, not to "kindle flame" in the building.

But Freshers' Fair is the maddest, most diverse event of the year. The Schools building on the High Street is invaded by stalls representing all the different university clubs and societies, hoping to sign up Freshers as new members. There are over 200 clubs to choose from, ranging from the sensible (the Strategic Studies Group, the Industrial Society) to the surreal (the Pooh Sticks Club, the Heterosexual Decadence Society).

sity Dramatic Society. Many colleges also have their own theatre groups, and during term-time there are at least three student productions a week. The standard varies, but the best is very good. The summer shows, held outdoors in college quads or gardens, are especially popular despite the frequently inclement weather.

Oxford journalism has long been dominated by the weekly newspaper *Cherwell* (founded 1920) and the literary magazine *Isis* (founded 1897). Several national newspaper editors are former *Cherwell* editors. Even Rupert Murdoch once worked on the paper. The usual stereotypes are that *Cherwell* is frivolous and *Isis* pretentious, but both regularly win national awards and are worth looking at if you can get hold of a copy (they are both distributed in college lodges).

But the Oxford Union debating society is by far the best-known student institution in Oxford, perhaps in the world. Five British Prime Ministers were once officers of the Union. The various political clubs are also well-trodden training-grounds for future politicians; the Conservative Association, for example, can point to Margaret Thatcher as just one of many of its ex-presidents who made the big time.

nowned events which still take place, but also because of the sheer numbers of students who are regular participants in one or other of the great range of sports played.

The highlight of the sporting year is the Boat Race. Held in early April, the race from Putney to Mortlake on the River Thames in London is the focus for the Oxford–Cambridge rivalry which dominates Oxford sport. It was first held in 1829, since when it has been raced 136 times, Oxford having won 66 and Cambridge 69, with a dead heat in 1877.

The Oxford versus Cambridge Varsity Matches first began with a cricket match in

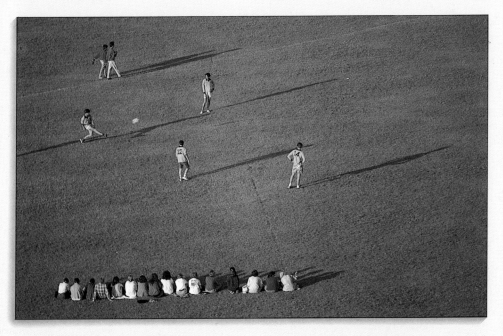

However, it must be said that Oxford students are generally quite apolitical. A recent survey showed that only 42 percent had attended political meetings or discussions. And, although most students go to plays, read *Cherwell* and *Isis* and attend debates at the Union, only a minority—known to the rest as "hacks"—seek to become involved.

Sporting life: Sport is a part of the very fabric of Oxford University, not just because of its long traditions or the nationally re-

1827. They are now held in every sport, and many are given wide coverage in the national newspapers. Two are televised: the Boat Race (second only to football's FA Cup final with 13 million viewers) and the Varsity rugby match, held at Twickenham in December. Training is deadly serious, as those who play in a Varsity Match are awarded a "Blue", which is perhaps as equally prestigious as gaining a First Class degree.

Sport is also taken very seriously at college level. Each college produces several rugby, cricket, hockey and football teams who compete in leagues and in an inter-college knock-out competition known as Cuppers, and up to 10 or 12 rowing eights, who compete in "Torpids" in winter and in "Eights" in summer, where the winning college is proclaimed "Head of the River". Oriel College has a remarkable rowing record, having been head of the river for 17 of the past 18 years.

But not all Oxford sport is taken so seriously. Brasenose College won Tortoise-racing Cuppers in 1989, their champion tortoise "Addington" beating Balliol's reigning queen "Rosa Luxemburg" by "inches". There are also Cuppers matches in Korfball, American Football, Croquet, Eton Fives,

by those which see balls as elitist. But are they? Yes, the balls *are* extravagant: dress is black tie and dinner jacket for men, brightly coloured ballgown for women—and the revellers enjoy a combination of dancing, drinking and mild debauchery until the obligatory 6 a.m. champagne breakfast. And yes, they *are* expensive: the equivalent of an average week's wages for a double dining ticket, and anachronistically priced in guineas (£1.05) rather than pounds. And yet, the vast majority of Oxford students go to at least one ball during their time at the University, considering them a harmless excuse for dressing-up and having a good time.

Sailing and Orienteering, among others. Perhaps all that cycling gives Oxford students a sporting disposition.

The social life: Predictably, Oxford students do most of their socialising at pubs and parties. But for a few weeks every summer they indulge in the unashamed opulence and extravagance of the summer balls. Some colleges have a ball every year, some bi-annually, and the bigger ones every three years. These are known as "Commemoration Balls" and are the most prestigious—and expensive. There are also minor balls and Events, held by the smaller colleges, or

The summer is generally the most active social season, as it brings students out on to the river to go punting, and out on to the streets to raise money for charity during Rag Week. But long gone are the extravagances of the 1930s when the "gilded youth" of Britain's great families supposedly squandered fortunes in a day and flitted from lunch party to cocktail party to dinner party.

Private dining societies with names like the Disraeli Society and the Russell Club still exist, but today's social scene tends to reflect the wider social mix of the Oxford of the 1990s. Parties are generally unpretentious and alcoholic—they are also becoming more infrequent as increased academic pressure takes its toll. However, Oxford is still alive on Friday and Saturday evenings with groups of students leaving their favourite pubs (the King's Arms, the Turf, the Bear or the White Horse) and heading for a party, easily recognisable by the alcoholic offering each clutches under his arm—today's party invitations invariably include the magic words "Please Bring A Bottle".

Students and the town: The relationship between the University and the city of Oxford has historically been one of hostility and mutual suspicion. This "Town versus

Turf are probably the most "studenty" pubs, while the Westgate and the Roebuck are still more or less "no-go areas" for students, especially at the weekend.

However, violent clashes are quite rare—except in Cowley. Because of its cheap housing, Cowley is very popular with students, but they do not always mix too well with the locals. Known to students as "The People's Republic of Cowley", the area's population includes many Caribbean and Indian immigrants, along with a large "alternative" or counter-cultural community.

But there are some institutions whose status doesn't quite fit the Town/Gown

Gown" rivalry has been the cause of many deaths in the course of Oxford's turbulent past, but nowadays is restricted to sports matches between university and city teams and the occasional scuffle outside a pub on a Friday night.

In some ways Oxford is two cities, with certain shops and pubs never visited by students because they are "too townie", and others shunned by locals on the grounds that they are "full of students". The Bear and the

Left, formal dinner in a college. **Above**, informal lunch at an Oxford pub.

stereotype. Principal among these are the numerous secretarial and tutorial colleges, which find it easy to attract both students and teachers because of the proximity of the University. Students at secretarial colleges are universally known to students as "seccies" and are often (perhaps unfairly) accused of coming to Oxford more to find an eligible bachelor than to learn to type. In the summer, many students make a little extra money by teaching at language schools or giving guided tours to tourists. This is generally considered to be the lowest known form of paid employment.

COLLEGES: THE GOOD, THE BAD AND THE UGLY

ALL SOULS
Founded: 1437
Number of students: Varies,
graduate students only.

All Souls is the only Oxford college never to have accepted undergraduate students. It stands on the High Street but can also be reached from Radcliffe Square, from where its famous twin towers are best viewed. The Front Quad has remained virtually unchanged since the college's foundation, as has the chapel, and the college boasts a sundial designed by Christopher Wren, a former All Souls bursar. To be elected a Fellow of All Souls is perhaps the highest academic honour in the University.

BALLIOL
Founded: 1263
Number of students: 350
Alumni: Harold Macmillan, Graham Greene, H.H. Asquith, Hilaire Belloc, Edward Heath, Roy Jenkins, Aldous Huxley, Denis Healey.

Occupying a huge area between Broad Street and Magdalen Street, Balliol is one of the oldest, biggest, wealthiest and most prestigious colleges in the University. Balliol's academic reputation is second to none, and its students tend to be dynamic and successful, both at Oxford and in public life. The great scholars Wycliffe and Jowett are associated with Balliol, as is Adam Smith.

The college has a strong political tradition, and went through an especially radical phase in the 1960s. Formal Hall, the saying of Grace and the wearing of gowns have all been abolished. It was also one of the first colleges to begin accepting large numbers of non public school-educated and overseas students, fostering a cosmopolitan atmosphere. The architecture is serious and uninspired, but the place buzzes with activity.

BRASENOSE
Founded: 1509
Number of students: 330
Alumni: Jeffrey Archer, John Buchan, Colin Cowdrey, William Golding, Michael Palin, Robert Runcie.

Situated right in the centre of the city, the college tends to be overshadowed by the surrounding splendour of the Bodleian and Radcliffe Camera libraries, though the Old Quadrangle is noted for its colourful sundial. Historically "middle-of-the-road", Brasenose has built up a reasonable reputation both for sport—mostly rowing—and on the academic side it is especially strong in Law. It acquired its name from a rather unusual door-knocker ("brazen nose") which now hangs in the hall.

CHRIST CHURCH
Founded: 1546
Number of students: 540
Alumni: Sir Robert Peel, William Ewart Gladstone, Anthony Eden, Lord Hailsham, Auberon Waugh, W.H. Auden.

Originally founded in 1525 by Cardinal Wolsey and re-founded by Henry VIII in 1546, "The House" is Oxford's largest and best-known college. It is the one college *every* tourist visits, if only to be shouted at by the bowler-hatted "Bulldogs" on duty there. The grandiose architecture is imposing to the point of being intimidating, especially Tom Quad, with its famous tower and fountain—and the college even has its own cathedral and picture gallery. For many years the cradle of the British aristocracy, Christ Church still produces its fair share of bishops and MPs, though there is a slightly wider social mix at the college today. It remains one of the top colleges both academically and in sport, despite not trying very hard at either.

CORPUS CHRISTI
Founded: 1517
Number of students: 200
Alumni: Sir Isaiah Berlin, William Waldegrave, Matthew Arnold, John Ruskin, Lord Beloff.

Sandwiched between Christ Church and Merton, Corpus is the smallest college but boasts a main quad which is among the most beautiful in Oxford—its most notable feature being the famous Pelican Sundial. In 1989 Corpus topped the "Norrington Table", the unofficial academic ranking of the colleges. Academic standards have traditionally been very high, but the college is also known for its tolerance and friendliness. It is the home of the annual tortoise races, the slowest spectator sport in the University.

EXETER
Founded: 1314
Number of students: 300
Alumni: Richard Burton, J.R.R. Tolkien, Sir Roger Bannister, Tariq Ali, Alan Bennett, Ned Sherrin, Russell Harty, William Morris.

One of the three Turl Street colleges, Exeter is an architectural mish-mash of styles, as bits were added on over the centuries. The Victorian chapel tends to look especially odd as only its tall spire is visible from the street, the rest being hidden inside the college. Exeter has historical links with the West Country, and has traditionally been an unpretentious, slightly unremarkable college.

HERTFORD
Founded: 1740
Number of students: 330
Alumni: Evelyn Waugh, Jonathan Swift, John Donne, Charles James Fox.

A hall for students known as Hart Hall was established as long ago as the year 1282, but the college has had a chequered history and has been plagued by financial problems, which remain to this day. Its most remarkable feature is the famous Bridge of Sighs (not the one in Venice), which connects the two halves of the college. This attracts hordes of tourists, partly because of its proximity to the Bodleian.

JESUS
Founded: 1571
Number of students: 300
Alumni: Harold Wilson, T.E. Lawrence (of Arabia).

Jesus was founded by Queen Elizabeth I, but much of the money behind the foundation was provided by a Welshman named Hugh Price, and the college retains very strong links with Wales. The joke is that if you run into the college and shout "Jones!" a hundred people will stick their heads out of their windows. Architecturally the least interesting of the Turl Street colleges, Jesus has fallen over backwards to keep a low profile over the years—except in 1974, when it became the first of the previously all-male colleges to admit women.

KEBLE
Founded: 1870
Number of students: 400
Alumni: Imran Khan, Andreas Whittam-Smith, Sir David Wilson.

Keble was originally founded with the intention of making an Oxford education more accessible to people from different social backgrounds. Links with the Church (John Keble was a leading figure of the High Church Oxford Movement) ensure the college retains a strong social conscience. Keble's buildings have aroused enormous controversy. The main quad is a neo-Gothic palace of red-and-white chequered bricks, with the appearance of a Victorian mental institution. Other quads are all-modern glass and steel—the notorious bar often being compared to a space ship in design.

Local rival St John's College boasts a "Demolish Keble Society", the membership requirement of which is to bring along a brick removed from Keble to your first meeting. It is a dynamic college, traditionally active in sport and politics (both Left and Right), with academic achievement especially strong in the sciences.

LADY MARGARET HALL
Founded: 1878
Number of students: 350
Alumni: Antonia Fraser, Benazir Bhutto.

Its out-of-town location and beautiful gardens make this college idyllic in summer, though it does look like a prison from the front. LMH was the first "academic hall" for women at Oxford—it became a full college only in 1960 and went mixed in 1978. It is known for its tolerance and unpretentiousness – though it was recently radical enough to stage an anti-pornography protest.

LINCOLN
Founded: 1427
Number of students: 250
Alumni: John Le Carré, John Wesley.

One of the most beautiful sights in Oxford is the view up Turl Street towards All Saints' Church (now Lincoln College library). The college itself is rather small, but picturesque. It was originally founded as a "small college" in order to create a friendly, cosy atmosphere—a tradition which is strongly adhered to. Lincoln enjoys long-standing rivalry with the other Turl Street colleges, Exeter and Jesus.

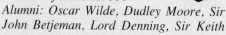

MAGDALEN
Founded: 1458
Number of students: 350
Alumni: Oscar Wilde, Dudley Moore, Sir John Betjeman, Lord Denning, Sir Keith Joseph, Desmond Morris, Cardinal Wolsey, Edward VIII.

Pronounced "*Maudlin*", Magdalen's academic traditions are as fine as its beautiful romantic buildings. They include the tower overlooking Magdalen Bridge from which the choir sings on May Morning, built in the 1490s, Cloister Quad and the Regency New Buildings. The gardens are as impressive as the buildings, with over a mile of riverside walks and the famous Deer Park. Magdalen probably captures the spirit of Evelyn Waugh's *Brideshead Revisited* more than any other college, and was for long the favourite choice for the sons of the upper classes. Traditionally weak in sport, the college's strength lies in the arts, and its members have always been among the most social and outgoing of Oxford students.

MANSFIELD
Founded: 1886
Number of students: 135
Alumni: C.H. Dodd, Nathaniel Micklem.

Originally a Congregationalist theological college, Mansfield has the advantage of beautiful and tranquil surroundings in a fairly central location off Holywell Street. The college is historically short of cash, and strong in the arts. In undergraduate life, it contributes more than its fair share to journalism, and its Women's Group has been notably active.

MERTON
Founded: 1264
Number of students: 250
Alumni: John Wycliffe, T.S. Eliot, Kris Kristofferson, Robert Morley, Jeremy Isaacs, Frank Bough.

Merton boasts the oldest quad in the University, large and beautiful gardens and a fine academic pedigree. From the cobblestones of Merton Street to the medieval library in Mob Quad to the old city wall which borders the garden, the eye is constantly delighted by this college. It is noted for high academic standards and a lively, outgoing collection of undergraduates.

NEW

Founded: 1379
Number of students: 380
Alumni: Tony Benn, John Galsworthy, Lord Longford, John Fowles, Richard Crossman, Hugh Gaitskell.

New College looks anything but new. In fact, it's one of the oldest colleges in the University, and many of the buildings, including the front quad, dining hall, chapel and cloisters, have survived from the original foundation and look positively medieval. The college has a kind of austere beauty—certainly one cannot fail to be impressed by its size and sheer solidity. It's a prestigious and well-known college, with links to the Civil Service and Winchester (it was founded by William of Wykeham). Strong in both sport (especially rowing) and academia, New is currently considered to be one of the main social centres of university life.

ORIEL

Founded: 1326
Number of students: 275
Alumni: Cecil Rhodes, Sir Walter Raleigh, Cardinal Newman, Beau Brummell, John Keble.

The Oriel rowing tradition is one of the strongest traditions in Oxford. The college has consistently dominated the river, especially in the past 20 years, and was the last college to remain all-male, admitting women only in 1985. The film *Oxford Blues* is considered an accurate portrayal of the college: hearty, traditional and not overly academic. However, things are beginning to change now that the women have arrived. Oriel Square is a fantastically picturesque place, and is probably the most-filmed location in Oxford.

PEMBROKE

Founded: 1624
Number of students: 310
Alumni: Michael Heseltine, Samuel Johnson, William Fulbright.

A middle-of-the-road college, tucked away behind Carfax, which suffers from being directly opposite Christ Church. Equally undistinguished in both sport and academia, Pembroke has the doubtful accolade of being the finest darts-playing college in the university. Architecturally as unremarkable as its undergraduates.

QUEEN'S

Founded: 1341
Number of students: 300
Alumni: Rowan Atkinson, Brian Walden, Edmund Halley.

Queen's takes its name from Philippa, wife of Edward III, whose chaplain Robert Eglesfeld founded the college. But the statue above the main gate, overlooking the High Street, is of Queen Caroline, wife of George II, who in the mid-18th century funded the building of its two unusual and impressive quads. The college has links with the north of England and is traditionally a sporting college, being especially strong in rugby (with appropriate beer cellar).

ST ANNE'S

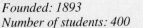

Founded: 1893
Number of students: 400
Alumni: Edwina Currie, Baroness Young, Naomi Mitchison, Dame Cicely Saunders.

This former women's college looks like part of the Polytechnic and many of its students certainly behave like Poly students. Even so, it has developed a fearsome rugby-playing reputation, providing more than half of a recent Blues team. One of Oxford's more "unpretentious" colleges, St Anne's does its bit for student drama and journalism.

ST CATHERINE'S

Founded: 1963
Number of students: 450
Alumni: Eric Partridge, David Hemery, J. Paul Getty.

Oxford's newest college is an architectural masterpiece or a sprawling modern monstrosity, depending on your point of view. Designed by Danish architect Arne Jacobsen and situated out of town by the River Cherwell, it is very pleasant in summer. "Catz" has yet to perform a feat remarkable enough to attract the attention of the rest of the University. But the liberal establishment of the college (for example, Catz has no chapel) makes it popular with students.

ST EDMUND HALL
Founded: c.1278
Number of students: 350
Alumni: Terry Jones, Sir Robin Day.

"Teddy Hall" is a compact college just off the High Street, whose buildings are an interesting combination of a typical 17th-century front quad and several 1970s tower blocks. It has always been famous for sport, especially rugby—the college won Rugby Cuppers for nine successive years in the 1980s. The college has an extraordinary library with a tall book-lined tower: it is in a converted church and students have to cross a graveyard to get to it.

ST HILDA'S
Founded: 1893
Number of students: 350
Alumnae: Barbara Pym, Hermione Lee.

Situated just over Magdalen Bridge, St Hilda's lies on the banks of the River Cherwell, with superb views over Christ Church Meadows. It is one of the only two all-women colleges, but "Hildabeasts" are anything but cloistered, and are known for their active participation in university life. However, its continued single-sex status may have contributed to a decline in academic standards. The buildings are not ugly—even the modern ones.

ST HUGH'S
Founded: 1886
Number of students: 400
Alumni: Barbara Castle, Brigid Brophy.

St Hugh's is a former women's college

which went mixed in 1987. It is sited far out in North Oxford, on the extreme edge of the university area, so St Hugh's students are noted cyclists. The college grounds are said to be quite pleasant, but no one except St Hugh's students have actually seen them.

ST JOHN'S
Founded: 1555
Number of students: 350
Alumni: Robert Graves, Kingsley Amis, Philip Larkin, A.E. Housman, Dean Rusk.

It is sometimes said that you can walk all the way from Oxford to Cambridge on land owned by St John's. It is the richest Oxford college, and is said to own a fair chunk of Switzerland as well as large tracts of London's West End. The college's extreme wealth means glorious buildings and luxurious accommodation for the students (there are rumours of jacuzzis). A new block—"a fish tank on stilts"—lets things down. Situated on St Giles (which it also owns), St John's has traditionally been the most academically successful college, consistently topping the "Norrington Table", the unofficial academic standings.

ST PETER'S
Founded: 1929
Number of students: 280
Alumni: Edward Akufo Addo.

St Peter's has long been considered a backwater of Oxford. Situated next to Oxford Prison, rooted firmly to the bottom of the Norrington Table, it was mostly noted for the great ugliness of its buildings and the beer-drinking exploits of its students. However, this picture is no longer so accurate nowadays, according to those who have dared enter.

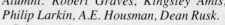

SOMERVILLE
Founded: 1879
Number of students: 350
Alumnae: Indira Gandhi, Shirley Williams,

Margaret Thatcher, Dorothy L. Sayers, Iris Murdoch, Esther Rantzen.

Mrs Margaret Thatcher's old college is not overly proud of its most illustrious graduate—in 1989 a bust of the Supreme Leader had to be taken off display and stored in a broom cupboard after being repeatedly daubed with graffiti. The college site up the Woodstock Road is grassy and pleasant, its members sociable, outward-looking and very dominant in most of the University's women's sports. It is, of course, an all-women college and its denizens like to point out that "Somerville girls can take care of themselves". Given their alumnae, who could doubt it?

TRINITY
Founded: 1554
Number of students: 250
Alumni: William Pitt the Elder, Jeremy Thorpe, Terence Rattigan, Anthony Crosland, Miles Kingston.

Trinity is a must-see. The path from the wrought-iron gates on Broad Street through the beautiful college buildings to the spectacular gardens is a pilgrimage for every tourist. Generations of Trinity students have spent their summers playing croquet or just relaxing on the lawn, with the result that, despite its long history, the college has never really distinguished itself. It is, however, a great place for a picnic.

UNIVERSITY
Founded: 1249
Number of students: 370
Alumni: Willie Rushton, Clement Attlee, Richard Ingrams, Percy Bysshe Shelley.

The college is reputed to have been founded by King Alfred the Great in the year 812, but this remains disputed—as does the existence of the college ghost, that of one Obadiah Walker, a former Master of the college. What is certain is that "Univ" was the first Oxford college to be founded, and has never ceased to set high standards for its students, whether in the library or on the

games field. The college has a particularly strong reputation in the sciences, and Univites have always been very active in university life—perhaps in order to escape the architecture of their own college, which has been likened by some to an Alcatraz on the High Street.

WADHAM
Founded: 1610
Number of students: 375
Alumni: Melvyn Bragg, Michael Foot, Sir Christopher Wren, Michael Checkland.

The self-styled "People's Republic of Wadham" has always been a centre for radical thought. In the early days of its foundation it was the meeting place for the leading figures of the Scientific Revolution, who went on to form the Royal Society. Today it is known as a left-wing college, the majority of students entering the public sector after graduating. The Parks Road college has a long tradition of political activism—it is the only college to have its own Student Union rather than a Junior Common Room. The college buildings are attractive, especially the original front quad, but the notoriously trendy Wadhamites are more likely to be found in the neighbouring King's Arms than in their own college.

WORCESTER
Founded: 1714
Number of students: 340
Alumni: Richard Adams, Sir Alastair Burnett, Rupert Murdoch.

Secluded Worcester is set in 26 acres (10 hectares) of grounds on the western edge of the university area. It stands on the site of the former Gloucester Hall, a Benedictine foundation of 1283 which was dissolved at the suppression of the monasteries. The college's front quad isn't really a quad at all—the money ran out after only three sides had been finished. However, Worcester is the only Oxford college to possess its own lake—complete with ducks. Its students are consequently a relaxed bunch.

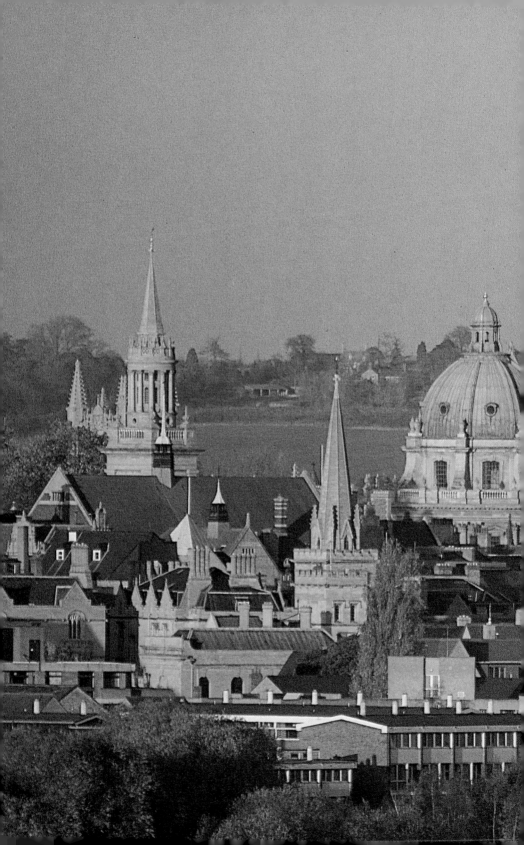

What, precisely, gives Oxford its special appeal? In 1856 the American writer Nathaniel Hawthorne, in his *English Note-Books*, put forward an appealing theory: "The quality of the stone has a great deal to do with the apparent antiquity. It is a stone found in the neighbourhood of Oxford, and very soon begins to crumble and decay superficially, when exposed to the weather; so that twenty years do the work of a hundred, so far as appearances go. If you strike one of the old walls with a stick, a portion of it comes powdering down. The effect of this decay is very picturesque."

Despite the subsequent destructive emissions of the internal combustion engine, Oxford's walls have yet to fall down. But the city retains its allure, seldom better expressed than by another 19th-century American writer, Henry James: "I walked along, thro' the lovely Christ Church meadow, by the river side and back through the town. It was a perfect evening and in the interminable British twilight the beauty of the whole place came forth with magical power. There are no words for these colleges. As I stood last evening within the precincts of mighty Magdalen, gazed at its great serene tower and uncapped my throbbing brow in the wild dimness of its courts, I thought that the heart of me would crack with the fulness of satisfied desire."

The setting is equally magical. Oxford is not a large town and you don't need to climb far up one of the dreaming spires in order to spy the green countryside which encircles it. Beyond the town centre traffic-jams and the undistinguished suburbs, the Cotswolds beckon, their showpiece villages appearing to grow out of the earth, so perfect is their relationship with the landscape. For some, Stratford-upon-Avon will be a place of essential pilgrimage. For others, the sleepy Thames-side towns will hold more attractions.

Oxford provides a convenient base for exploring this rich part of England – that is, if you can drag yourself away from the dreaming spires. As Nathaniel Hawthorne put it: "The world, surely, has not another place like Oxford; it is a despair to see such a place and ever to leave it."

Preceding pages: the dreaming spires; graduation day at Queen's College; a familiar figure in cosmopolitan Oxford. **Left,** serious studies.

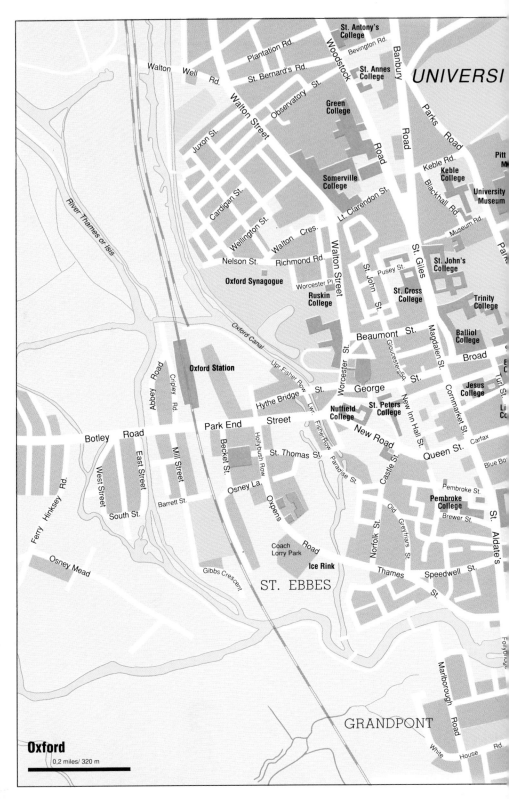

Oxford

0,2 miles/ 320 m

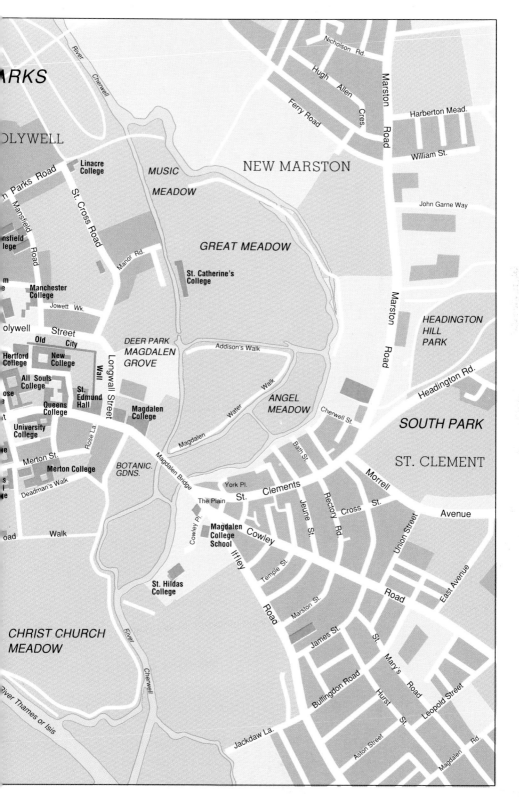

ARKS

OLYWELL

Linacre
College

MUSIC

MEADOW

NEW MARSTON

Nicholson Rd.

Hugh Allen Cres.

Ferry Road

Marston Road

Harberton Mead.

William St.

John Garne Way

n Parks Road

St. Cross Road

Mansfield Road

nsfield
lege

m
e

Manchester
College

Jowett Wk.

olywell Street

Old City

Hertford College

New College

All Souls
College

ose
e

St. Edmund Hall

Queens
College

University
College

Merton St.

Merton College

Deadman's Walk

GREAT MEADOW

Manor Rd.

St. Catherine's
College

DEER PARK
MAGDALEN
GROVE

Longwall Street
Wall

Magdalen
College

Rose La.

BOTANIC.
GDNS.

Addison's Walk

Walk

Water

ANGEL
MEADOW

Cherwell St.

HEADINGTON
HILL
PARK

Headington Rd.

SOUTH PARK

ST. CLEMENT

Bath St.

Morrell

Avenue

Union Street

Magdalen

Magdalen Bridge

York Pl.

The Plain

St. Clements

Jeune St.

Rectory Rd.

Cross St.

we
s
we

oad

Walk

Cowley Pl.

Magdalen
College
School

Cowley

Iffley

Temple St.

Marston St.

Road

St. Mary's Road

East Avenue

St. Hildas
College

CHRIST CHURCH
MEADOW

River Thames or Isis

River

Cherwell

James St.

Bullingdon Road

Jackdaw La.

Aston Street

Hurst St.

Leopold Street

Magdalen Rd.

River Cherwell

THE UNIVERSITY

A precious and rather feeble Oxford joke is sometimes told about the American tourist who stops an undergraduate in the High Street and asks to be directed to the University. At this point, those in the know are supposed to chuckle over their port for—"as every educated person is aware"—Oxford does not have a central university campus. Like Cambridge (known to Oxford people as "the other place"), these two ancient universities differ from others in Britain in that they constitute a federation of independent colleges.

And yet, if our American tourist had stopped a helpful student instead of an insufferable prig, he would have been pointed down Broad Street, to the heart of Oxford, where there is an impressive group of buildings that might loosely be termed "the University"—in the sense that they provide central facilities for all college members.

Heads of stone: As one walks eastwards, down **Broad Street**, the eye is drawn to the curious set of railings, jutting out into the road, that separate "the town" from the realm of ceremony and scholarship. Towering above the railings is a series of 13 outsize stone busts, known as the **Emperors' Heads**. They follow the curve of the apsidal end of the Sheldonian Theatre, and were put up in 1669, the same year that the Theatre was completed.

Armless busts like these have been used to surmount gateposts since antiquity, and are called "terms", from the Latin *terminus*, a boundary, or "herms" if they represent Hermes, the messenger of the gods. Nobody knows what these splendid giants represent. Max Beerbohm, in his Oxford-based novel *Zuleika Dobson*, wrote that "they are, by American visitors, frequently mistaken for the Twelve Apostles"—making yet another dig at the poor, untutored tourist from the New World. He

also calls them "the faceless Caesars", and perhaps from that developed the current nickname, the Emperors.

Faceless they were until recently; the original terms were replaced in 1868 but in such poor quality stone that time and the weather had reduced their features to what John Betjeman called "illustrations in a medical textbook on skin diseases". Then, in 1970, and despite Henry Moore's objection that the eroded heads had their own awesome power, the Oxford sculptor Michael Black was commissioned to carve new heads. Having completed the work in 1972, and after exhaustive research into the form of the original heads, Michael Black added his own theory, that the 13 represent the history of fashions in beards.

In any event, the Sheldonian terms make an impressive approach to the buildings beyond, starting with the **Sheldonian Theatre**. This was commissioned by Gilbert Sheldon, Chancellor (or honorary head) of the Univer-

Left, doorway to the Divinity School. Right, after Encaenia, the degree-conferring ceremony.

sity, in 1662. Sheldon chose, as his architect, the young Christopher Wren. Wren, who was then 30, had been appointed Professor of Astronomy the previous year and was regarded as one of the most brilliant mathematicians of his day. He had not yet, however, designed any buildings, and the Sheldonian Theatre was the first commission that launched him on an architectural career. It is fashionable among art historians to describe the Theatre as the work of a young amateur. Most of us would give this exuberant building, with its rich honey-gold coloured stone, far higher praise. It was also revolutionary in its time, for Wren rejected the popular Gothic-Jacobean style and chose instead to follow classical antecedents.

Wren modelled the Sheldonian on the antique open-air Theatre of Marcellus, in Rome. The English weather made it necessary to roof the Theatre and Wren devised an ingenious timber structure (since replaced) that dispensed with pillars and allowed all 2,000 spectators an uninterrupted view of the proceedings. In place of the open sky, Robert Streeter was commissioned, in 1669, to paint the ceiling with a depiction of the *Triumph of Religion, Arts and Science over Envy, Hate and Malice*.

The Theatre was built for university ceremonials, rather than for stage drama, and is still used for this purpose, as well as for concerts and lectures. Here successful students receive their degrees and, at the "Encaenia" ceremony in June, scarlet-gowned dons meet to honour the university founders and bestow honorary degrees upon the worthy and famous.

At other times of the year the Theatre is open to the public and well worth visiting for the original woodwork of the Chancellor's throne and the two Orators' pulpits—but most of all for the fine views over the heart of Oxford from the rooftop cupola.

The building to the right (east) of the Sheldonian is the **Old Ashmolean Museum**, built between 1678 and 1683 to

Student propulsion.

The University

0,1 miles/ 160 m

house the "cabinet of natural curiosities" inherited by Elias Ashmole from the Tradescants. Designed, perhaps, by Thomas Wood, the master mason who supervised its building, it picks up motifs and ideas from Wren's building alongside, and is equally ornate.

The contents of the museum were transferred to the newly built Ashmolean in Beaumont Street in the late 19th century and the building now houses a **Museum of the History of Science**, a comprehensive but little visited collection of early instruments. The museum may at first seem daunting, with its cases packed with complex astrolabes, quadrants, armillary spheres and clockwork models of the planetary system, but there is much to enjoy, even for the non-scientist.

The ground floor, for example, has a collection of very early photographs, dating to the experimental period of the 1840s; they include one of John Ruskin's views of Venice, used as reference material by the artist for his own hand-drawn illustrations for his pioneering work on Renaissance architecture, *The Stones of Venice*. There are some novelties among the serious exhibits: George III's ornate silver microscope and an extraordinarily elaborate machine turning handwriting into minuscule engravings on glass, so small that the result can only be seen under a microscope.

In the former chemistry laboratory in the basement, a blackboard covered with Einstein's neatly chalked theorems is carefully preserved, a memento of his first Oxford lecture on the theory of relativity, given on 16 May 1931. It is partnered by an odd assortment of gruesome medical and dental instruments, early radios, gramophones and phonographs, and a display on the war-time work of Oxford scientists racing against time to prepare penicillin (discovered by Alexander Fleming in 1928) for large-scale production, using improvised materials such as milk churns, tin baths and animal feed containers.

The degree ceremony moved in 1669 from St Mary's into the secular Sheldonian.

Early publishing: On the other side of the Sheldonian is the **Clarendon Building**, created to provide the first permanent home for Oxford University Press. Originally, the Press occupied odd rooms in the Sheldonian Theatre, an inconvenient arrangement.

Between 1702 and 1704 the Press published the Earl of Clarendon's account of the English Civil War, and this three-volume *History of the Great Rebellion* proved to be a best-seller. Despite the fact that some of the profits were embezzled by the University Vice-Chancellor, sales of Clarendon's work were sufficient to provide the Press with a new home next door.

The Clarendon, a rather severe classical building, was designed by Nicholas Hawksmoor, Christopher Wren's brilliant pupil, and completed in 1715. The Earl of Clarendon himself occupies a niche on the west wall, where he gesticulates proudly at the building he paid for. Around the roofline are gracious figures, by James Thornhill, of the nine

Muses (1717); seven are cast in lead but two are fibre-glass replicas, made in 1974 to replace the originals that had blown down.

The Press moved out of the Clarendon Building in 1830 and the space vacated by the compositors and printers is now filled by part of the Bodleian Library's vast collection of books. As a copyright library, the Bodleian is entitled to a free copy of every book and journal published in the UK. Even by being selective in what it accepts, the Bodleian is expanding at a record pace, and is running out of space for a collection that already occupies over 80 miles (130 km) of shelving.

In 1939, the **New Bodleian** was completed to take some of the overspill. This fortress-like building opposite the Clarendon, on the corner of Broad Street and Parks Road, has three floors of underground storage beneath Blackwell's bookshop. A conveyor belt beneath Broad Street links the new library to the old.

The original Bodleian lies south of the Clarendon Building, in **Old Schools Quadrangle**. Stepping into this stone-paved quad, you leave behind the noise and bustle of Oxford and enter an enclosed courtyard with an atmosphere of calm and sobriety. Discreet signs request silence, and one suspects that bowler-hatted Bulldogs (the University's four-man police squad) might leap from the shadowy doorways and admonish anyone churlish enough to disobey. Above these doorways, painted in letters of gold, are the names of the original schools, or faculties, of the University. The complex was designed to provide lecture rooms on the lower floors, and library space above.

Three sides of the quad are regular in composition, built in the Gothic-Jacobean style that characterises many Oxford buildings of the early 17th century. James I was on the throne when the building was completed in 1624, and the monarch sits in a niche between allegorical figures representing Fame

Oh for a muse... this is the Clarendon Building's.

and the University, in the gate-tower at the east end. This splendidly carved work is called the **Tower of the Five Orders** because it is ornamented with columns and capitals of each of the five orders of classical architecture—Doric, Tuscan, Ionic, Corinthian and Composite—in ascending order.

Opposite, on the west side, a 17th-century statue by Le Sueur of the Earl of Pembroke, a former Chancellor of the University, stands guard outside the entrance to the **Divinity School** and the **Bodleian Library**. The Divinity School predates the rest of the quadrangle by two centuries. It was begun in 1420 and proceeded, fitfully, as funds permitted, over the next 70 years. The facade, covered in panel tracery, is considerably more ornate than the rest of Old Schools Quad—appropriately enough, since Divinity, or theology, was the principal subject at Oxford until well into the 19th century and the subject for which all other studies were merely a preparation.

Beyond the entrance door is a small vestibule, and then the magnificent vaulted Divinity School proper, regarded by many as Oxford's finest interior. The stone ceiling, completed in 1488, resembles a fan vault, and at each rib intersection there is a rounded protuberance, carved with Biblical subjects, real and mythical beasts, and the coats of arms of university benefactors. It was beneath this gorgeous ceiling that the Oxford Martyrs—Cranmer, Ridley and Latimer—were cross-examined on their religious beliefs in 1554, then condemned as Protestant heretics.

Until recently, the Divinity School was used to display rare manuscripts from the Bodleian collection. Now it is empty, except for an iron-bound chest, with its elaborate lock mechanism, that once belonged to Thomas Bodley, the library's founder. The chest is used to collect donations towards a £10 million appeal for vital restoration work that will eventually allow books back on display in a temperature and humidity-

The Sheldonian Theatre and the Clarendon Building.

controlled environment. In the mean-time, there is a small display of exhibits, ranging from early copies of Chaucer's *The Canterbury Tales* to Victorian playbills, in the School of Natural Philosophy, on the south side of Old Schools Quad.

The oldest part of the Bodleian Library lies above the Divinity School and can be visited by signing up for a guided tour, in the vestibule. The highlight of the tour is **"Duke Humfrey"**, the central reading room in which precious, leather-bound books are stored in early 17th-century bookcases beneath an elaborate ceiling decorated with coats of arms. Humfrey, Duke of Gloucester and younger brother of Henry V, was an important benefactor whose collection of manuscripts, given in the 1440s, formed the core of the earliest library. Thomas Bodley, however, gave his name to the Bodleian because he rescued it from "ruin and waste", paid for its refurbishment and assembled a new collection of 2,000 books.

This new library opened officially in 1602 and soon needed more space. The extension, known as the "Arts End", was completed in 1612, and the "Selden End", named after John Selden, who gave 8,000 volumes to the library, was added around 1650, both with beautiful panelled and painted ceilings. Sometimes visitors are also shown the top floor of the library, with its painted frieze of 200 famous men, executed in around 1620 and only rediscovered in the 1960s.

You will find many more heads (binoculars are essential to appreciate them fully) carved in stone all around the battlement line of Old Schools Quad—grotesques and demons, angels and men, all convincingly medieval in appearance but, in fact, the inspired work of masons who restored these buildings in the 1950s. At ground-floor level as you pass through the passageway between the Schools of Music and Natural Philosophy, look for the portraits of two recent Librarians, carved into the stone.

Emerging the other side, the splendid sight of **Radcliffe Camera**, rising from a perfect green lawn, meets the eye. "Camera" simply means chamber, and John Radcliffe was the physician who, despite his renowned ill temper, made a huge fortune by treating the wealthy—including the monarch, William III. Radcliffe Camera was built after his death in 1714 to house a library devoted to the sciences—just one of the Oxford projects that was funded from his estate.

The gracious round form of the Camera was suggested by Nicholas Hawksmoor, but it was another great 18th-century architect, James Gibbs, who was asked to produce the detailed designs, and the building (not open) was completed in 1748.

Hawksmoor did, however, get his fair share of Oxford commissions, including the great North Quad of **All Souls College**, to the left (east) of Radcliffe Camera. This college, founded in 1438, is unique because it does not admit

Statue of the Earl of Pembroke in the quadrangle of the Bodleian.

either graduate or undergraduate students. Instead, it retains the medieval tradition of restricting membership to Fellows, and there are several means of entry: distinguished scholars from all over the world may be elected as visiting Fellows, while others sit a highly competitive examination. The system is, in theory, designed to provide facilities for the brightest and best minds to pursue their research, but it has not always been so, and in the 16th century fellowships were bought and sold, and the college was notorious for the drunkenness and corruption of its members.

A century or so later, the winds of reform were sweeping through the college and, as if in a symbolic break with the past, the medieval cloister was cleared away, and new accommodation planned. Then, in 1710, before the work began, Christopher Codrington, a Fellow and Governor of the Leeward Islands, died, leaving much of his sugar-wealth to the college, and a large collection of books. Thus the building plans

were changed, and Hawksmoor designed the grand library block and the imposing twin towers of the east side of the North Quad.

The **Codrington Library** is an ingenious piece of work; outside it is all Gothic, designed to match the existing college chapel, while the interior is fully classical—even the windows are Venetian within but with lancets and tracery on the outside. The sundial on the library wall, moved from the chapel, is renowned for its accuracy; Christopher Wren is reputed to be the designer.

The chapel is essentially 15th-century, with its original hammerbeam roof, carved with gilded angels, and misericords, which include depictions of a mermaid and a man playing the bagpipes. The floor to ceiling reredos, behind the altar, is a *tour de force*, although the statues are all replacements, installed in 1870, for the originals that were smashed by Puritan iconoclasts. The surviving 15th-century niches were once brightly painted

The Radcliffe Camera in winter.

and even now a few retain traces of the original pigment.

Returning to Radcliffe Square, the huge church of **St Mary the Virgin** closes in the south side, fronting on to the High Street. St Mary's is also considered to be part of the University—indeed, before the Sheldonian, the Bodleian and the Old Schools were built, this church was the centre of university ceremony and administration. St Mary's also housed the university library, and the side chapels were used as lecture theatres.

Now, instead of disputatious students sharpening their wits in learned debate, the church is often full of visitors queuing to climb the 188-ft (62-metre) spire-topped tower, which dates to the late 13th and early 14th centuries.

The rest of the church was rebuilt in Perpendicular style in the early 16th century and is really rather dull, except for the eccentric south porch, added in 1637 and designed by Nicholas Stone. Fat barley-sugar columns support the curvaceous pediment and angels surround the central niche containing a statue of the Virgin and Child. Perhaps the Virgin's rather startled look is a legacy of the English Civil War, for her head was shot off by a soldier in 1642—but replaced 20 years later.

Inside the church, the pillar opposite the pulpit in the north side of the nave has been cut away; this was done to build a platform for the final trial of Thomas Cranmer, Archbishop of Canterbury, in 1556. His fellow martyrs, Nicholas Ridley, Bishop of London, and Hugh Latimer, Bishop of Worcester, had both been executed at the stake the previous year for their support for the Protestant Reformation. Cranmer, however, was given leave to appeal against his sentence, and signed several statements recanting his earlier beliefs. This was not sufficient for his accusers, the Pope's commissioners and the zealous supporters of the Catholic Queen Mary. Cranmer was brought to St Mary's to make a public statement of his errors; but he refused to do so, and instead repudiated his former recantations. Like Ridley and Latimer before him, he went to the stake.

Nearly three centuries later, St Mary's was again at the centre of religious controversy: in 1833 John Keble preached his famous sermon here, which led to the foundation of the Anglo-Catholic Oxford Movement. John Henry Newman, Vicar of St Mary's at the time and a leading supporter of the Movement, brought down a storm of indignation for his increasingly pro-Catholic views; his sillier supporters affected an ascetic appearance, fasted on toast and water and smoked Spanish (because Catholic) cigars—while some colleges altered the times of compulsory chapel services to keep impressionable students away from Newman's sermons. In the end, Newman resigned, became a Catholic and ended up a Cardinal—and to this day Oxford remains a centre of High Church Anglo-Catholicism.

St Mary the Virgin, from the church of the same name.

A Beginner's Guide to Oxford Architecture

Oxford is a city of crazy architectural juxtapositions, a rag-bag of buildings that reflects the changing tastes of every age from Saxon times to the present. Gothic, Jacobean, Palladian and neo-Grecian stand cheek by jowl with some of the most quirky buildings ever put up: Wren's pepper-pot gate-tower to Christ Church, Hawksmoor's bristling All Souls and Nicholas Stone's twisting baroque columns fronting the porch of St Mary's Church.

All that binds this haphazard *mélange* together is the colour of the limestone, an aristocrat among building materials. The oolite once quarried in the hills around Oxford— at Headington and Wheatley, Taynton and Barrington—is very accommodating. When freshly dug, it is plastic and easily sawn, dressed and carved into any shape. Once dry, it is a strong, hard-wearing material, ranging in colour from honey gold to white, with shades of pink and blue. The Normans, themselves from a limestone region, were the first residents of Oxford to see the potential of this versatile stone.

As English masons, copying their Continental counterparts, grew in confidence, they developed their own variations on the Gothic style. Early English, characterised by tall, pointed lancet windows, clusters of shafts in place of monolithic columns and capitals carved with stylised leaves, is well exemplified at Christ Church Cathedral.

Merton College Chapel shows the transition that took place in the late 13th century to the Decorated style, with its huge east window divided by flowing and curvaceous tracery. The same college claims to have established the pattern for collegiate buildings in Oxford, and further afield, with its enclosed quadrangle surrounded by communal dining hall, library, nave-less chapel and accommodation wings.

The Perpendicular style was invented in Gloucester in the 1350s along with the fan vault, England's greatest contribution to Gothic architecture. Oxford has several splendid examples, notably in the vestibule of Christ Church Hall and in the Divinity School—the latter a late example, completed in 1488, and pushed to the extremes of decorative flamboyance.

In the 17th century, Oxford developed its own hybrid Jacobean-Gothic style, exemplified by the Old Schools Quadrangle and Wadham College. These buildings retain Gothic features—traceried windows, blank arcading and stone vaulting—alongside classical columns and entablature, and it has been argued that the reluctance to let go of the Gothic represented a deep-seated conservatism, with antiquarian leanings.

Yet, within less than a century, the best-known architects of their age were to give the city some of Europe's most radical and adventurous buildings. Wren's Sheldonian Theatre, Gibb's Radcliffe Camera and Hawksmoor's Clarendon Building transformed central Oxford from a place of reserved cloisters to a city of boisterous and assertive buildings.

The architectural rot began to set in with the 19th century when zealous proponents of the neo-Gothic style, satirised by Lewis Carroll as "the very climacteric and coronal of all our architectural aspirations", swept away many serviceable medieval buildings and replaced them with their own "perfected Gothic", as often as not in harsh brick.

Our own age has done even worse, with its taste for building in concrete and steel, but stoneworking skills do still survive; many college buildings, stained by coal smoke and pitted by acidic rain, have undergone major surgery since the 1950s and modern masons have left their mark all over the city in the form of humorous gargoyles.

Wherever you look in collegiate Oxford, around doorways, beneath parapets and over drainheads, you will see carvings that look medieval—until you spot the anachronisms: a rugby player on the High Street frontage of Brasenose, or a bespectacled librarian in the Old Schools Quadrangle. Hundreds of new sculptures have been added to college buildings in the past four decades, and spotting them is part of the fun of a ramble round the city. Ironically, Oxford's ancient quarries closed just about the time that the tradition of carving was revived; today's masons have to import their limestone from France.

COLLEGES SOUTH OF HIGH STREET

The centre of Oxford is called **Carfax**, derived from the Latin *quadrifurcus* (four-forked). Here the four main roads of Oxford meet at a chaotic, noisy crossroads. On rare occasions, such as early Sunday morning, you can stand at this point, beneath Carfax clock tower, and enjoy an uninterrupted view of Oxford's beautiful High Street, or look down St Aldate's to the great pepper-pot tower of Christ Church.

For the rest of the time, the streets of Oxford thunder with the restless noise of people and traffic—or so it seems until you escape into the quiet college cloisters, where high walls deflect the sounds of the modern world. Following narrow lanes and threading through little-used pathways, it is still possible to tour much of Oxford without ever stepping into the bustling main streets.

Heading down St Aldate's, you pass the **Town Hall** on the left, a fine neo-Jacobean building, opened in 1897, with Queen Victoria seated in the apex of the central pediment. Above, the three-tiered belvedere on the roof is topped by a weathervane in the shape of a horned ox—for Oxford was originally called Oxenford. Tea dances are still regularly held in the Town Hall Assembly Room, beneath a large and incongruous painting of the *Rape of the Sabines* by Pietro da Cortona (1596-1669) and portraits of former mayors and Members of Parliament.

Better flavour: This fine building enlivens an otherwise dull stretch of street—the 1879 Post Office on the right is only of interest for the brass-bound wooden posting box in front. **Pembroke Street**, the first turning on the right, provides a better flavour of old Oxford, before Victorian improvers and modern developers set to work—lined as it is with jettied and bay-windowed houses, painted pastel colours.

It leads to **Pennyfarthing Place** and

the **Museum of Modern Art**, occupying a former brewery warehouse, which mounts highly regarded exhibitions of contemporary work. Also here is the **Church of St Ebbe's**, dedicated to a 7th-century Northumbrian abbess. The church was demolished and rebuilt in 1816, but the 12th-century west doorway, ornamented with beakheads, has survived.

By turning left down Littlegate, and immediately left again, you enter the North Quad of **Pembroke College**. This quad, formerly Beef Lane, has attractive flower beds and is used by those who know of its existence as a short cut from the city centre eastwards to Christ Church Meadow.

A passageway on the right leads into the Chapel Quad, with the splendid hall on the right. The projecting tower contains a statue of James I, who founded the college in 1624, and the hall is reached by means of a steep stone staircase. The hammerbeam roof, and tall Perpendicular windows, all look con-

receding ages: **ollege ustodians onferring at hrist Church. eft, lercury's tatue at hrist Church. ight, after ne exams...

vincingly of the 15th century, but the hall was actually built in 1848 by John Hayward.

The chapel, on the opposite side of the quad, was completed in 1732 and the stalls and screen are of that date—but the richly painted ceiling and the Renaissance-style stained glass is all the work of Charles Kempe, a former student of the college; it was executed between 1884 and 1900.

Another former student, the celebrated lexicographer Samuel Johnson, had rooms in the entrance tower of the Old Quad, to the east. He entered Pembroke in 1728 but stayed only four terms, unable to afford the fees. He was, at his own admission, a lazy and rebellious undergraduate, contemptuous of authority. Once fined for not attending a lecture, he complained at being "sconced twopence for something not worth a penny". Later in life, in recognition of his achievements in compiling the first English dictionary, he was awarded an honorary degree by the University, and

Pembroke has his portrait, by Reynolds, hanging in the Senior Common Room.

On emerging from Pembroke gate-tower, you enter the cobbled Pembroke Square, with **St Aldate's Church** on the left and a fine view of Christ Church tower ahead. St Aldate's was virtually rebuilt in 1832, and is the centre of the city's lively young evangelical congregation—services are noisy affairs, at which hymns are sung with much *joie de vivre* and to the accompaniment of guitars and tambourines.

A far different sound is often heard if you turn right into St Aldate's and right again into Brewer Street, for the buildings on the left house **Christ Church Cathedral Choir School**, and the delightful music of boys rehearsing for evensong is often carried on the breeze. Further down, on the left, is **Campion Hall**, a rather austere building of 1935 and Oxford's only example of Sir Edwin Lutyens' architecture.

Campion Hall was founded in 1895 as a place of study for Roman Catholic

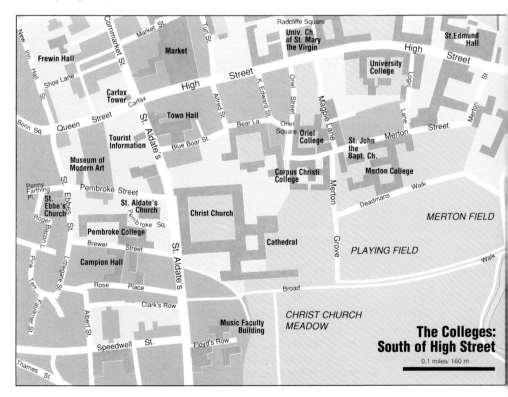

**The Colleges:
South of High Street**

0,1 miles/ 160 m

priests. The chapel has a striking set of Stations of the Cross painted by Frank Brangwyn.

The friendlier-looking garden wing of Campion Hall, built in Cotswold vernacular style, can be seen by turning left into Littlegate and left again into Rose Place. At the end of Rose Place, on the right, is the **Old Palace**, built for the first Bishop of Oxford in the 16th century. The oriel windows, supported by carved wooden grotesques, are dated 1628. The Palace now houses the Newman-Mowbray bookshop, and some of the rooms have 17th-century panelling and ornate plaster ceilings.

Alice again: Back in St Aldate's, the little shop on the right (No. 83) is known as "The Sheep Shop", for it is here that the real-life Alice Liddell used to buy her favourite barley sugar, before setting out on river trips with Charles Dodgson, better known as Lewis Carroll. In *Through the Looking Glass*, Alice visits the shop and is served by a bad-tempered sheep.

At the very end of St Aldate's, some distance south, is **Folly Bridge**, which crosses the Thames. Although this was rebuilt in 1827, a few fragments of the original Norman bridge, built by Robert d'Oilly around 1071, can be seen by anyone passing under in a boat.

Opposite the Sheep Shop is the **War Memorial Garden**, laid out in 1926, whose raised perennial beds are beautiful and colourful for most of the year. Beyond lies Broad Walk *(see page 179)* and, to the left, the turnstyle entrance to **Christ Church**. After paying your admission fee to a bowler-hatted college custodian, you pass through the 19th-century Gothic Meadow Buildings and enter the 15th-century cloisters of **Christ Church Cathedral**.

On the right, the Chapter House with its Norman doorway and tall Early English lancet windows is now the cathedral shop, and the next room beyond is used to present an audio-visual history of the cathedral.

This occupies the supposed site of a

The Memorial Garden at Christ Church.

nunnery founded by St Frideswide, the daughter of a Saxon nobleman, in the early 8th century. According to accounts of her life, written in the 12th century, Frideswide refused to marry the king of Mercia and fled to Abingdon, where she hid for three years in the woods, working as a servant to a swineherd. When the king discovered her hideout and tried to take Frideswide by force, he was struck and blinded by a lightning bolt.

Frideswide died not long afterwards, and Danish raiders destroyed the convent; but a new Augustinian priory, dedicated to the saint, was re-established here by the 12th century. The present church was begun towards the end of the 12th century when Norman architecture was giving way to the new Early English style—hence the interesting marriage between the massive round and octagonal piers of the nave, with later pointed arches in the clerestory above.

The church was improved and embellished over the next 300 years and the magnificent fan vault of the choir, similar to that of the Divinity School, was added around 1500. In 1524, Cardinal Wolsey dissolved St Frideswide's Priory, and used the endowments to found a new college; he intended to demolish the church and build a new chapel, but fell from power in 1529, partly because he had failed to achieve the speedy annulment of Henry VIII's marriage to Katharine of Aragon. Henry, who refounded the college in his own name in 1532, kept the priory church and in 1546 made it the cathedral of the newly created diocese of Oxford. Thus it is unique in being both a college chapel and a cathedral—the smallest in England.

North of the choir, a black marble slab simply inscribed "Frideswide" marks the spot where the remains of Oxford's patron saint are buried. Alongside, fragments from a tomb canopy, carved in the 13th century, when her bones were "discovered" and laid to rest here, have been reconstructed.

In the **Latin Chapel**, to the north, is a Burne-Jones window of 1859, depicting the life of the saint. This is one of Burne-Jones's earliest works, and the crowded scenes are full of dramatic detail—especially where the king of Mercia is struck by a red-hot thunderbolt—though the calamine-lotion colour of the faces is less successful. Nearby is a monument to Robert Burton (died 1640), author of *The Anatomy of Melancholy*.

There is more excellent stained glass around the cathedral, much of it designed by William Morris and Edward Burne-Jones. One of the finest is the **St Catherine window**, in the southeast corner of the choir, which depicts Edith Liddell, sister of Lewis Carroll's Alice, as the saint, and was designed by Burne-Jones in 1878.

Further west, the **St Lucy's Chapel** contains a wealth of early 14th-century glass, including a scene showing the martyrdom of St Thomas à Becket. This has survived, despite Henry VIII's in-

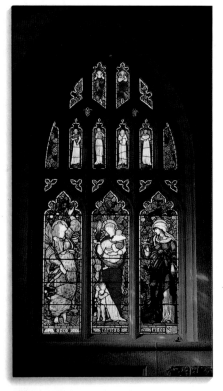

The Burne-Jones window in Christ Church Cathedral.

struction that all monuments to Becket be destroyed: here, only the head of the saint was removed and replaced with plain glass. He keeps company with a number of lewd and grotesque beasts that inhabit the tracery lights.

As one returns from the cathedral to the west side of the cloister, a flight of steps leads up to the high vestibule of **Christ Church Hall**, with its delicate fan-tracery ceiling, and a view over the extensive Great Quadrangle.

Here it is worth stopping to consider the history of the college and its architecture. Wolsey intended everything about his foundation, originally called Cardinal College, to be built on the grandest scale. However, all that was completed when he fell from grace in 1529 was the hall (rarely open to visitors), with its carved and gilded hammerbeam roof, the kitchens behind, and three sides of the Great Quad, including the lower stage of the gate-tower.

The college remained in this half-finished state for more than a century.

Building work began again around 1640, when Samuel Fell (the Dean, or head, of the College) commissioned the splendid fan vault, with its slender central column, under which we now stand. Shortly afterwards, Charles I made Christ Church his residence and work stopped during the Civil War.

After the monarchy was restored, John Fell (Samuel's son) was appointed Dean. He completed the fourth side of the Great Quad, adding the north range, copying Wolsey's work exactly, even down to the truncated pillars and arches that had been intended to support a vaulted cloister all around the perimeter. At the focal point of this spacious courtyard—Oxford's largest, measuring 264 by 261 ft (roughly 80 metres square)—Fell commissioned Christopher Wren to finish the great gate-tower, which he did in adventurous style, adding the bulky octagonal tower with its lead-covered cupola in 1681.

At the same time, the huge bell called Great Tom, weighing more than seven

Tom Quad, Christ Church.

tons, which had come to Christ Church from Osney Abbey at the Dissolution of the Monasteries, was recast and hung in the tower. Every night at 9.05 pm, Great Tom rings out from Tom Tower, tolling 101 times to signify the number of students admitted to the college at its original foundation. The bell also signalled the hour at which, in theory, all students in Oxford were supposed to be in bed.

The central fountain, dug originally to supply water to the college, is also contemporary with this work. A statue of Mercury was put up in 1695 but was removed in 1817 after being damaged. The current statue, a copy of Giovanni da Bologna's *Mercury*, was donated in 1928 and is sometimes to be seen clothed in sports kit or academic dress when students play their pranks in the relaxed post-exam weeks of summer.

At the northeast corner of Great Quad is **Fell Tower**, built between 1876 and 1879, with its statue of John Fell who, for all that he did to improve Christ Church, was a strict disciplinarian and far from popular. The poet Thomas Brown wrote of him:

I do not love thee, Dr Fell,
The reason why I cannot tell,
But this I know, and know full well,
I do not love thee, Dr Fell.

Passing beneath Fell Tower, you pass **Killcanon** on the left, built in 1669 and so called because of the icy winds that blow around the block in winter, and enter **Peckwater Quad**, named after an inn that stood on the site until these grand classical buildings were constructed in 1705. On the south side, the **New Library**, with its giant Corinthian columns, was completed in 1772. It is not open to the public but you can, with discretion, peer through the windows at the ceiling-high bookstacks, leather-bound volumes and fine stucco ceiling.

Canterbury Quad, housing the **Christ Church Picture Gallery**, lies to the southeast. The gallery contains an outstanding collection of paintings and drawings—mainly Italian of the 14th to 17th centuries, as well as a famous

Left, watching the birdie outside Oriel. Right, gateway to Corpus Christi.

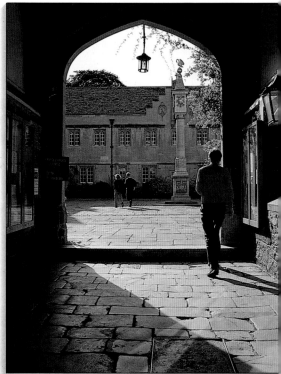

Holbein portrait of Henry VIII (painted *circa* 1545).

On to Oriel: As one leaves Christ Church by the Canterbury Gate, there is a fine view ahead of Merton Street and, to the left, of the wide Oriel Square, lined with 18th-century houses. **Oriel College**, on the east side of the square, was founded in 1324 and originally occupied a house called La Oriole, because of its prominent upper bay window (medieval Latin: *oratoriolum*).

Nothing medieval survives now, but Oriel does have a splendidly ostentatious Front Quadrangle, built in 1620-42 in the Jacobean-Gothic style. This form of architecture is peculiar to Oxford and combines beautifully shaped gables, rather in the Dutch manner, with traceried windows of medieval appearance. Dominating the quad is the staircase entrance to the hall, with its open strapwork cresting, and its inscription *Regnante Carolo* making a bold statement of Royalist support for Charles I. In the niches above are statues of Char-les I and Edward II (Oriel's founder, Adam de Brome, was one of Edward's civil servants) as well as a plump and matronly Virgin and Child.

On the south side of Oriel Square is **Corpus Christi College**, founded in 1512 by Richard Foxe, Bishop of Winchester. This small college has always been somewhat radical. Foxe, a friend of the great humanist Erasmus, encouraged the study of "pagan" classical texts in Latin and Greek, so aligning the college with contemporary Renaissance thought. In 1963, the college took the radical step of allowing women to dine as guests in hall: women were not finally admitted as students until 1979.

The intimate Front Quad of the college contains a famous sundial of 1581, topped by the emblem of the college, a pelican wounding her breast to feed her young, a symbol of Christ's sacrifice. The plinth below is inscribed with an ingenious perpetual calendar, dating to 1606. A passageway on the left leads to the chapel, with its colourful Arts and

Oxford's student intake remains impressively international.

Crafts window depicting St Christopher, designed by Henry Payne in 1931. The brass eagle lectern is Oxford's oldest, and was given to the college in 1537.

If Corpus Christi is one of Oxford's smallest colleges, next-door **Merton** is one of the largest and grandest. It also claims to be the earliest, having been founded in 1264 by Walter de Merton. Two other colleges dispute this primacy: University College on the spurious grounds that it was established by Alfred the Great, and Balliol, which was certainly in existence as a community of scholars by 1263 but was not formally endowed until 1282. It is generally accepted, however, that the constitution of Merton (the statutes) served as the model for all the other subsequent colleges of Oxford and Cambridge.

The chapel of Merton, running parallel to Merton Street, dates to around 1290, and so was begun soon after the college was founded. The massive gargoyles that leer from the battlements are

another example of brilliant modern masonry—put up in the 1960s to replace the eroded stumps of the originals.

The statues of Walter de Merton and Henry III, in the gate-tower, are also recent, but the mysterious woodland scene carved above the arch is 15th-century. It probably depicts St John the Baptist in the wilderness—but it is a wilderness populated by numerous rabbits and bears while the fruit-filled trees are crowded with a chorus of nesting birds. In the foreground, Walter de Merton kneels before the Book of Seven Seals from the Revelation of St John, perhaps a reference to the fact that Merton was founded for the study of theology, while a lamb and a unicorn, representing Christ, look on.

Passing through, into the Front Quad, the hall lies ahead. This was the first building on the site to be completed, but was virtually rebuilt in 1794 and again in 1874 when Sir George Gilbert Scott added the fine roof. Remarkably, the original 13th-century door, with its ornate scrollwork, has survived.

To the left of the Quad is the **Fitzjames arch**, built by the Warden (head of the college), Robert Fitzjames, in 1497. He had a horoscope cast in order to find the most propitious date on which to begin building, and his astrological interests are reflected in the Signs of the Zodiac carved in the vault of this arch. It leads through to the 17th-century **Fellows' Quadrangle**.

A passageway to the west leads into **Mob Quad**, enclosed by 14th-century buildings and the oldest quad in Oxford. The origin of the name is not known, but members of Merton like to think that the characteristic form of the Oxford and Cambridge enclosed quadrangle owes its origin to this group of buildings. The Old Library on the south side still has an original 14th-century reading stall, with chains to protect the valuable manuscripts from theft, while most of the panelling and bookcases are 16th-century. An astrolabe, an instrument for measuring the altitudes of stars and

Merton: its claim to have been the first college is disputed.

reputed to have belonged to Chaucer, is sometimes shown to visitors, who are admitted during vacations. There is a collection of cartoons bequeathed by the caricaturist Sir Max Beerbohm.

Huge and lofty: To the north of Mob Quad is Merton's splendid 13th-century chapel. Again, the plan of the chapel, consisting of an ante-chapel, screen and choir, set the pattern for all the other colleges—although this form evolved by accident: Walter de Merton intended a massive building, with an extensive nave, that was never built. Even so, the choir alone is huge and lofty. The magnificent east window, with seven lancets, meeting to form a wheel with 12 spokes at the apex, is one of the finest in Europe.

Nearly all the windows retain original late 13th-century glass, representing apostles and saints in gorgeous colours. The choir screen is made up of pieces salvaged from one designed by Christopher Wren, sadly broken up in 1851, of which parts were recently re-discovered. Of the many monuments to Fellows and benefactors, the finest is to Thomas Bodley (died 1613) on the west wall; the founder of the Bodleian Library is surrounded by allegorical figures representing the arts and sciences.

As one re-emerges into cobbled Merton Street, there is a good view of Magdalen College tower to the east. On the left, **Logic Lane** is so called because there used to be a school of logicians at the High Street end.

Almost the whole of the block of land to the right of the lane is occupied by the **Examination Schools**, completed in 1882. These were built to replace the Old Schools, now inadequate to accommodate all the students attending lectures and sitting examinations. Jackson, the chosen architect, built in neo-Jacobean style and the result, especially the High Street facade, has sometimes been described as heavy-handed—designed, perhaps, to intimidate the poor exam candidates.

Equally portentious on the High

Merton as Loggan saw it in 1675 in his *Oxonia Illustrata*.

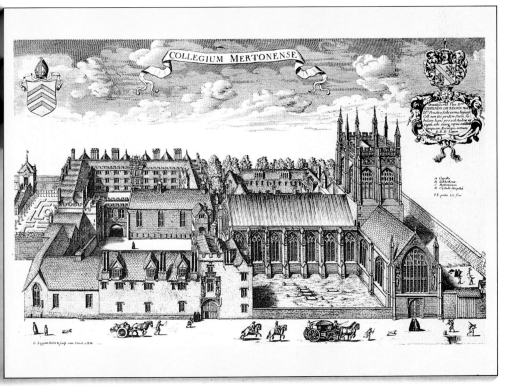

Street front is **University College**. The claim that "Univ" was founded by King Alfred was invented by medieval lawyers, but it did not stop the College celebrating its millennium in 1874. Even without this fiction, Univ is respectably ancient: money was left for its foundation in 1249, and on this basis it can claim to be the oldest college.

Changing statues: Substantial benefactions in the 17th century meant that all the medieval buildings were swept away, and the college rebuilt in the now familiar Oxford Jacobean-Gothic style. The plump, bird-bespattered statue of Queen Anne on the gate-tower replaced a statue of King Alfred in 1700. On the inner face of the tower is one of only two surviving statues of James II. It was erected in 1676 by the then Master, Obadiah Walker, who supported the monarch's Catholic religious views.

The chapel, refurbished by Sir George Gilbert Scott in 1862, retains its original stained glass, designed by the German artist Abraham van Linge in 1641, his last known work and full of exotic details. The ante-chapel contains fine monuments by Flaxman, including that of Sir William Jones (died 1794), judge in the Calcutta High Court, shown compiling his digest of Hindu law and watched by a group of Indians.

Another monument, to the poet Shelley, occupies a domed chamber reached via the passageway in the northwest corner of the quad. Shelley spent less than six months as an undergraduate at Univ, having been expelled in 1811 for his joint authorship of a pamphlet on *The Necessity of Atheism*. Some 80 years later, in 1894, Lady Shelley presented the monument to the college. Designed by Edward Onslow Ford, it was intended for the poet's grave, in the English Cemetery in Rome, but was found to be too large. The life-sized sculpture of the naked drowned poet, supported by winged lions and the Muse of Poetry, is shockingly pathetic; sadly, it attracts the attention of the graffiti brigade.

Left, Shelley's vulnerable memorial. Right, University College.

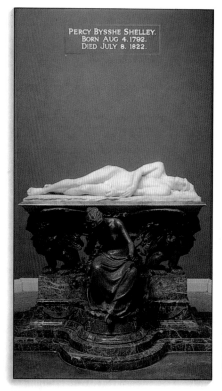

PERCY BYSSHE SHELLEY.
BORN AUG 4. 1792.
DIED JULY 8. 1822.

THE CYCLIST'S CITY

Each working day, about 26,000 trips are made in and out of Oxford's central area by bicycle, and an estimated 20,000 cycles can be on the streets at any one time. Not surprisingly, mishaps occur—though the number has been falling, from 200 reported accidents in 1984 to 136 by the end of the decade. And, even less surprisingly, many cycles are stolen: just under 3,000 a year.

Cycling has always played an important part in Oxford's transport system. William Morris, the car magnate who became Lord Nuffield, began his career building and racing pedal cycles. In 1922 Morrell's Brewery produced a *Hunting and Cycling Road Map of Oxford and District* over-printed with a list of hotels and inns within circles representing distances from Oxford. It was not then necessary, as it is today, to publish maps highlighting accident black-spots.

Nor was theft as prevalent then. Bikes are mostly taken from colleges and cycle parks, particularly those at Westgate and Magdalen Street East (which were installed in 1935 by Oxford City Council, one of the first local authorities to provide for the needs of the urban cyclist). Most are recovered, with some being fished out of the river, having been thrown from Magdalen or Folly Bridges.

A thief's favourite is the ATB (All Terrain Bicycle) which, with as many as 21 gears, can be ridden almost anywhere and costs up to £6,000. Cycles costing £600 regularly disappear. The thieves are rarely students; they are mostly young men, occasionally schoolchildren, sometimes professionals who come in vans from other cities and are not deterred by even a £25 U-bolt steel lock. The professionals are likely to repaint the bikes, first erasing the coded serial numbers and then stamping them with new ones.

To counter such crime, the Police Cycle Department keeps records of all cycles manufactured and can produce serial numbers, colours, decoration, modifications and accessories for almost every model. Ron Orman, a retired detective, runs the department, which keeps two detectives and a constable fully employed in an office behind the Central Police Station. Bikes are kept in two cycle stores: one for the "found" and "miscellaneous" and the other for "crime" bikes (being held pending court cases). The ingeniously designed store holds 200–300 cycles hanging from S-hooks at any one time. The "found" bikes are kept for at least six weeks to see if anyone claims them. Unclaimed cycles are auctioned; the average price is £20.

In addition to third-party and theft insurance, cyclists are recommended to have a Green Card—a record issued by the Cycle Department on which an owner can list the bicycle's frame size, type, number and distinguishing marks. The police ask the city's cycle dealers to accept secondhand cycles only if a certified Green Card is presented. A useful free service provided by the Cycle Department is postcoding bicycles, which can be done any Saturday morning between 9 and 11 a.m.

Oxford City Council is committed to making travel by bicycle safer and easier, and has produced a comprehensive *Cycling Guide*. Three signed cycle routes use minor roads and purpose-built tracks totally free from motorised traffic. The North and South Oxford routes provide quiet alternatives to main roads into the city and the Donnington route links Cowley Road and Iffley Road.

Almost all the cycle lanes are advisory; this means that motorists should avoid driving in them, although it is not illegal to do so. Cycle lanes provide a reminder to motorists to look out for cyclists and to give them space. Cyclists are allowed to use all bus lanes.

The junction with Parks Road and Broad Street has one of the highest cycle flows in the country. To ease congestion, the Advanced Stop Line, the first to be introduced in Great Britain, allows cyclists to wait at the traffic lights in front of motor vehicles. Other streets in Oxford restrict motor vehicle access for safety and environmental reasons but cyclists are usually exempt.

Racing remains popular and there are three local clubs for national and international road races, time trials, cyclo-cross and track races. The Oxford University Cycling Club is Britain's oldest surviving cycling club.

COLLEGES NORTH OF HIGH STREET

William of Waynflete, Bishop of Winchester, originally intended to build **Magdalen College** (pronounced *maudlin*) on the site now occupied by the Examination Schools. His plans were delayed for 10 years, during which time he was promoted to the office of Chancellor of England; in 1458 he acquired the current, much larger site. It was not quite a greenfield location—Waynflete first had to obtain permission to suppress the Hospital of St John that occupied the land—but, because it was outside the city walls, there were few constraints on growth, and the land included substantial stretches of parkland alongside the River Cherwell.

May Morning: For that reason, Magdalen today is one of the most spacious colleges, and delightful to explore, as much for the gardens, deer park and river walks as for the buildings themselves. The famous **Bell Tower**, which dominates the view as you enter Oxford over Magdalen Bridge, was one of the first buildings to be completed. The practice of singing from the tower on May Morning may have begun when the structure was inaugurated in 1505. Nobody is certain whether the custom continued in unbroken succession since that date, but the ceremony was in full swing in the 18th century, when spectators were pelted with eggs by unruly undergraduates from the tower.

Today, when the Magdalen College School choristers sing Latin grace from the top of the tower at 6 a.m. on 1 May, the ceremony initiates a morning of revelries: bells ring out, Morris men dance, and students take their lovers off by punt for champagne breakfasts along the banks of the Cherwell.

The Bell Tower and High Street front of Magdalen display an extensive collection of grotesques and gargoyles, completed in 1981, and there are many more enjoyable caricatures inside, on

the buildings on the right-hand side of **St John's Quadrangle**. Note, too, immediately on the right, the outdoor pulpit from which a sermon is preached on the nearest Sunday to the feast of St John the Baptist.

Crossing St John's Quad ahead and to the right, you enter the low **Muniment Tower** of 1485, which shelters the west doorway to the chapel, carved with figures of St John, Edward VI, Mary Magdalene, St Swithun and William of Waynflete. Again, much that you can see here, including the stone vaulting and ornamental screens, is the result of improvements carried out in 1829–34, but it is pleasing enough, especially when seen by candlelight at choral evensong. The ante-chapel contains some medieval stalls with carved misericords and a good selection of monuments, including that of the founder's father, Richard Patten (died 1450).

Leaving the chapel, the **Founder's Tower**, ahead and to the right, was the original front gate of the college and

eft, Magdalen's famous Bell Tower. Right, side Magdalen's chapel.

leads into the peaceful **Cloister Quad**, dating originally to 1490. Parts were rebuilt in the 19th century but are now gracefully clad in the branches of a magnificent wisteria.

The allegorical figures on the buttresses, called "hieroglyphicals", were added in 1508. One is free to speculate what they represent, for nobody really knows—though in the 1670s, Dr William Reeks produced a 60-page treatise arguing that they symbolised the virtues (sobriety and temperance) and vices (gluttony, lust and pride) of academic life. The grotesques of the cloister walls include more dark, mysterious subjects, and several that are explicitly erotic—a surprising fact, given that most are the work of Victorian carvers.

A narrow passageway in the north range of the cloister debouches into a vast expanse of green lawns, with the stately colonnaded New Building straight ahead—begun in 1733 and intended as one range of an enclosed quad that was never completed. To the right,

a bridge across the Cherwell leads to the leafy deer park, while, to the left, a massive plane tree, planted in 1801, stands beside the path that leads to the open fields of Magdalen Grove. It is worth following this path a short way in order to look back, southwards, over the fine jumble of towers, pinnacles and Cotswold tile roofs of the college—Oxford's dreaming spires in miniature.

Golden glow: Back in the High Street, there is a good view eastwards, up the slight rise, with the soaring spires of St Mary and All Saints forming the focal point. As far as the eye can see, the street facades are nearly all of honey-coloured stone—best seen as the low light of the setting sun adds its own golden glow.

One of the few non-stone properties is that of **Frank Cooper**, a delicate neo-Grecian shop with a balcony. Here, the makers of the famous Oxford marmalade have a small museum in the grocer's shop from which Sarah Jane Cooper first began selling her home-made products in 1874.

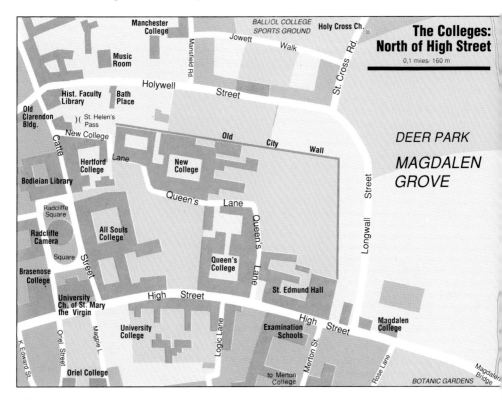

On the opposite (right-hand) side of the High Street is a run of antique shops and outfitters; one shop, number 48, was once the bicycle repair shop of William R. Morris, who later progressed to servicing and, finally, to manufacturing motor cars. Further on, on the corner of Queen's Lane, is one of Oxford's oldest coffee houses, established in 1654, where students still linger for hours over hearty breakfasts or mugs of coffee, perched on high stools around a communal table, sorting out the problems of the world.

Queen's College lies beyond, its long and beautiful Baroque facade best appreciated from the opposite side of the road. Facade is, perhaps, the wrong term, for the High Street front is no more than a screen, with a handsome domed gatehouse, containing a statue of Queen Caroline. All this work was once attributed to Nicholas Hawksmoor, but is now thought to be by the local Oxford mason, William Townesend, and was completed around 1735.

Queen Caroline occupies pride of place because she donated substantial funds to the 18th-century rebuilding of the college, which swept away all the original buildings. The college is, however, named after Queen Philippa, wife of Edward III, whose chaplain, Robert of Eglesfeld, founded it in 1340. Queen's still celebrates the memory of its founder with an ancient ceremony whereby dinner guests are presented with a needle and thread—the French for which (*aiguilles et fils*) is a pun on Eglesfeld's name. The more famous Boar's Head Feast, celebrated in December, commemorates a Queen's student who is said to have killed a wild boar by thrusting a copy of Aristotle's works down its throat.

As one passes through the centre of the Front Quad, the north range ahead has the hall on the left and the chapel on the right. The latter, consecrated in 1719, re-used the colourful stained glass windows from the old chapel, designed by Abraham van Linge in

1636, and is notable for the bold and exotic foliage framing the Biblical scenes.

Beyond lies the Back Quad, with its splendid library of 1696 on the left, lit by a great expanse of glass, through which the stucco frieze and ornate bookcases may just be glimpsed. A narrow passage to the left of the library passes between high walls into a tiny rose garden known, for reasons now forgotten, as "the Nun's Garden".

From this peaceful haven it is a shock to return to the noisy High Street, but one of the best and quietest parts of Oxford lies ahead. Turn into Queen's Lane and right into the unimposing entrance door to **St Edmund Hall** (known to students as Teddy Hall).

This pretty college, with its small, flower-filled quads, achieved independent status as late as 1957. Before that, it had been controlled by Queen's, next door. It is, however, the only surviving example in Oxford of the medieval halls that pre-dated the foundation

of the colleges. By tradition, it dates to the 1190s, when St Edmund of Abingdon resided and taught here, and therefore has every right to be considered Oxford's oldest educational establishment—although, since the medieval halls had no formal statutes, it has no official date of foundation.

Everything about St Edmund Hall is built on a diminutive scale, including the chapel, on the east side of the Front Quad. Note that the pillars supporting the 1682 door pediment are carved to resemble a stack of leather-bound books. Inside, there are stained-glass windows (and the original paper cartoons) by Morris, Burne-Jones and Philip Webb, and a bold modern altar painting of *Christ at Emmaeus* (1958) by Ceri Richards.

A passage in the north wing of the quad leads to the churchyard of **St Peter in the East**, where, in summer, students study beneath the sombre yews, leaning against the tombstones, for the church is now the college library. One of the tombstones, on the left of the path to the porch, commemorates James Sadler, described as the "first English aeronaut". Sadler's inaugural flight, by hydrogen-filled balloon, began in Oxford on 4 October 1784.

St Peter's itself is one of Oxford's oldest and most interesting churches. Sadly, only the crypt is open to the public (key from the Porter's Lodge). This dates to about 1130, and the capitals are carved with dragon-like beasts.

Mice and frogs: From St Edmund Hall, the narrow, traffic-free Queen's Lane passes between high walls. The walk is enlivened by Michael Groser's series of corbels on the New College buildings to the right, carved in the 1960s with harvest mice, beetles, frogs, lizards and other zoological subjects.

The entrance to **New College** is easily missed, tucked down an alley to the right, at the junction of Queen's and New College Lane. The narrow gatetower, with statues of the Virgin, an angel and the founder, William of

During the May ball season, a string quartet in the cloisters.

Wykeham, belies the spaciousness and grandeur of what lies beyond.

Wykeham, Bishop of Winchester, founded New College in 1379, having acquired land in the northeast corner of the city wall, which, according to contemporary accounts, was "full of filth, desolate and unoccupied".

Building work proceeded speedily—in part because Wykeham was a very wealthy man and funds were not in short supply; indeed, his other great foundation, Winchester College, was being built simultaneously. Wykeham intended New College to draw its scholars from his school, and so close was the link that Fellowships were restricted to former Winchester scholars until the 19th century.

The range of buildings surrounding the Great Quadrangle was largely completed by the time of Wykeham's death in 1404. What is more, it has survived largely intact, although a third storey was added to the accommodation range in 1674.

On the left of the gate-tower is the spacious chapel, a fine example of Perpendicular architecture. A dramatic stone figure of Lazarus, struggling to break free of his funeral bonds, dominates the ante-chapel and was carved by Sir Jacob Epstein in 1951.

It stands beneath a controversial window designed by Sir Joshua Reynolds and painted by Thomas Jervais between 1778 and 1785 (the two artists appear as shepherds in the Nativity scene). The chiaroscuro effect is achieved by painting the dark areas in shades of brown, with almost clear glass for the highlights. Sir Horace Walpole called it "washy" and Lord Torrington described the figures of the Virtues as "half-dressed languishing harlots". As models, Reynolds used society beauties of the day, including Mrs Sheridan, wife of the playwright; she appears as the Virgin.

There is no glass in the east end of the chapel; instead, a great 19th-century stone reredos rises from floor to ceiling,

filled with life-size statues, in four tiers, of apostles, saints and martyrs. The soaring hammerbeam roof is also Victorian, the work of Sir George Gilbert Scott, as is the stone sedilia (group of three seats) to the left of the altar, one of which is used to display the founder's gilt and enamelled episcopal staff.

Scott also designed the woodwork of the choir stalls, but incorporated original armrests and 38 misericords that provide a glimpse of 14th-century life, with bishops preaching, acrobats tumbling, knights in combat and menacing monsters with multiple heads.

On the left, as you emerge from the chapel, is the cloister, dominated by a vast and ancient holm oak tree, that evokes medieval Oxford with its original 14th-century waggon roof and atmosphere of tranquillity.

At the northeast corner of the Great Quad is the **Muniment Tower**, again with statues of the Virgin and William of Wykeham. The steep stone staircase within leads to the hall, lined with 16th-

century linenfold panelling under Scott's roof of 1877.

The wall above the high table is hung with portraits of former benefactors and Wardens (heads of the college). Among them (bottom right) is the white-haired figure of William Spooner, elected Warden in 1903, whose inadvertent habit of transposing the initial letters of words gave rise to many humorous "Spoonerisms". Many are thought to be apocryphal, made up subsequently to nurture the myth. There is no evidence, for example, that he once proposed a toast to "our queer Dean". It is also said that he expelled one undergraduate with the words "Sir, you have tasted two whole worms, you have hissed my mystery lectures and you were found fighting a liar in the quad: you will leave at once by the town drain."

An archway in the Great Quad east range leads through to the Garden Quad, lined with 17th-century neo-Palladian buildings and separated from the gardens beyond by a curvaceous

New College with part of the ancient city wall.

wrought-iron screen—a replica of the original designed by Thomas Robinson in 1711. The gardens contain a substantial stretch of Oxford's medieval town wall, begun in 1226. The college was made responsible for maintaining it under the terms of the original land purchase; consequently, it is one of the best-preserved examples of a town wall in England and forms a magnificent backdrop to the deep, colourful perennial borders.

The tree-covered Mound, in the northeastern angle of the wall, looks like a Norman castle motte but was thrown up in the 16th century as a prospect from which to view the gardens. In former times a knot garden occupied the lawn space between the Mound and the college.

Student digs, a cosy alternative to living in college rooms.

Through a breach in the wall made in 1700 you pass to the north side, with fine views of the chapel to the left, past a range of 19th and 20th-century buildings and out into **Holywell Street**. This is one of Oxford's quietest and most charming streets, closed to traffic and lined with a mixture of pastel-painted, timber-framed houses and Cotswold-stone vernacular; most are now student lodgings. Here also is **Holywell Music Room**, opened in 1748 and reputedly the world's oldest surviving concert hall. Restored in 1959–60, it can seat around 250 people and has acoustics which do particular justice to solo recitals and chamber concerts.

In Holywell Street, too, you can see how effectively the town wall marked the limits of the city, for, apart from the 17th and 18th-century houses of Holywell Street itself, everything to the north belongs to another age, part of the 19th-century expansion of the city.

Some few ramshackle houses—former slums but now picturesque leaning cottages and inns—were built outside the town wall, backing up against it. These can be seen by turning left down **Bath Place**, a narrow, cobbled alley with many a right-angled bend, past the rambling 18th-century Turf Tavern.

THE COLLEGES: CENTRAL OXFORD

Midway down Broad Street, on the south side, **Turl Street** marks a boundary of sorts between Town and Gown, for most of the colleges lie to the east and the shops and markets to the west. The street is thought to be named after a pedestrian turnstile or twirling gate that stood in the city wall at the Broad Street end. Looking south, you can see how the street gradually narrows down to its original medieval width, where it appears to be blocked off by the splendid tower of All Saints' Church (now Lincoln College Library), rebuilt after the original tower collapsed in 1700, partly to the designs of Nicholas Hawksmoor.

A short way down Turl Street, on the right, is **Jesus College**. It is said that college porters hate being on duty on Christmas Day because of the stream of telephone calls from pranksters ringing to ask "Is that Jesus?"—to which, if the answer is yes, the caller responds by singing "Happy Birthday to you".

Jesus is also known as the Welsh college because it was founded, in 1571, by Brecon-born Hugh Price, and took many of its students from the grammar schools of Wales until 1882. T.E. Lawrence, "Lawrence of Arabia", was one of the non-Welsh alumni, admitted in 1907, although he resided only a term in college and spent most of his time studying medieval military architecture in a shed in the garden of his parents' North Oxford home (2, Polstead Road). There is a bust of Lawrence in Jesus College Chapel, a replica of the one in St Paul's Cathedral.

The chapel itself, consecrated in 1621, contains a High Victorian altar reredos so out of keeping with the surviving 17th-century woodwork that it is usually curtained-off from view. In the same north range of the first quad, the Principal's Lodging has a delicate shell hood of 1700 over the doorway.

Exeter College, directly opposite Jesus, was founded in 1314 by the Bishop of Exeter, Walter de Stapledon. Much of the college now looks Victorian, due to rebuilding, and the first quadrangle is dominated by the over-large chapel. This was built in 1854–60 to the design of Sir George Gilbert Scott, and the resemblance to a miniature French cathedral is no accident— Scott borrowed freely from the Sainte Chapelle in Paris.

The interior is bathed in the rich colours of stained glass, even on a dull day, and the sense of opulence is enhanced by the mosaic work of the apse. On the right of the altar, the large tapestry of the Adoration of the Magi was made in 1890 by the firm founded by William Morris, and designed by Burne-Jones. The two artists met in 1853 as fellow students at Exeter College, and their shared interest in the ideas of Ruskin and the pre-Raphaelites led them to devote their lives to the revival of medieval arts and crafts.

Another Exeter man was J.R.R. Tolk-

Off-duty in Turl Street: off to the ball (left) and afternoon tea.

ien, author of *The Lord of the Rings*, who much enjoyed the magnificent chestnut trees of the Fellows' Garden, beyond and to the rear of the front quad. The vast tree, "Bishop Heber's chestnut", seems as ancient as the college itself, and members of the Exeter boat club watch its growth in spring with interest. It is said that if the foliage of the branches, arching over the garden wall, succeed in touching Brasenose College opposite, Exeter will beat its neighbour in the Bumping Races.

Lincoln is the last of the colleges fronting on to Turl Street. It was founded in 1427 by the Bishop of Lincoln, Richard Fleming, but he died only four years later, leaving the college with little income and few endowments. Because it remained relatively poor, many of the original 15th-century buildings escaped "improvement", and much of the charm of the Front Quad is due to its small scale and unspoiled character.

The Chapel Quad, to the south, was added in the 17th century as the college began to expand. The chapel exterior, of 1629, is conservatively built in the Perpendicular style of the previous century, but the fine carved woodwork inside is much more typical of its age. The richly coloured stained glass, showing prophets, apostles and Biblical scenes, is attributed to Abraham van Linge, and was probably painted soon after the German artist's arrival in Oxford in 1629.

One of the ironies of Lincoln College is that, founded during an age of heresy specifically to train priests in orthodox church teachings, it nevertheless elected John Wesley to a fellowship in 1726. Members of the Holy Club—nicknamed "the Bible moths" and "Methodists" because of their regular and methodical devotions—used to meet in his college rooms, in Chapel Quadrangle. Another room in the Front Quad, erroneously thought to have been Wesley's, was restored as a memorial by American Methodists in 1925.

Brasenose Lane, shaded by the chestnuts of Exeter, has a leafy, rural feel and the cobbled gulley down the middle marks the line of the original open sewer. Undergraduates use the lane as an unofficial cycle path.

Brasenose College is entered from Radcliffe Square. The college is named after the "brazen nose", a bronze door knocker that once hung on the gates of Brasenose Hall. Anyone who was fleeing from the law could claim sanctuary within the protective walls of the Hall if they could get their hands firmly round the ring of the knocker.

Perhaps because of the protective powers of the brazen nose, a group of students stole the ring in the 1330s and took it with them to Stamford where they intended to establish a rival university. Edward II refused to sanction the breakaway institution but, while some of the students settled in Cambridge, and others returned to Oxford, the brazen nose got left behind. Here it remained, serving as a door knocker, until Brasenose House in Stamford came on

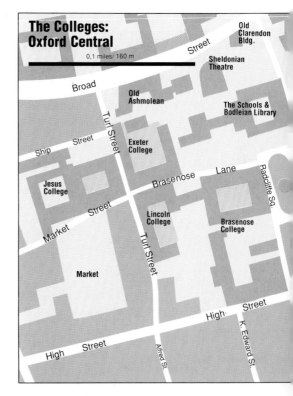

The Colleges: Oxford Central

0,1 miles/ 160 m

Old Clarendon Bldg.

Sheldonian Theatre

Broad Street

Old Ashmolean

The Schools & Bodleian Library

Ship Street

Turl Street

Exeter College

Jesus College

Brasenose Lane

Radcliffe Sq.

Market Street

Lincoln College

Brasenose College

Turl Street

Market

High Street

High Street

Alfred St.

K. Edward St.

the market in 1890, and, even then, the college had to purchase the whole house in order to secure the return of the symbolic piece of bronze—now hung behind the High Table in the dining hall.

In the meantime, a new knocker was commissioned for Brasenose, on the occasion of its official foundation as a college, as distinct from the pre-existing academic hall, in 1509. Shaped like a human head, this is now fixed at the apex of the main gate of the college.

Passing through, you enter the Old Quad with its Tudor buildings, completed shortly after the foundation; the third storey, with its fine dormer windows, was added in the early 17th century. The splendid sundial on the right-hand side was painted in 1719. The dining hall, on the left (eastern) side, is usually open, so that the original brazen nose can be seen. First mentioned in a document of 1279, the Romanesque feline head and ring could have been made as early as the 12th century.

A passageway in the southeastern corner leads into Chapel Quad, with its delightful library, carved with a frieze of exuberant swags, and lit below by pairs of oval windows. This work dates to the mid-17th century and is surprisingly innovative for its date, foreshadowing the 18th century's Baroque style.

The chapel is of the same date and mixes Gothic with classical motifs. The unusual fan-vaulted and painted roof is made of plaster. In the ante-chapel is a bronze plaque with a Greek inscription celebrating Walter Pater (died 1894), the writer and aesthete. He is portrayed at the centre of a tree whose other branches bear portrait medallions of Plato, Dante, Leonardo da Vinci and Michaelangelo. The implication that Pater was a scion of the same stock as these great artists reminds us that his precious and overblown style was once considered the epitome of fine writing.

As you turn to leave the college, you realise what a splendid view the students and fellows enjoy, being so close to Radcliffe Square.

Left, Ackermann's *Brazen Nose College*. Right, Brasenose today.

COLLEGES NORTH OF BROAD STREET

Spacious **Broad Street**, wide in the centre and narrowing at each end, was originally a horse market just outside the city walls. Even now, despite the car park in the central island, it is still a place where the countryside seems to meet the town—for much of the north side is open, with only 18th-century iron gates separating the street from the ample, tree-filled grounds of **Trinity College**.

Unlike most other colleges, you do not enter Trinity by means of a castle-like gate-tower, but through a narrow gate beside a row of humble, leaning cottages. Originally built in the 17th century, these were dismantled and rebuilt almost entirely in 1969.

Next comes an expanse of lawn, scattered with trees, and a path that leads northwards to Durham Quad, so called because it occupies the site of the origi-

nal Durham College, founded in 1286 by the monks of Durham Abbey. When the monasteries were dissolved by Henry VIII, the property was purchased by Sir Thomas Pope, a wealthy Treasury civil servant, and he re-founded the college in 1555.

Durham Quad is fronted by the elegant Baroque chapel—so much like Christopher Wren's City of London churches that the design has been attributed to him, although all the college records that could prove or disprove this theory are missing. Certainly the chapel, which attracts the highest eulogies from architectural historians, was the first in Oxford to break away from the backward-looking Gothic style. Completed in 1694, the tower is carved with swags of fruits and flowers, and the pinnacles consist of allegorical figures representing Theology, Medicine, Geometry and Astronomy.

Inside, the panelling, stalls and screen, carved with figures of the Evangelists, are principally of juniper wood, with walnut veneer. The beautiful reredos, all cherubs and foliage, is certainly good enough to be the work of the great 17th-century master of wood carving, Grinling Gibbons. The centrepiece of the plaster ceiling is painted with an Ascension by the Huguenot artist, Pierre Berchet.

All change: A passageway on the north side of Durham Quad leads through to the peaceful Garden Quad. Here the north range, of 1668, is known to be Wren's work, but 19th-century alterations have obscured his design beyond recognition.

Four handsome lead urns, of 18th-century date, form a prelude to the long college garden, to the right, entered through a wrought-iron gateway, made as a World War II memorial. The expansive gardens stretch all the way to Parks Road, creating a fine vista that is closed at the far end by 18th-century wrought-iron gates. By taking the central path, and turning right, you reach a group of buildings added in the 19th and 20th

Preceding pages: Trinity chapel. Left and below, May Day entertainers.

centuries, tucked into the rear of Blackwell's bookshop. The paving of Cumberbatch Quad, built 1964–68, actually forms the roof of Blackwell's vast underground Norrington Room.

Adjoining Trinity, towards the town end of Broad Street, is **Balliol**, a college that has produced a greater number of eminent men—in particular, statesmen and politicians—than any other. One of their number, Lord Asquith (Prime Minister 1908–16), characterised Balliol men as distinguished by their "effortless superiority".

The liberal traditions and academic prowess of the college in its heyday were due to the reforming measures of Benjamin Jowett (Master 1870–93), who believed that his students should not merely be filled with facts but educated for life. His self-proclaimed mission was to "innoculate England with Balliol"—which he sought to do by encouraging his charges to devote their lives to public service.

Jowett also supervised the near-total rebuilding of the college and, sadly, it is difficult to find much of merit in the result. William Morris, who watched the demolition of the medieval Balliol buildings with dismay, later founded the Society for the Protection of Ancient Buildings with the avowed aim of seeking means to repair and protect old buildings rather than replacing them.

The Fellows of Balliol, however, considered the buildings to be too decayed to be rescued. They had stood for a long time; Balliol claims to be the oldest Oxford college (against the counter-claims of University College and Merton) on the grounds that John Balliol founded it in 1263, as penance for insulting the Bishop of Durham; the statutes, drawn up under the patronage of Balliol's widow, Dervorguilla, date to 1282.

The college was never very wealthy, however, until some ancient estates in Northumberland were discovered to be a rich source of coal. Three major Victorian architects were employed in the

Balliol College Hall.

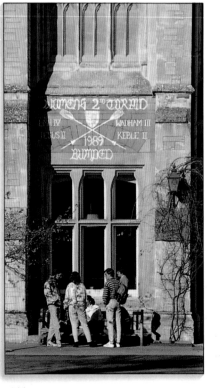

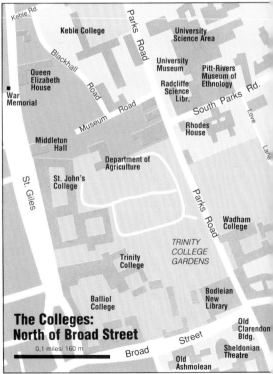

The Colleges: North of Broad Street

0,1 miles/ 160 m

rebuilding that resulted—Salvin, Butterfield and Waterhouse—yet all produced second-rate work.

The Front Quad, entered from Broad Street, contains the former hall, now the library, and one of the few surviving pre-Victorian buildings, last remodelled in the 18th century. The chapel, Butterfield's work of 1856–57, was once lavishly decorated with Gothic furnishings—too ornate for the taste of Balliol dons who had them removed in 1937. The silver-gilt altar frontal commemorates college members who died in World War I.

The chapel exterior, partly clad in ivy and Virginia creeper, is built in alternating bands of buff and red stone and is best appreciated from the Garden Quad. Here things begin to improve slightly: a group of trees and rose beds softens the appearance of the ill-harmonised buildings, and the steep flight of stone steps up to the porch of the dining hall—the work of Waterhouse, 1876—makes a dramatic statement.

Spoiled for choice: Sometimes it is possible to leave Balliol by the gate-tower in the northwest corner of the Garden Quad, emerging in St Giles; alternatively, you go back to Broad Street and turn right into St Giles, following the long Balliol facade to the point where it meets the considerably more varied frontage of **St John's**.

This college was originally founded by Archbishop Chichele, in 1437, for Cistercian monks and named after St Bernard. After the Dissolution of the Monasteries, it was re-founded, in 1555, by Sir Thomas White, a wealthy member of the Merchant Taylor's Guild. A statue of St Bernard, flanked by the two founders, occupies a niche on the gate-tower. The niche on the inner side contains Eric Gill's splendid *St John the Baptist* (1936), commissioned in belated recognition of the renaming of the college by White, in honour of the patron saint of tailors.

The buildings of the Front Quad survive from the original St Bernard Col-

*Gargoyles
n St
John's.*

lege. The hall, though, was remodelled in the 18th century and given its stone screen, designed by James Gibbs, in 1742. The chapel, on the left, was comprehensively spoiled, internally, in the 19th century. More interesting is the Baylie Chapel to the north, with its plaster fan vault. This was built in 1662 and houses the monument of Richard Baylie (died 1667), the Royalist President (head) of St John's, who was forcibly ejected from the college by Parliamentary troops during the 17th-century Civil War but was reinstated at the Restoration.

In remaining staunchly loyal to Charles I, Baylie was following the example of his predecessor, Archbishop Laud, who was President from 1611 to 1621 and Chancellor of the University from 1629. During his time as Chancellor, Laud drew up a long list of rules governing the behaviour of Oxford scholars, which, for all that Laud was strongly opposed to the Calvinist doctrines of his day, could have been written by a

staunch puritan. Under the Laudian Code, as it is known, professional actors were forbidden to enter the University and scholars were forbidden to hunt, gamble, smoke, drink or wear their hair long or in curls—and these rules remained the basis of university discipline until 1854.

It is all the more remarkable, therefore, that Laud also financed the construction of the **Canterbury Quad** at St John's—a group of buildings unmatched in Oxford for their showy exuberance. The passage linking Front Quad and Canterbury Quad is fan vaulted, a last touch of late Gothic before the Baroque splendours beyond.

We emerge to face a bold, two-storey portal containing a bronze statue of Charles I (by Le Sueur) under the Royal coat of arms. To either side, the delicate arcade, carried on slender Tuscan columns, has medallion busts of female figures (by Anthony Gore), representing the Virtues and the Liberal Arts, beneath a running frieze of foliage. Crossing the quad and, turning round, we find that the opposite range is similar but with a statue of Queen Henrietta Maria, wife of Charles I, in the niche. For long the design was attributed to Inigo Jones or Nicholas Stone, two of the greatest architects of their day, but now the credit goes to Adam Browne, a craftsman-architect so obscure that you will search in vain for his name in architectural reference books.

When the quad was completed in 1636, Charles I and his Queen were invited to view the buildings and watch a play in the hall (despite the Laudian Code!). It is said that the cost of the king's entertainment was almost more than that of the buildings.

Posthumous move: The library on the south side of Canterbury Quad (not open) contains memorabilia of both Laud and the monarch, both of whom died on the scaffold—Charles, famously, in 1649 and Laud in 1645, accused by the Long Parliament of high treason. Originally buried in Barking,

Snowflakes fall on St John's.

his bones were quietly re-interred in St John's chapel in 1663.

The east side of Canterbury Quad leads out to the extensive gardens, arguably the richest and certainly the most naturalistic in Oxford, for many wild flowers are encouraged to grow here, among the woodland groves that were first planted in 1712.

The North Quad contains modern buildings: The Beehive, built in 1958, so called because the plan is based on clusters of interlocking octagons, and the Sir Thomas White Building of 1975.

From St John's turn right, up St Giles, and look for a passageway on the right, by the Lamb and Flag—a tavern which opened in 1695 and takes its name from the St John's College coat of arms. The passage takes you, in a matter of a few yards, from medieval Oxford straight into the 19th century, leading as it does to Museum Road, lined with 1870s villas, and out into Parks Road, first laid out in the 1830s.

On the left-hand side is the unmiss-able bulk of **Keble College**, a byzantine riot of red, yellow and blue brick. The college was founded in 1868 as a memorial to John Keble, leading light of the Oxford Movement.

At a time when the other Oxford colleges were becoming more liberal and preparing to abolish ancient rules that excluded all non-Anglicans from membership, Keble set out to be assertively different. Committed to turning out clergymen formed in the strict High Church mould, Keble demanded that its students lead an almost monastic life of poverty and obedience.

Fortunately for the students, this objective, the antithesis to intellectual freedom, was soon modified and, while remaining primarily a theological college, Keble began to adopt more progressive attitudes—accepting, for example, that Darwin's evolutionary theories were not necessarily incompatible with Christian teaching.

The buildings of Keble, however, were put up during the first flurry of

he first day f the rest of neir lives.

evangelical zeal, with William Butterfield, himself a committed supporter of the Oxford Movement, as architect. In an attempt to explain their raw ugliness, architectural critics have argued that Butterfield was at least consistent to the aims of Keble: how better to emphasise Keble's difference from the rest of Oxford than to build in harsh brick, an alien material in a city of stone; how better to keep the minds of Keble's students on spiritual matters than to deny them the sight of beautiful architecture? Lovers of High Victorian architecture might disagree, and argue that there is a certain splendour to the exterior, at least, of the huge chapel (nicknamed "the Fair Isle Jersey" for its interwoven patterns of coloured brick).

The chapel interior could only appeal to connoisseurs of kitsch, for the stained glass is lifeless and the mosaics of Biblical scenes around the walls (inspired by Giotto's great fresco cycle at Assisi!) are sickly sweet, like illustrations from a child's *Life of Jesus*.

A small side chapel to the south was added in 1892, specifically to house Holman Hunt's famous painting *The Light of the World*. Butterfield refused to allow the picture to be hung in the main chapel on the grounds that it is "a place of worship, not a gallery". Holman Hunt, on the other hand, was so angry when he learned that the college was charging visitors to see the picture that he painted another and gave it to St Paul's Cathedral in London. The side chapel also contains a painting by William Keys, *The Dead Christ Mourned by His Mother*.

Opposite Keble is another assertive Victorian building, a cross between a French château and London's St Pancras railway station, that houses the **University Museum**. This, however, is in an entirely different class, a delightful and innovative building that often induces a smile for the ingenious, half-humorous, half-serious details.

The University Museum was begun in 1855 at a time when Oxford was beginning to teach experimental science. Unlike the old humanities, which could be taught in a room, or even while strolling around the river meadows, science teaching required laboratories, and the block of land to the east of Parks Road was set aside for this purpose.

The museum was the first building to be erected, together with the Inorganic Chemistry Laboratory alongside (to the right)—curiously enough, designed to resemble the medieval Abbot's Kitchen at Glastonbury Abbey. The aim of the museum was didactic and all-embracing: to tell the history of life on earth.

Monkey business: Such an objective was bound to be controversial in an age that still clung to Biblical ideas of Creation—and when the building was completed in 1860, it was inaugurated by the now-famous debate between the Bishop of Oxford, Samuel Wilberforce, and Professor Huxley on Darwin's evolutionary theories.

The Bishop, according to contemporary accounts, thought that he had won

Keble College: set up as a memorial to an Oxford Movement founder.

the day when he asked Huxley "was it through his grandfather or his grandmother that he claimed his descent from a monkey?" At least one lady fainted and the meeting degenerated into a near-riot when Huxley said that he was "not ashamed to have a monkey for his ancestor, but he would be ashamed to be connected with a man who used great gifts to obscure the truth".

Other controversies surrounded the building itself. Critics called the design "indecent" and "detestable", because to them the Gothic style should be reserved for religious buildings, not one devoted to a secular purpose. The Dublin firm of builders employed to erect the museum hired as stone masons two brothers who have passed into Oxford legend. The brothers O'Shea, who carved all the animals and birds of the corbels and window surrounds, were not only renowned for their fondness for drink but also for their irascibility. Dons who continually interfered with the brothers' work, objecting to the subjects portrayed, were likely to find themselves featured in unflattering caricature in stone. Sadly, the brothers were ordered to destroy this work.

The interior of the museum is delightfully eccentric. It is lit by a glass roof, supported by slender columns and a wrought-iron vault that makes you feel as if you are inside the rib cage of one of the great dinosaurs displayed on the floor below. The ironwork is ornamented with representations of trees and shrubs, and the columns of the side aisles are each made from a different form of stone or mineral, all labelled.

Statues of eminent scientists line the walls, looking down on cases of stuffed animals and skeletons of creatures living and extinct. There is a splendid painting of a Dodo, by John Savery, described as an over-size flightless dove with a hooked beak—this same painting inspired Lewis Carroll's famous character in *Alice in Wonderland*. Another area is devoted to Oxford dinosaurs—not reactionary dons, but fossil

skeletons found in the Jurassic rocks of the Oxford area as the city began to expand rapidly in the 19th century.

The back corridor of the University Museum leads to the **Pitt-Rivers Museum of Ethnology**, another wonderfully unspoiled example of 19th-century museum display. This was built in 1885 to house the collection of Lieutenant-General Augustus Henry Lane Fox Pitt-Rivers, built up during his service at the frontiers of the Empire with the Grenadier Guards.

The museum is literally packed with case after case of splendid objects— demons, fertility figures, totem poles and masks—as well as practical objects such as boats, tents, saddles and snowshoes. A remarkable theme of the museum is the continuity and similarities that exist between cultures; illuminating parallels are drawn between the use of magical charms amongst the tribes of Asia and similar practices among Christians in "civilised" Europe.

The heart of Oxford is easily reached again by turning left down Parks Road, stopping first to admire the 18th-century gates, on the right, that separate the road from the long vista of Trinity College Gardens.

Directly opposite is **Wadham College**, regarded as the youngest of the "old" (i.e. pre-Victorian) foundations. Nicholas Wadham, a retiring and obscure Somerset landowner, left his considerable wealth for the foundation of a college at his death in 1609. Wadham's widow, Dorothy, proved an energetic executor, despite being over 75 years old, and by 1613, less than five years later, the college was virtually complete.

Thus Wadham is the only ancient college to have been built at one go, and it has scarcely changed since. The buildings are strictly symmetrical and were designed by the West Country builder William Arnold, who borrowed motifs from other Oxford Jacobean-Gothic buildings but put them together in a highly accomplished manner.

Wadham College from the Parks, as seen by Ackermann.

The Front Quad is entered through the fan-vaulted gate-tower. Directly opposite, the fine portal is similar to the exactly contemporary Tower of the Five Orders, in Old Schools Quadrangle: here, though, the statue of James I is joined by the founder and foundress. The chapel is entered by the passageway on the far left (northeast) corner of the quad, and has some of Oxford's finest 17th-century stained glass.

The east window, depicting the Passion and Resurrection, is the only one in Oxford painted by Bernard van Linge (dated 1622), brother of the more prolific Abraham, whose work is found in several college chapels. The other significant object is the fine screen of 1613, with its strapwork, slender columns and cresting.

To the left of the chapel is the **Fellows' Garden**, filled with rare and ancient trees, including a striking copper beech, planted in 1796. The garden completely surrounds the chapel, and the **Cloister Garden**, to the rear, con-

tains a modernistic bronze statue of Sir Maurice Bowra by John Doubleday. Bowra, a literary scholar who presided over Wadham as Warden (head) from 1938 to 1970, was renowned for his ascerbic, and often bawdy, wit. ("Awful shit, never met him," is one of his renowned judgements. Of the Master of Balliol, he once remarked: "He has been ill but unfortunately is getting better. Otherwise deaths have been poor for the time of year.")

The southeast side of Wadham's Front Quad is an exact match of the northeast, with the hall a mirror of the chapel but with a splendid original hammerbeam roof. The garden of the adjacent Back Quad contains a giant lime tree of considerable, though unknown, age. The heady scent of its summer flowers is not only irresistible to bees but spreads, on a still day, to fill the air as far as the city centre, which, for all that it seems a long way off in Wadham's quiet precincts, is only a few steps away.

Rubbish removal from Wadham today.

THE TOWN

Oxford's principal medieval streets meet at **Carfax** *(see page 115)*, which was always a chaotic crossroads and resolutely remained so despite the demolition of St Martin's Church as part of a street-widening scheme in the 1890s. All that is left of St Martin's now is the tower, with its 17th-century clock and jacks, mustachioed figures in Roman military costume, who strike the quarter hour.

Shakespeare's godson, William Davenant (later himself a playwright), was christened in St Michael's Church in 1606, and Shakespeare is known to have stayed regularly with Davenant's father, landlord of the Crown Tavern. This building, just across the street (No. 3, Cornmarket), was changed almost beyond recognition in the 1920s, but the **Painted Room** on the second floor (open during office hours) has well-preserved mid 16th-century wall paintings of fruits and flowers.

Next door, on the left, is the **Golden Cross Inn**. The 15th-century gateway leads into an enclosed courtyard, surrounded by timber-framed ranges with projecting upper storeys. The buildings were meticulously restored in 1987 to create a stylish shopping precinct, and the restaurant on the left occupies a 15th-century range, with more well-preserved 16th-century wall paintings on the upper floor.

Old-style selling: Golden Cross Way leads into Oxford's **covered market**, a paradise for gourmets, though no quarter is given to the sensibilities of vegetarians, who will find haunches of meat, plump turkeys and game of every kind, hung in great quantities outside the butchers' stalls in true Edwardian style. The market was originally built in 1774 as part of a campaign to rid Oxford of its untidy and often foul-smelling street markets. Fish and meat sellers, later to be joined by butter and fruit retailers,

were brought into one place under the supervision of a beadle.

The present structure dates largely from the 1890s when the market was rebuilt and roofed over. It retains its turn-of-the-century atmosphere, and it is possible to buy a great range of locally produced "poor man's meats"—haggis, brawns, faggots, raised pies, black puddings and Oxford sausages—not to mention fresh fruit and fish, cheeses and rich pastries.

The south side of the market leads out into the **High Street**, with the **Mitre** a short way down on the left.

The Mitre is one of Oxford's most ancient inns and was, until converted (many would say downgraded) to a restaurant in 1967, a favourite haunt of over-indulgent scholars. The German clergyman, Pastor Moritz, relates in his *Travels in England* (1795) that he was taken there by a companion and found it full of convivial parsons debating whether or not a passage in the Book of Judges ("wine cheereth God and man")

meant literally that God was a wine tippler.

On the opposite side of the High Street is a fine run of buildings. The premises of **Oxford University Press** are at number 116, selling only the books that it publishes, including complete sets of the *Oxford English Dictionary* at a mere £1,500. Next door, number 117/118 has a fine Art Nouveau shop window, while the Regency bow-fronted shop window of Hall Bros., University Tailors, is used to display silk-lined academic gowns and clothing embroidered with multi-coloured college crests. The front of Russell, Acott & Co.'s music shop is carved with cherubs, and a little further up, at number 137, is Savory's fragrant pipe and tobacco shop, in a medieval building that was once the Fox Inn.

In between these shops, scarcely noticeable, are the narrow entrances to three alleys, known as yards. One leads to the Wheatsheaf Inn, the middle one to Oxford's best-known French restau-rant, La Sorbonne, and the third to the Chequers, a characterful pub with 16th-century oak panelling and a splendid 18th-century tavern clock. All link up with Blue Boar Street, named after an inn, pulled down in 1893 to build the public library, now the Oxford Museum, on the corner of St Aldate's.

The **Oxford Museum** is excellent for an easy-to-digest history of the city's development, illustrated by recent archaeological discoveries. Best of all are the reconstructions of typical Oxford houses, contrasting the working-class district of Jericho *(see page 171)* with the stylish drawing rooms of North Oxford's spacious villas, decorated in the latest William Morris textiles.

Other highlights are the Keble College Barge, an example of one of the ornate floating boathouses of the late 19th century from which spectators watched river races during Eights Week, and the reconstruction of a 1930s living room in the newly built Morris Motors suburb of Cowley.

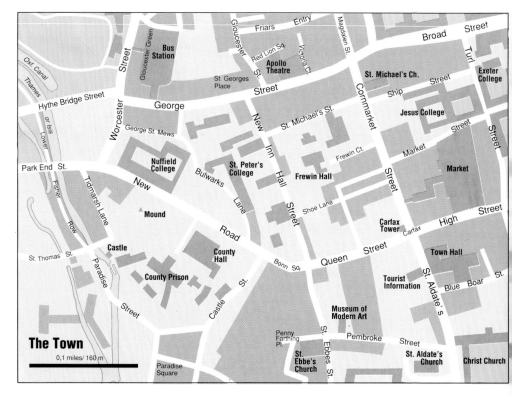

The Town

0,1 miles/ 160 m

From the museum, turn right up St Aldate's to return to Carfax, and then left down **Queen Street**, the shopping heart of the city. This part of the city has not been well treated by developers over the years, and this semi-pedestrianised street, where buses force a slow and resentful route through the crowds of shoppers, exhibits shop architecture at its most utilitarian. The designers of the **Clarendon Centre**, to the right (completed in 1984), and the Westgate Centre (1972) both show a preoccupation with post-modernist decor constructed of blue tubes.

At the far end of Queen Street is **Bonn Square**, named after Oxford's twin city, site of a memorial to men of the Oxfordshire Regiment who died in various campaigns on India's northwest frontier.

Open-top admiration for Carfax Tower and Cornmarket Street.

Beyond, in New Road, is the distinctive tower of **Nuffield College**, built as a library and containing 70,000 books on 10 floors. The tower was intended to be part of a large college chapel but this plan was altered as a consequence of the delays and financial problems surrounding the whole project. When Viscount Nuffield, better known as William Richard Morris, founder and proprietor of Morris Motors, proposed founding a new college, he had in mind one specialising in the practical skills of engineering and accountancy.

He was persuaded, instead, to fund a post-graduate college of social studies. Formal agreement was reached in 1937, but progress was slow because Nuffield disliked the original "un-English" designs for the college, and, by the time new designs were completed, war was declared.

In the event, work did not begin until 1949, and this Lutyens-inspired, Cotswold-style college, very much a product of 1930s architectural thinking, was not completed until 1960. Nuffield had devoted the best part of his wealth to the project, but still referred to it as "that bloody Kremlin, where left-wingers study at my expense".

Nuffield is, except for the tower, much like a Cotswold country house on a large scale, with two courtyards, linked by steps, surrounding lily ponds and rose beds. The lower quad is built on the site of the Oxford Canal basin, once used to unload coals from Staffordshire to warm many a cosy set of college rooms. The chapel of Nuffield, scaled down from its original grand proportions because of escalating costs, is now no more than a room on the top floor of L staircase, entered from the lower quad. John Piper, the artist, designed the glass and the simple wooden box pews, modelled on those of Ivychurch in the Romney Marshes.

Opposite Nuffield is the grass-covered mound, or motte, of **Oxford Castle**, thrown up about 1071 by the Norman Robert d'Oilly. **Oxford Prison** and **County Hall** now occupy the bailey. A small stone keep, four storeys high, can be seen by turning left up Tidmarsh Lane, where it stands by the side of a weir on the River Thames; indeed, it was probably built to defend the river crossing and may pre-date the castle mound itself.

Park End Street leads eastwards, out of the town, and was known in the 1930s as the "Street of Wheels" because of the number of garages lining both sides. One is now used as an auction room, while another forms the rambling premises of Waterfield's second-hand bookshop—a good place to look for unwanted review copies, sold by dons, or collections of books sold from the estates of deceased fellows. Beyond, recognisable from afar by the smell of malt, is Halls' Oxford and West Brewery—a subsidiary of Allied Breweries formed in 1980 but reviving the name of an old-established Oxford brewery that closed in 1926.

Beyond, **Oxford railway station** is visible in the distance, deliberately kept well out of the centre of Oxford because, among other reasons, the railway was thought likely to corrupt young students—making it easy for them to

Selling in the rain in Cornmarket Street.

travel to places of ill-repute, such as Ascot racecourse. The existing station lies on the former Great Western Railway line to London. Another line, closed in 1967, terminated at the junction of Park End Road and Hythe Bridge Street: part of the old station, painted red, white and blue, is now a tyre and exhaust depot.

Linking Park End Road and Hythe Bridge Street is a short footpath along the River Thames, known as **Fisher Row**. The original fishermen's and canal bargees' cottages have gone, but it remains a picturesque spot, overhung by a pendulous willow and often frequented by swans.

Hythe Bridge itself dates, in its current form, to 1861, and marks the point where the Oxford Canal *(pages 216-19)* stops today. The rest of the canal's route into the city is now filled in, but an ambitious scheme has been mooted to create a new canal basin on the Worcester Road car park site, to the right.

Opposite, fronting on to Worcester Street, is an adventurous brick building, with three lead-covered angle towers, completed in 1989 and enclosing Gloucester Green. This is a welcome new addition to the Oxford townscape, tidying up an area that had served as a windswept and litter-strewn bus station ever since 1932, when the cattle market on the site was closed down.

Of the pubs that once served the thirsty cattle drovers, only the **Welsh Pony**, in George Street, now survives, a student haunt popular for its inexpensive food. Further up, the 1894 Corn Exchange and Old Fire Station are due to be redeveloped as an Arts Centre. Opposite, the delicate neo-Jacobean Social Studies Faculty was originally built in 1880 as the City of Oxford High School, and numbered T.E. Lawrence among its pupils.

New Inn Hall Street marks the eastern boundary of the medieval city, and was once just inside the walls. The original New Inn Hall has gone but **St Peter's College**, halfway up on the

Swanning around at Fisher Row.

right, now occupies part of the site. St Peter's was founded in 1929, and did not achieve college status until 1961, but the buildings are much older. The college is entered through **Linton House**, built in 1797 as the headquarters of the Oxford Canal Company which then moved, in 1828, to the neo-classical **Canal House**, which now serves as the Master's Lodge. The college chapel is the former church of St Peter-le-Bailey, built in 1874 to the design of Basil Champneys on the site of the original Norman church.

Opposite St Peter's, **Frewin Hall** is an attractive house, set well back from the street, of 16th and 18th-century date, converted to student accommodation in the 1970s. It backs on to the red-brick Gothic premises of the **Oxford Union Society** (closed to the public), built in 1857 as a permanent home for the debating club that was founded in 1823. Harold Macmillan, Britain's Prime Minister from 1957 until 1963 and later Chancellor of the University,

called it "an unrivalled training ground for debates in the Parliamentary style". The list of past Presidents reads like a Who's Who of the political and journalistic world—and not merely of the UK, since Benazir Bhutto, President in 1977, went on to become Prime Minister of Pakistan.

The Union Society fronts on to St Michael's Street, with the Saxon tower of **St Michael's Church** framed at the Cornmarket end. The sturdy tower is Oxford's oldest surviving building and dates to around 1050. It exhibits characteristic late Saxon features, having double belfry windows, each with a fat baluster shaft supporting the arched window heads.

The tower was once built up against the north gate of the city walls, and the gate itself was enlarged in 1293 to create a prison known as the Bocardo. Scholars debate whether Bocardo simply means "boggard", a privy, or whether it derives from the medieval logician's term for a syllogism, imply-

The former New Inn in St Michael' Street.

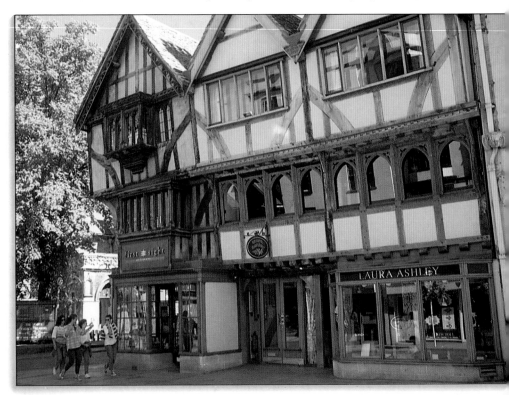

THE OXFORD UNION

"Again and again in its history, the young speakers who catch the President's eye have gone on to catch the eye of the country, even the eye of the world," wrote political journalist David Walter in his book *The Oxford Union*. It's a fair claim: the Oxford Union Society, founded in 1823, is the most famous student-run body in Britain, possibly in the world, and seven of its officers have become prime ministers.

Like most such student organisations, the Oxford Union runs discos and jazz evenings and operates a cheap bar. But what sets it apart are its weekly showpiece debates. Modelled on Westminster's parliamentary procedure, these constitute nothing less than a top-notch political training ground. They give students a chance not only to hear leading public figures defend their views but also to hone their own debating skills in preparation for the anticipated day when they themselves will be leading public figures.

Richard Nixon and Jimmy Carter have spoken here. British Cabinet Ministers regularly make the 50-mile trek from London. Preachers, playwrights and popular comedians have all pitted their wits against the difficult acoustics and an unusually discerning and frequently rowdy audience. Hitler was given hope in 1935 when the Oxford Union carried the motion that "This House would not fight for King and Country". (Strangely, he failed to appreciate that what people say they would do in certain circumstances often bears little relation to their actual behaviour.)

The Union's training for the rough and tumble of real politics is ruthlessly practical. To become President of the Union, a student must clamber up the proverbial greasy pole by winning various elections, perhaps becoming initially a committee member and later secretary, treasurer or librarian. Just to make things just that little bit more interesting, the Society's celebrated Rule 33 forbids a candidate from informing anyone, with the exception of "close personal friends", that he or she is running for office.

This awkward handicap spurs candidates to find ingenious ways of circumventing the rule. They are thus liable to buy drinks for total strangers, casually letting slip in the conversation the fact that they just might be standing for election this term. This practice, known as "hacking", is scorned by non-political students, thereby affording them the opportunity to rehearse the contempt they will doubtless display in later life towards professional politicans.

Once elected, the President assumes significant responsibilities. Four speakers have to be found for each of the eight debates held every term, and the Union, which has a staff of 30 and a turnover of around £500,000 a year, has to be managed efficiently and profitably.

It is no small task. In the mid-1980s, the Union's fine Victorian buildings, including a library with Pre-Raphaelite murals, were in serious disrepair and bankruptcy seemed a possibility. But company sponsorship of debates and events helped swell the coffers and a Japanese bank donated £1 million towards restoration. The resulting new-found vitality boosted university membership to 6,500 (two students in three) and there are 60,000 members worldwide. Dues are £70 a year.

Even for non-debaters, this is good value. The Union's library, for example, houses over 75,000 volumes, making it the city's largest lending and scientific library. It has the best collection of 19th-century books in Oxford. The New Library houses a collection of classical, political, philosophical, economic and scientific periodicals and a large selection of literary classics. The Old Library is said to have the most comfortable leather armchairs in the city.

The bar, open from 9 a.m. to 11 p.m. each day, serves snacks as well as drinks, while the intimate Jazz Cellar is the only place in Oxford for drinking into the small hours without an entrance fee. Those wishing to escape college food or to entertain their parents can dine at the Union's own licensed restaurant, the Macmillan, at rock-bottom prices. There are other rooms for sitting, reading or watching television. Not least important, the Union has the only two full-sized snooker tables in central Oxford.

BLACKWELL'S: PICTURE OF A PHENOMENON

Blackwell's, one of the world's most famous bookshops, first opened its doors in October 1879. Situated at the end of Broad Street, it was (and still is) in one of the most beautiful parts of the city, surrounded by Trinity, Balliol, Exeter, Hertford and Wadham Colleges and opposite Christopher Wren's Sheldonian Theatre.

Benjamin Henry Blackwell's shop was just 12 ft (3.6 metres) square and was criticised by many for its situation—at the end of Broad Street furthest from the city centre and with two well-established bookshops opposite. Frederick Macmillan, proprietor of the famous publishing house of Macmillan and forebear of Harold Macmillan who became Prime Minister and Chancellor of Oxford University, said: "Well, Mr Blackwell, we shall be pleased to open an account with you but I fear you have chosen the wrong side of the street to be successful."

This pessimism was soon disproved. Blackwell's devotion to books—he characterised bookselling as "the infinite capacity for taking pains"—quickly became legendary. Professors, dons and undergraduates hastened to his door. The shop was originally so small that, when more than three customers came in, the apprentice had to be sent outside.

Right from the start the tradition was established that customers should be allowed to browse among the books, undisturbed by the staff. The custom continues today.

Naturally enough, famous literary figures have always been among Blackwell's customers and the shop itself has been the subject of many writings. In *Summoned by Bells*, John Betjeman wrote:

I wandered into Blackwell's, where my bill
Was so enormous that it wasn't paid
Till ten years later, from the small estate
My father left.

Other well-known customers have included Hilaire Belloc, A. E. Houseman, Oscar Wilde, Bernard Shaw and Charles Dodgson (better known as Lewis Carroll).

From the first tiny room, Blackwell's gradually expanded in order to meet the steadily increasing business and took over more space behind the shop. After World War II, this need became more urgent and some departments were moved to nearby premises. The most notable part of this continual expansion was the development of a vast underground room when further sideways and upwards growth proved impossible. Known as the Norrington Room and opened in 1966, it was named after the then president of Trinity College, under which it extended.

Still a family firm, Blackwell's is also a publisher in its own right. Benjamin Henry Blackwell started to publish poetry in the 1880s, and this was continued by his son, Basil, publishing early works by many who subsequently became famous, among them J.R.R. Tolkien, Robert Graves, and L.P. Hartley. From these small beginnings, two major publishing companies have grown: Basil Blackwell Ltd, which specialises in humanities, and Blackwell Scientific Publications, which concentrates on scientific and medical titles. Basil Blackwell, known to everyone as "the Gaffer" [*boss*], was knighted in 1956 for his services to bookselling.

Today, Blackwell's has nine shops in Oxford. The main store, with its front on the original site, is at 48–51 Broad Street and houses most academic subjects and general titles, including secondhand books. At number 53 is the Map and Travel Shop, a treasure trove of information for both practical and armchair travellers. Across the street are three more shops. At number 27, the Art and Poster Shop has a huge range of books, posters, postcards, calendars and cards. The Paperback Shop at number 23–25 includes a Science Fiction department. The Children's Bookshop at number 8 stocks books and toys.

A few yards from the main shop at 38 Holywell Street is the Music Shop which offers not only books but also sheet music and recordings. A shop in the Museum of Modern Art at 30 Pembroke Street reflects the museum's specilisation in the history and development of 20th-century art. Away from the city centre are two more shops, one at Oxford Polytechnic and one in the academic centre of the John Radcliffe Hospital.

ing a difficult trap from which to escape. The Oxford martyrs, Cranmer, Latimer and Ridley, were all imprisoned here before being taken outside the city wall to be executed.

St Michael's Church was substantially restored after a fire in 1953 but some good 15th-century glass has survived, including, in the south aisle, a window showing Christ crucified on a lily flower (symbolising purity). The treasury in the tower is used to display a beautiful silver chalice of 1562, and a lustful sheela-na-gig, a late 11th-century erotic stone carving. Opposite the church is one of Oxford's finest timber-framed buildings, originally built in 1389 as the New Inn, and recently restored to its 18th-century appearance, with jettied upper storeys.

In the opposite direction, **Dillon's bookshop** occupies the handsome William Baker House on the corner of Broad Street. This is the latest arrival (opened in November 1987) in a street famed for its bookshops. **Thornton's bookshop**, at number 11 Broad Street, is a rambling antiquarian bookshop, no longer quite so idiosyncratic since "improvements" were made in 1985 to meet fire regulations. It is now possible to reach the upper floors without climbing over stacks of unsorted books. At the far end of Broad Street is **Blackwell's**, the doyen of Oxford bookshops, founded in 1879 and still regarded as the largest in the world. The underground Norrington Room, with its murals of Oxford life painted by Edward Bawden in 1973, alone contains more than 3 miles (5 km) of shelving—enough to win it a place in the *Guinness Book of Records*.

Other features of Broad Street include **The Oxford Story**, at number 6, relating the history of the city by means of tableaux (with authentic sounds and smells) and taped commentaries, and number 17, the first permanent shop to be opened by the charity **Oxfam** (Oxford Committee for Famine Relief) in 1948.

Blackwell's Norrington Room has a world-beating 3 miles of shelving.

Theology

Somerville College comes next, founded in 1879 specifically for the education of women. The first "ladies" college, Lady Margaret Hall, had been founded the previous year but under the aegis of the Anglican Church. A group of breakaway liberal nonconformists founded Somerville, named after the scientist and suffragette Mary Somerville (1780–1872), to take women of all religious persuasions—or none.

Women at Oxford were at first patronised rather than welcomed. They were not allowed to attend lectures; instead, tuition was provided by the AEW, the Association for Promoting the Higher Education of Women. They were not allowed to take degrees until 1920, and Somerville, along with the other four women's halls founded in the late 19th century, was not recognised as a full college until 1959.

The buildings of Somerville are small and homely in scale, some built in the "Queen Anne" style of the late 19th century, others in 1930s neo-Georgian.

Somerville, along with St Hilda's College, still does not admit men, and has always been regarded as rather high-brow or "blue-stocking". Yet its former students include an extraordinary number of public figures, not least Shirley Williams, Indira Gandhi and Margaret Thatcher.

Top hospital: Further up Woodstock Road is **Radcliffe Infirmary**, built from the estates of John Radcliffe, the 18th-century physician, but now surrounded by an accretion of later hospital buildings. The adjacent **Radcliffe Observatory**, completed in 1794, is now part of **Green College**, founded in 1979 for graduate medical students. The Observatory, mostly designed by James Wyatt, does not have the expected dome; instead, it is topped by an elongated octagon, carved with personifications of the four winds and modelled on the ancient Greek Tower of the Winds in Athens.

St Anne's College, opposite, traces its origins to the "Society of Oxford

Serious girls studying at Somerville.

172

Home Students", an organisation formed in 1879 to provide higher education for Oxford women—the daughters and wives of dons and students from the local girls' high schools. Because they lived at home, rather than in one of the two women's halls of residence (Somerville and Lady Margaret), they were known as "unattached students", and opponents of women's education were fond of referring to the Society as "Soc. mul. Ox. priv. stud." (abbreviated from the Latin name *Societas mulieram Oxoniae Privatum Studentium*).

The Home Students were taught and supervised in the houses of sympathetic Oxford dons and their friends until, in the 1930s, the numbers of students became so great that more permanent arrangements became necessary. To the existing Victorian houses on the current site, the library and lecture rooms were added. Designed by Sir Giles Gilbert Scott, son of the Victorian Gothicist Sir George, they were completed in 1937.

During World War II, so many Oxford families were involved in war work that it became increasingly difficult to accommodate students at home and find suitable "hostesses" or chaperones; so hostels were built and by 1942 St Anne's had been transformed into a residential institution like any other, achieving full college status in 1959. A number of buildings were added postwar, notably the **Founder's Gatehouse** (1966), a building in the modernist idiom reflecting medieval precedents in its polygonal turrets, and the **Dining Hall** (1958–60), with its glass walls and rooftop lantern.

Heading back towards Oxford city centre, the **Church of St Giles** sits at the apex of the fork where Woodstock and Banbury Roads take their separate ways. The church is largely 13th-century and sits in an island of green, facing down the wide, tree-lined thoroughfare, best seen in early September when the traffic is excluded for the annual St Giles' Fair (Monday and Tuesday fol-

ess serious
rls
elebrating
lay Day.

lowing the first Sunday in September).

Originating as a toy fair with side shows for children in the 1780s, the fair survived attempts to suppress it in the 19th century because of alleged rowdy and licentious behaviour. Today's fun fair is no different to any of those that are held up and down the country except for the poignant contrast between the flashing lights, candy floss and bingo stalls set against the sedate and ancient college buildings.

The east (right-hand) side of St Giles' Street is lined with a pleasing mixture of mainly 17th and 18th-century buildings, many of them owned by religious bodies who, in this century at least, seem to co-exist in neighbourly harmony: at number 34–36, the Christian Scientists, at number 38, St Benet's Hall, Catholic Benedictine monks, and at number 43, the Quakers, while at Pusey House and **St Cross College**, beyond Pusey Street, theological scholars train for the Anglican ministry.

One pub, the **Eagle and Child** (known locally as the Bird and Babe), sits amongst these religious houses. It has been an inn since 1650, and was the meeting place from the 1930s to the 1960s of the informal literary group known as the Inklings. Led by C.S. Lewis (described by his pupil John Betjeman as "breezy, tweedy, beer-drinking and jolly"), the Inklings included amongst their fraternity such luminaries as Charles Williams, Nevill Coghill and J.R.R. Tolkien.

It was here, in these cosy, fireside surroundings, that Tolkein began reading instalments of his saga *The Lord of the Rings* to the assembled company, little realising that it would become such a success that Tolkien himself would be forced, by a torrent of letters, phone calls and visits from fans, to exchange the comforts of Oxford for a life of seclusion in Bournemouth. Eventually, however, after his wife died in 1971, he returned to Oxford's womb, taking rooms in Merton and becoming an Honorary Fellow.

Soft sales pitch at St Giles' Fair.

ST GILES' FAIR

The Fair (as it is always called) is one of Oxford's most cherished annual events. Of course, there are hard-headed citizens who complain that it disrupts trade and traffic, but most people would spring to the defence of an occasion enjoyed by people of every age and type. Like Christmas, it is age-old but perennially fresh.

St Giles' Fair was originally a parish wake, a religious event. The first record of the wake dates from 1624, but its existence through the period of the Civil War and the Protectorate would have been fitful. The association with St Giles, the patron saint of beggars and cripples, fixed both the date of the Fair (the Monday and Tuesday following the first Sunday in September) and the location, the splendidly wide street that links the Martyrs' Memorial and St Giles' Church. By the 18th century, the occasion was known as St Giles' Feast, and was well established as a time for feasting, sporting events, and the selling of "small wares".

The Fair really came into its own in Victorian times, when "wonders of art and nature" were added. Menageries and freak shows were the earliest sights: an elephant was a regular visitor, as were the Bear Lady and the Double-bodied Hindoo Boy. An account of the Fair in 1838 mentions "the galloping horses, the Fat Woman, the dwarves, and Jonah's Whale", where one " went in at his head and out at his tail".

New inventions always found their way to the Fair: the photographer with his three-for-a-shilling portraits; the Biograph exhibitions; the miniature railway; the Chairoplane rides. Towards the end of the 19th century, the Fair was a dazzling event, with the great traction engines called *Alexandra* and *General Buller* providing brilliant illuminations. Taylor's Bioscope Show was adorned with 4,000 coloured lights, while the rival establishment, run by Jacob Studt, was approached through Corinthian pillars and graced by troupes of lady dancers.

More surprisingly, females also appeared at the Fair as wrestlers, wearing corsets and black tights, as we know from the photograph of them taken by the great Oxford photographer Henry Taunt. Little wonder, with such attractions on offer, that St Giles' Fair became, by 1900, the major holiday for not only Oxford city, but the county beyond. The huge caravan of wagons, caravans and engines gathered in Woodstock Road—then open country—on Sunday, providing a fine spectacle, and at 5 a.m. on Monday morning, the procession moved into the city.

The Fair had its problems, of course. In 1838, the Mayor of Oxford issued an order for the exclusion of gipsies from the site because of their pickpocketing. Horseplay was firmly dealt with in 1898, when the Mayor decreed a penalty of two months' imprisonment or a £5 fine for anyone found assaulting another person with "a Squirt, Scratch-back, Cracker, Whip, or Brush".

Particularly dramatic events occurred in 1830, after a year of trouble on nearby Otmoor, where the local people were opposing the enclosure by landowners of their common land. Matters came to a head in September, when the militia were called in to stop the systematic destruction of drainage and enclosure works by the moormen. About 50 were arrested and taken by wagon into Oxford for trial. But the crowds gathered for the Fair were sympathetic to the villagers' cause, the soldiers were pelted with stones, and the prisoners freed to cries of "Otmoor for Ever".

In many ways, the Fair today looks much as it did in Edwardian times. The traction engines still provide power, and an ancient and splendid roundabout always occupies pride of place by the Martyrs' Memorial. There are still coconuts as prizes if you can knock one off its perch, shooting galleries, stalls selling candy floss and toffee apples.

Nowadays there are much more elaborate and terrifyingly fast rides, taking the place of the freaks and theatre shows. But the wide street is still gaudy, crowded, and full of exciting noise and smells, the Fair still a local occasion enjoyed by all who come.

There's an old saying: "A town without a fair is like a body without a heart." Oxford's heart still beats strongly for those two cheerful days each September.

THE RIVERS

To many towns and cities built by a river, the water is simply an obstruction to be bridged, or a convenient sewer. To Oxford, the Rivers **Thames** and **Cherwell** and their surrounding meadows are far more: they provide a large, semi-wild playground for the competitive instincts of energetic oarsmen or for the more sybaritic pursuits of picnics, punting, bathing and courtship.

Philosophers have resolved complex syllogisms while walking the river banks, in true Platonic fashion. Poets, painters and storytellers—notably Lewis Carroll—have been inspired by the calm, scenic beauty of the meadows, and, in our own age, ecologists have come to realise that the meadows, regularly flooded but never ploughed or fertilised (except by cows), are a haven for rare plants and insects.

Protest poem: Less sensitive souls have often proposed plans to tame or use these "wastelands": a four-lane highway, crossing Christ Church providing an inner city relief road, was first proposed in 1933 and revived in 1968. W.H. Auden penned a poem in protest at the proposals ("may the Meadows be only frequented by scholars and couples and cows").

The combined efforts of Oxford's townspeople and the academic population brought a halt to these plans, proving with what affection everyone in the city holds their river landscape. The threat has not entirely disappeared: science parks are the latest rage, and although the more picturesque meadows of Christ Church and Magdalen are virtually sacrosanct, developers continually seek to swallow up the wilder wastes of Osney Mead and Port Meadow, west of the city.

Christ Church Meadow is the principal focus of Oxford's summertime sport and recreation. Most people enter via the wrought-iron gates off St Aldate's and through the colourful Christ Church War Memorial Garden. There is, however, another way in, used by those who want to slip into the meadows for a quiet walk, without meeting the tour groups who congregate at the Christ Church entrance. It is the narrow pathway, off Merton Street, between Corpus Christi and Merton colleges.

If you take this route, you come out beneath the walls of Merton College, with **Deadman's Walk** to the left—so called because funeral processions used to pass this way to the Jewish cemetery in what is now the Botanic Garden. **Merton Grove** comes next, and its playing fields used by Christ Church choirboys and Merton students.

The path then joins **Broad Walk**, a wide avenue once planted with ancient elm trees. The stump of one giant remains, but old age and Dutch elm disease carried them off in 1976; plane trees have now been planted in their place. Oxford families used to promenade here on Sunday afternoons, and

even now it is a popular setting-off point for boat trips.

Turning right, then first left, you enter **Poplar Walk**, lined with tall trees planted by the head of Christ Church, Dean Liddell, in 1872, turning a muddy pathway into an avenue down to the river boathouses. The Dean's daughter, Alice, came this way with "Lewis Carroll" in July 1862, on the way to a boat trip during which Charles Dodgson began to tell the stories that resulted in *Alice's Adventures in Wonderland*.

Poplar Walk leads to a wide, straight stretch of the River Thames—also called the **Isis** within Oxford, a Latinate name first coined by John Leland in 1535 who seems not to have been at all happy with the pre-Roman Celtic name (from *tam*, meaning "broad" and *wys*, "water").

This part of the river is the focus for the main boating event of the summer, Eights Week—also a great social event, with partisan crowds either celebrating or drowning their disappointment in wine, depending on the performance of their college eights.

College members and their guests watch the races from the verandahs of bank-side boathouses. Until the turn of the century, ornate floating barges were used instead—the last of these, Keble College barge, remained in use until 1958 and part of it is now displayed in the Museum of Oxford *(page 156)*. In his satirical novel, *Zuleika Dobson*, Max Beerbohm has the entire student population of Oxford commit mass suicide by leaping from their barges into the river, all hopelessly in love with Zuleika—not, perhaps, so far from the truth as one might think, since romantic emotions still run high as the summer term draws to a close and final-year students either cement or break their Oxford liaisons on these banks.

Tree-hung backwater: It is possible, from here, to follow the Thames for some 2 miles (3 km) down to the lock at Iffley *(see page 194)*. Otherwise, take the leftward path that follows the bank

Limbering up on the Ergometer.

of the River Cherwell from the point where it meets the Thames. The Cherwell, which rises in Northamptonshire, is a narrow and shallow river, used for punting rather than races, with many a tree-hung peaceful backwater, rich in bird and plant life.

Occasionally, as you walk eastwards, you catch glimpses of the city skyline through the trees to the left. After a short stretch, the Cherwell divides—the right hand (southernmost) branch is the **New Cut**, dug during the Civil War in the 1640s as part of the city defences, intended to halt Parliamentary troops approaching from the London side.

The Cherwell path eventually returns to meet Broad Walk, on the left, and Rose Lane to the right, which leads to the **Botanic Garden**. At around 5 acres (2 hectares), this garden is small but packed with interest. It was founded in 1621 by Henry Danvers, Earl of Danby, and is the oldest physic garden in Britain (third in the world, after Pisa and Leyden).

The first keeper, or head gardener, was a retired German soldier and publican named Jacob Bobart, but he certainly understood what was needed to create a good growing environment. He ordered 4,000 loads of "mucke and donge" to be spread on the original 3-acre site to raise it above the Cherwell floodwaters, and built the 14-ft (4.3-metre) wall that still encloses three sides of the garden.

The fourth side is enclosed by laboratory buildings and the massive stone triumphal arch, designed by Nicholas Stone as the main entrance in 1632 (the statues of Charles I, Charles II and the Earl of Danby were added later, at the end of the century).

Within this sheltered, well-drained and fertilised plot, Bobart laid out a series of rectangular beds, each one devoted to one of the principal plant families. This arrangement, designed to serve the scientific objectives of the garden, has survived, although the regularity is softened now by the many fine

The Botanic Garden, Britain's oldest.

specimen trees that have grown up between the beds.

At the far end of the central path, on the right, is a huge yew tree, sole survivor of an avenue of yews planted in 1650 by Jacob Bobart. Beyond, the triangular New Garden, enclosed in 1944, contains a lily pond, bog garden and two rockeries for lime-loving plants. Another part of this garden is planted with roses illustrating the development of hybrid varieties in the 19th and 20th centuries.

Instant change: Much of this can look bleak in winter, but the third part of the garden, the glasshouse area, provides an instant change of climate and the sight of luxuriant palms and lotuses, ferns and alpines, and a special collection of carnivorous plants.

To reach the **Water Walks** on the opposite side of the High Street you have to enter Magdalen College, cross St John's Quad, pass through the Cloister to the right and out into the green expanse, facing New Building, that lies

beyond. On the left, beyond the huge plane tree, is **Magdalen Grove**, winter home of the famous college herd of fallow deer. The grove once looked considerably more leafy than it does at present: massive elm trees, planted around 1689, succumbed to disease and were felled in 1978. The deer park was probably also first stocked in the late 17th century to supply the college with meat—as it does today, for when the herd grows too large, surplus animals are culled for the college kitchens.

To the right, through the wrought-iron gates, is a bridge over a branch of the Cherwell. Here, if you watch on a sunny day, you are quite likely to see brown trout, or even larger fish, such as perch or pike, basking in the clear, warm waters below, ready to dart back into the shadows created by the overhanging chestnut tree branches beyond if they are disturbed.

Beyond the bridge, the narrow path turns left to follow a raised bank beside the Cherwell, with Long Meadow, **Magdalen Deer Park.**

MESSING ABOUT ON THE RIVERS

Punts, as much a feature of Oxford as the bicycles and spires, have come to embody the timeless romance of the privileged university world. Yet long before the first student ever skipped lectures in favour of punting up the slow-flowing Cherwell, the punt played a vital part in the lives of watermen up and down the Thames. River dredging, fishing, ferrying, transporting and delivering were all duties once carried out by this humble craft.

Decline in river transport in the mid-19th century could have led to the disappearance of the punt altogether. Fortunately, the Victorian Society, recognising the delights of punting days on the river, claimed it as its leisure craft. Punts were modified from broad pontoons which could carry cattle to the slender "saloon" comprising two back-rests for passengers—a design still in use today.

Increased use of power craft on rivers has resulted in a sharp decrease in punting and it has survived as an almost unique feature at Oxford and Cambridge. As a Thames craft, the punt was not introduced to Cambridge until the early Edwardian era, when it was imported from Oxford. The Oxford tradition is to punt from the slope, stern first, whereas in Cambridge, punting from the deck end is the norm.

Some Oxford colleges retain their own punting fleets and most have private hiring arrangements. Punts can be hired throughout the summer from 10 a.m. to sunset from three stations: Folly Bridge on the Thames, and at Magdalen Bridge and the Cherwell Boat House, Bardwell Road (both on the Cherwell). They cost £4 to £5 an hour and can take up to five people, but their use is restricted to swimmers. Paddles are provided in case poles get stuck in the mud. For the less adventurous, rowing boats can also be hired from each station.

Those new to punting might find that the Cherwell provides far fewer hazards than the Thames and is notable for its absence of rowing crews and power boats. The Cherwell is navigable by punt up to Islip. The stretch of Thames from Folly Bridge to Iffley Lock is the congested province of the University rowing crews.

Numerically, rowing is by far the most popular sport amongst students and a large proportion of rowers are women. Participants range from non-competitive water lovers exploring the river to the elite University team. Each college has its own rowing society and the societies are brought together under the umbrella of Oxford University Boating Club (OUBC), founded in 1939.

Rowing was listed among students' major pursuits as early as 1793. The original rowing boats were six-oared and the eight-oared boats in use today are believed to have been introduced from Eton. The first mention of eight-oar racing occurred in 1815.

Since then, rowing has flourished at Oxford. From early morning until dusk throughout the year, Eights, Fours and Sculls can be seen accompanied by coaches who cycle along the towpath, megaphone in hand. On the stretch of river beyond Christ Church Meadow are the college and OUBC boathouses. Just before Iffley Lock is the Isis Tavern, watering hole for many a rower and home to much boating regalia. The two main events in the rowing calendar are Torpids in Hilary term and Eights in Trinity. Torpids involve inter-college matches and, despite the name, the event is far from sluggish. In Eights, rowers of all standards compete to provide the highlight of Oxford's rowing year.

But by far the most glamorous event in rowing is the inter-Varsity race, first staged in 1829. Oxford "dark blues" take on Cambridge "light blues" in the annual Putney-to-Mortlake race. The Blue is awarded in rowing and other sports to those competing in a University team against Cambridge. The extensive media coverage awarded to this race makes the rowing Blue among the most coveted of all sporting awards. At Oxford this elite team trains downstream from Iffley Lock on longer, wider reaches of water.

Between Folly Bridge and Isis Lock at Donnington Bridge is Oxford City Rowing Club. The Town's answer to the Gown. Its aim is to promote men's and women's rowing at national and international levels, thus continuing Oxford City's long association with the river.

summer grazing home for the Magdalen deer, to the right. The raised causeway, almost completely enclosed by a tunnel of tree foliage, was partly created out of the remains of Civil War defensive embankments. It is known as **Addison's Walk**, after Joseph Addison (1672–1719), poet and *Spectator* essayist, whose rooms in Magdalen College overlooked these meadows.

The walk was not laid out in its present form, nor called after Addison, until the 19th century, but the name is appropriate since Addison was a pioneer of naturalistic landscape design, arguing in his *Spectator* essays that the works of nature are often superior to the artificial creations of man.

Ironically, the verdant beauty of the walk was almost changed for ever by one of Addison's later followers. Humphry Repton proposed, in 1801, to dam the Cherwell and create an artificial lake out of the meadows. We must be thankful that the plan was not executed for the meadows now are famous for a far more beautiful sight than a blank sheet of water: in late April, or early May, the grass is filled with the graceful nodding flower heads of purple and white snake's head fritillaries, one of the largest colonies of these rare wild flowers in Britain. Almost picked to extinction in the last century, the Magdalen fritillaries have been carefully protected since 1908. The grazing fallow deer are part of a careful management programme, introduced to the meadows to keep down the buttercups that were threatening to crowd out the vulnerable fritillaries.

At the northern end of Addison's Walk, there are views across to the modern buildings of St Catherine's College (not accessible from this point). The path turns to the right and, at the eastern angle, a bridge over the Cherwell leads into a secluded area known as the **Fellows' Garden**, a delightful spot in spring when the ornamental trees are in flower and the grass is covered in daffodils and anemones. To complete

Addison's Walk, looking towards Christ Church tower.

the circuit, return to the bridge and turn left, following the river bank to Magdalen Bridge and right to return to the college grounds.

The stretches of river north of Magdalen can be reached by crossing Magdalen Bridge to the triangular road junction known as **The Plain**. This busy traffic junction marks the divergence of the Headington, Cowley and Iffley roads, fanning out to the suburbs of Oxford and beyond. Isolated in the island in the centre, the **Victoria Fountain** was built in 1899 and paid for by Morrell's Brewery as a drinking trough for thirsty horses.

Off to the right, in Cowley Place, is the **Magdalen College School**, originally founded in 1480 but relocated to this new site in 1894. A little further down is **St Hilda's College**, founded in 1893 but occupying a fine 18th-century house that looks over the river back to the city.

The founder of St Hilda's was the formidable principal of Cheltenham Ladies' College, Dorothea Beale, and she named the new institution after the 7th-century Abbess of Whitby, who had been the first great educator of women in England. Miss Beale stated, in documents relating to the aims of the college, that "I want none to go for the sake of a pleasant life", and the strict chaperonage system, along with measures such as iron grilles fitted on the hall windows, were all designed to prevent encounters between ladies at the college and members of the opposite sex.

A contemporary wit penned a few immortal lines of protest on behalf of Miss Beale's charges:

Miss Buss and Miss Beale
Cupid's darts do not feel.
How different from us
Miss Beale and Miss Buss.

The road to the left, off The Plain, forms the main street of the suburb of **St Clement's**. A few 17th-century timber-framed buildings survive from the time when St Clement's was a village, but most now date to the early 19th century,

when speculative developers laid out a network of new streets. The area now has many characterful pubs and shops selling everything from near-antiques to theatrical costume, and the **Penultimate Picture Palace**, a cinema in Jeune Street, is a popular student haunt.

Where St Clement's Street divides, take the left-hand fork into Marston Road and look for the lane that leads to the river, opposite the government buildings. This path leads to **Mesopotamia Walk**; the name derives from the Greek, meaning "between the rivers", as in the ancient kingdom that lay between the Tigris and Euphrates. Here the path follows a narrow strip of land between two branches of the Cherwell, a popular stretch of the water for punting and picnics.

At the northern end of the river, punters have to disembark and manhandle their boats over the metal rollers to one side of a weir. Hidden in the bend beyond is the bathing place known as **"Parson's Pleasure"**—traditionally a

male-only resort, where swimming clothes are not worn. It was once customary for ladies to disembark from their punts and walk round the rear of the pool to avoid the sight of naked sunbathers. Another bathing place nearby, called Dame's Delight, was opened in 1934 for the use of ladies and children, but closed in 1970 after flood damage.

From the weir, a path to the left crosses a concrete bridge to meet South Parks Road. On the right is the **University Parks**; part of this is a nature reserve, part forms the grounds of the Oxford University Cricket Club, and the rest is occupied by science faculties and laboratories.

Linacre College, on the left, is for students studying for higher degrees and was founded in 1962 for graduates of universities other than Oxford— many of whom, it was felt at the time, had difficulty in adjusting to the strange ways of Oxford's more traditional colleges.

St Cross Road, left at Linacre, leads past **Holywell Manor** (right), originally 16th-century but remodelled as student accommodation in the 1920s, and the massive brick cubes of the **Law Library** (1964), opposite.

Functional and dull: The turn left into Manor Road, and right into Manor Place, brings you to another problematical example of 1960s architecture, **St Catherine's College**, designed by the Danish architect Arne Jacobsen and completed in 1964.

While modern architects rave over its pioneering "functional" style, most visitors will find the unadorned yellow-brick buildings rather dull. However, the landscaping, also planned by Jacobsen, is now mature and does much to compensate—especially the long vista between the Cherwell and the water gardens, backed by the splendid trees of Magdalen College meadows. From St Catherine's, the city centre is a short walk away, down St Cross Road and Longwall Street.

Left, St Catherine's College. **Right**, strong-arm tactics by Corpus Christi.

OUTER OXFORD

Oxford began to spread out from its medieval walled core in the early 19th century. There was not much room to expand, however, for the city lies on a long north–south gravel terrace, an island between the two rivers, Thames and Cherwell. Once off this island, the terrain was, and still is, wet and marshy. Inevitably, perhaps, as the population began to grow, the poorer housing was built on the wet, low-lying ground, while the wealthier citizens were able to afford large villas on the high ground north of the city.

North Oxford has come to mean something more than just an address: it means wealth and culture, for the splendid houses of this garden suburb were built for Oxford's elite: professors and professional men. Even the peculiar form of "refined" pronunciation once affected by Oxford dons, and still sometimes heard (whereby "o" is pronounced "u", so that college is pronounced *cullage*), was known as "North Oxford".

This suburb begins north of University Parks. **Norham Gardens** was laid out from 1860, and although Italianate villas feature in early plans, neo-Gothic was all the rage by the time the estate came to be developed. Built of brick, with high gables, ornate stone dressings sculpted with fruits and flowers and the occasional turret, these houses were praised by Ruskin as "human and progressive" but ridiculed by others, as were their inhabitants: the Rev. W. Tuckwell disapproved of the fact that professors, tutors and fellows now lived family lives in the "interminable streets of villadom", rather than residing in college "celibate and pastoral".

At the end of Norham Gardens is **Lady Margaret Hall**, founded in 1878 as a women's hall of residence and itself occupying one of the newly built villas. Strong connections with the Church of England distinguished this college, named after Lady Margaret Beaufort, the scholarly mother of Henry VII, from its contemporary, Somerville.

The original villa, Old Hall, is the undistinguished yellow-grey brick building to the right of the entrance. Better by far is the "Queen Anne" style red-brick extension, designed by Basil Champneys and similar to the splendid work he did at Newnham College, Cambridge—more domestic in scale, more endearing than the assertive Gothic.

For the chapel, yet another style was employed—Byzantine, with an external octagon that, inside, forms a dome, and designed by Sir Giles Gilbert Scott in 1931. The beautiful triptych was painted by Burne-Jones around 1863. The Hall is also blessed with gardens that stretch to the River Cherwell, where remnants of old water meadows are carpeted with daffodils, cowslips, fritillaries and primroses in spring.

North Oxford also has its own school,

eft, an old-
yle postbox
North
xford. **Right**,
e new-style
rchitecture
f Lady
largaret
all.

founded by a committee of local residents in 1877. Originally called the Oxford Preparatory School, it is now known as the **Dragon School** after the college badge which was, itself, modelled on the George and Dragon motif that appeared on the coinage of the day.

The Dragon adjoins Lady Margaret Hall, while to the north, off Charrington Road, is **Wolfson College**, founded in 1965 for science graduates. The buildings, on the banks of the Cherwell, are regarded by some as examples of the best modern architecture, by others as the worst, especially now that the concrete and pebble-dash has accumulated so many streaks and stains.

By contrast, the streets of **Park Town**, entered off Banbury Road, to the southwest, are much admired examples of late Regency style—so late (built in 1853–55) that they might almost be called neo-Regency. Built around crescents, these stucco-fronted houses, with attractive iron railings, remind us more of Cheltenham than of Oxford.

Slightly earlier than the development of North Oxford, the boggy meadows of Osney and St Ebbe's became the focus of new industrial and working-class suburbs. **St Ebbe's** was chosen as the site for the town's new gasworks in 1818, and the extension of the railway to east Oxford in 1851 further stimulated speculative building.

Much of St Ebbe's has again been redeveloped in recent years. One of the few good buildings left is the 19th-century group of mill buildings, beside the River Thames in Becket Street, now the **Oxford Business Centre**.

Osney lies on the opposite bank, reached over the bridge built in 1888, with its ornamental railings and coat of arms of the Oxford Local Board. Now a conservation area, Osney Town, with its characterful waterside pubs and 1850s terraces, is completely surrounded by water. From Ferry Hinksey Road there is an attractive short walk over the meadows, via a bridge over the Thames that marks the county boundary

A casual walk by the canal.

between Oxford and Berkshire, to the village of **North Hinksey**.

This village, with its thatched cottages, riding stables, Norman church of St Lawrence and pub, still manages to retain a rural feel. John Ruskin is commemorated on one of the picturesque cottages. In 1874, Ruskin organised teams of undergraduates to work on road improvements in the village—with the intention of convincing his students (who included Oscar Wilde) of the "pleasures of useful muscular work".

Alice again: Back in Osney, the church of St Frideswide on Botley Road contains a door panel, with a relief of the saint praying by the Thames, carved by Alice Liddell, herself a pupil of Ruskin, in 1890.

Other reminders of the saint and of the heroine of *Alice's Adventures in Wonderland* can be seen in the remote church of St Margaret, in **Binsey**. The church is reached down Binsey Lane and, once past the messy builders' yards

and the golf club, the suburbs give way to a patchwork of small fields surrounded by high hedges and tall trees. Binsey itself is a tiny farming hamlet but with a renowned pub, The Perch, beside the Thames, a favourite lunchtime retreat for weekend walkers.

Beyond the village, a single-track road leads to the little late-Norman church. Just beyond the west end, almost covered by ivy, ferns and moss, is the Treacle Well that features in the story told by Lewis Carroll's Dormouse at the Mad Hatter's Tea Party. In Middle English, *triacle* meant any liquid with healing or medicinal powers—only later did it come to mean a syrup.

This well is said to have sprung up at the command of St Frideswide. The king of Wessex, her suitor, was struck blind by thunder when he tried to carry the saint away forcibly. Frideswide agreed to cure him on condition that he leave her in peace; the well appeared miraculously and its waters restored the king's sight.

A brisk walk in the suburbs.

Hundreds of pilgrims used to visit the church. Few come now and the rustic nave, lit only by oil lamps, has been colonised by pipistrelle bats. The simple wooden pulpit has a carving of St Margaret trampling on a dragon set into the front.

If you look inside, you will find another relief of St Margaret on the inner face—not by Eric Gill, though it has been attributed to him, but with clearly delineated breasts. Regarded as too sensual for public display, she is condemned to face the feet of the incumbent preacher rather than risk arousing the passions of the congregation.

Binsey seems remote from all the bustle of central Oxford, even though the nearest suburbs are only half a mile away. It sits in the great expanse of **Port Meadow**, much of which is common land; this fact has so far helped to preserve the meadows from development, even if some of the unspoiled charm has been compromised by electricity pylons and the continual background noise of traffic on the Oxford by-pass.

Even so, the meadows are much frequented by local people: in winter, when the flooded fields freeze over, skaters come out to test the strength of the ice. The bird life is rich at all times of the year, and in summer you can often make out the outlines of Iron Age farming enclosures and hut circles, delineated by the buttercups that grow taller over buried features such as ditches and foundation trenches.

One attractive walk through the meadows follows the right-hand bank of the Thames up to **Godstow**, where a 15th-century bridge leads to the scant remains of the medieval **Godstow Abbey**. The nearby Trout Inn, originally a fisherman's cottage, was rebuilt in 1737, and is famous for its peacocks that wander freely around the attractive riverside terrace garden.

For the route back, you can take the Godstow Road until it meets the Oxford Canal, and follow the towpath all the way to its end at Hythe Bridge.

Port Meadow

Further out of Oxford, you do not have to travel far before you meet the wooded hills that almost completely surround the city. Visually, the most rewarding of these is **Boar's Hill**, 3 miles (5 km) out to the southwest and famous for its views.

Saving the view: Large houses line the complex of narrow lanes that lead to Boar's Hill, and such was the pressure of development that the Oxford Preservation Trust purchased the remaining land in 1928 to ensure that the views would not be destroyed.

One Boar's Hill resident, Sir Arthur Evans, famous for his archaeological discoveries at Knossos, worked with the Trust to build an artificial mound at the summit of the hill. Evan's intention was partly to provide work for the local unemployed during a period of economic depression, partly to provide a vantage point from which to admire the views, famously immortalised in Matthew Arnold's poem *Thyrsis*, where he describes the winter scene:

Humid the air! leafless, yet soft as spring,
The tender purple spray on copse and briers!
And that sweet city with her dreaming spires,
She needs not June for beauty's heightening.

The tumulus that Evans built, known as **Jarn Mound**, rises to 50 ft (15 metres), and the summit is 530 ft (162 metres) above sea level. It was completed in 1931 and the surrounding area planted with trees to create a wild garden. Now it is overgrown with bracken and scrub, and the topograph on the summit is gone, the column on which it stood broken. Even so, the views are unchanged: to the northeast the ancient buildings of Oxford appear, framed between ancient trees that seem deliberately planted to hide the modern suburbs—if you go at dusk, the setting sun adds its own rich colouring to the scene.

Turn round and you see another extensive view, stretching southwest-

Boar's Hill: the classic view of Oxford's dreaming spires.

wards over the Vale of the White Horse to the Berkshire Downs.

From this point, which Arnold called "a shy retreat", it is 2 miles by the thundering ring road to **Iffley**, a village on the southern edge of the city worth seeking out for its Norman **parish church of St Mary the Virgin**. In the whole of England there is scarcely a more complete example of the late 12th-century Romanesque style. Only the rose window of the west end is later (inserted in 1856). All the remaining doorways, windows and arches—covered in sawtooth ornament and carved with beakheads, the signs of the Zodiac, fighting horsemen and symbols of the Evangelists—date to around 1180.

After Iffley comes the extensive suburb of **Cowley**, dubbed "Motopolis" by John Betjeman who hated this industrial town on the doorstep of his beloved Oxford devoted to producing the motor car that "roars down the lanes with its cargo of cads, poisons the air, deafens the ears and deadens the senses".

Cowley was responsible for a massive 43 percent increase in the population of Oxford between 1921 and 1939, as the success of the Morris motor attracted labourers from the depression-hit Midlands and South Wales. They were accommodated in what John Betjeman called "strips of shoddy houses... indistinguishable from Swindon, Neasden or Tooting Bec".

Passing through Cowley, for there is nothing really worth stopping to see, Rover Group, the modern successor to the Morris Motor Works, lies either side of the eastern by-pass, as it heads towards Headington, with the woodland of Shotover Country Park rising behind.

Headington consists of several distinct "villages". Headington Quarry, as its name suggests, originally supplied the limestone and roof tiles from which much of medieval Oxford was built. The current suburb developed around the quarrymen's cottages, some of which still remain, dating from the 17th and 18th centuries. This village is home to one of England's best-known teams of Morris dancers, the Quarrymen.

Old Headington lies on the opposite side of the London Road, and was once the resort of undergraduates seeking illicit pleasures in alehouses, beyond the jurisdiction of the Proctors or Bulldogs. In the 18th and 19th centuries, wealthy tradesmen built large houses on the leafy hillside. One of them, Bury Knowle House, is now the Headington Library and occupies attractively landscaped grounds. Just to the north, restored 17th-century cottages surround St Andrew's Church, which has a Norman chancel arch and 15th-century chancel roof.

Headington Hill, which plunges steeply down into central Oxford, was largely built up in the 19th century. Oxford United's football ground is on the right, off Sandfield Road, and further down is part of Robert Maxwell's international publishing empire, the Pergamon Press, occupying Headington Hill Hall.

Left, even he can't keep the traffic moving. **Right**, exuberant cinema in New High Street, Headington.

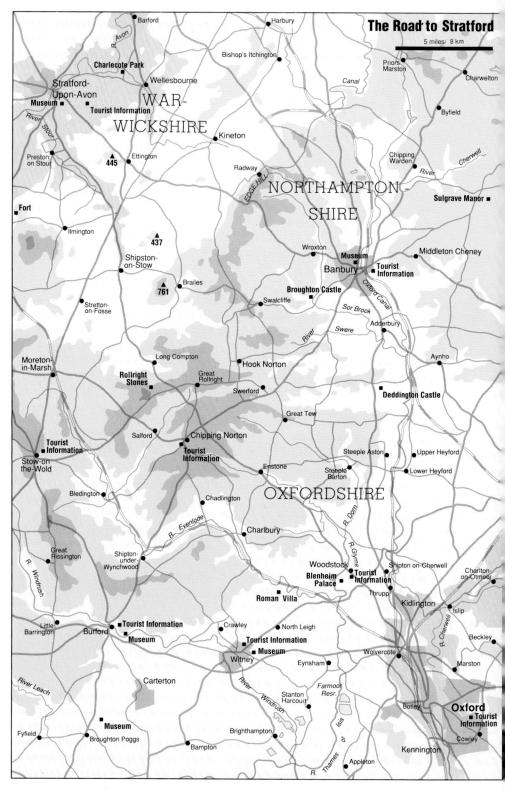

The Road to Stratford

5 miles/ 8 km

Barford
Harbury
Bishop's Itchington
R. Avon
Priors Marston
Charwelton
Charlecote Park
Wellesbourne
Stratford-Upon-Avon
WAR-WICKSHIRE
Byfield
Museum
Tourist Information
River Stour
Kineton
Preston on Stour
Ettington
445
Radway
EDGE HILL
Chipping Warden
R. Cherwell
River
NORTHAMPTON-SHIRE
Fort
Ilmington
437
Sulgrave Manor
Shipston-on-Stow
761
Brailes
Wroxton
Museum
Middleton Cheney
Stretton-on-Fosse
Swalcliffe
Broughton Castle
Banbury
Tourist Information
Oxford Canal
Sor Brook
Swere
River
Moreton-in-Marsh
Long Compton
Hook Norton
Adderbury
Aynho
Rollright Stones
Great Rollright
Swerford
Deddington Castle
Salford
Great Tew
Chipping Norton
Tourist Information
Steeple Aston
Upper Heyford
Tourist Information
Stow-on-the-Wold
Enstone
Steeple Barton
Lower Heyford
Bledington
Chadlington
OXFORDSHIRE
R. Dorn
Great Rissington
R. Evenlode
Charlbury
R. Glyme
Woodstock
Shipton on-Cherwell
Chariton-on-Otmoor
Shipton-under-Wynchwood
Blenheim Palace
Tourist Information
Thrupp
R. Windrush
Roman Villa
Kidlington
Islip
R. Cherwell
Little Barrington
Burford
Tourist Information
Crawley
North Leigh
Beckley
Museum
Tourist Information
Wolvercote
Marston
Carterton
Witney
Museum
Eynsham
River Leach
R. Windrush
Stanton Harcourt
Farmoor Resr.
Botley
Oxford
Tourist Information
Museum
Isis or Thames
Fyfield
Broughton Poggs
Brighthampton
Bampton
R. Thames
Appleton
Kennington
Cowley

198

THE ROAD TO STRATFORD

Stratford-upon-Avon lies 30 miles (48 km) northwest of Oxford and exerts a magnetic attraction, having acquired an international status as a tourist attraction. It would be a mistake, though, to rush to Stratford along the busy main highways, missing out the scores of memorable sights along the route.

Leaving Oxford on the A34, it is a matter of minutes only before you reach the handsome market town of **Woodstock**. The main street lies off the main road, to the left, and the large, stone houses, many of them older than their Georgian fronts suggest, speak of a prosperity built on glove-making; one glove factory, in Harrison's Lane, still operates, the sole survivor of this ancient industry.

In Park Street, Fletcher's House, now the Oxfordshire County Museum, provides an overview of the region's archaeology, agriculture and domestic life, and the gardens to the rear are used to display contemporary sculpture. Opposite, the church of St Mary Magdalene was lavishly restored in 1878, but the best part is the 18th-century tower, carved with swags of flowers around the clock and parapet.

At the far end of Park Street, a triumphal arch announces the entrance to **Blenheim Palace**. There is still half a mile to go before you reach this monumental building, for it lies at the heart of a vast estate, covering 2,700 acres (1,100 hectares)—the palace alone occupies an area of 7 acres (2.8 hectares). Not for nothing is it called a palace, rather than a mere manor, although that is what it was originally.

For Woodstock was, as far back as records go, a royal manor, frequented by a succession of monarchs for the deer hunting, when the land was still part of the great forest of Wychwood. Henry II installed his mistress, Fair Rosamund Clifford, at Woodstock, until Queen Eleanor discovered her hunting lodge hideaway. By the 16th century the original royal palace was decayed, and the last remaining buildings were demolished after the Civil War.

In 1705, Queen Anne gave the manor, and the funds to build the palace, to John Churchill, 1st Duke of Marlborough. This was his reward for defeating the French army at Blenheim, on the Danube, the previous year, a major victory that temporarily thwarted Louis XIV's desire to dominate Europe.

The Queen made it quite clear that the palace was to be no mere private house, but a national monument, a symbol of Britain's supremacy—by implication, a building to outshine even Louis XIV's own splendid palace at Versailles. Consequently, the best architects of the day were consulted on the designs. Christopher Wren was the obvious candidate, and many of his masons, men who had worked on St Paul's, were employed on the project. But Wren was rejected in favour of John Vanbrugh,

whose designs for Castle Howard were greatly admired by Churchill. Vanburgh is therefore credited as the architect of this Baroque masterpiece, but his assistant, Nicholas Hawksmoor, ought to share at least equal credit—for it was he that supervised a great deal of the work, taking day to day decisions about the details.

In the event, it is remarkable that the building was completed at all, let alone on such an heroic scale. Parliament quibbled about the cost, funds ran out, and the Duchess of Marlborough constantly opposed the grandiose scheme, declaring "I mortally hate all gardens and architecture", and insisting that all she wanted was "a clean, sweet house and garden, be it ever so small".

The Duke ended up bearing a great deal of the cost himself, and such was the enmity between architect and client that Vanbrugh never saw the finished building; when he tried to visit in 1725, the Duchess refused him entrance, even to the grounds.

Even when completed, Blenheim continued to be controversial: Horace Walpole called it "execrable" and Alexander Pope, with an eye to practicalities, quipped "'tis very fine; but where d'ye sleep and where d'ye dine?" Yet now Blenheim excites the imagination and invites superlatives. The skyline, with its bizarre chimneys, its pinnacles resembling stacks of cannon balls and its ducal coronets, creates a wonderful silhouette, viewed across the lakes and avenues of the park, landscaped by "Capability" Brown.

Symbols of soldiery: Everywhere you look there are symbols of military prowess—over the main entrance, Britannia stands supreme in armour above the Marlborough coat of arms. Chained slaves writhe on the upper pediment, and the gates to the side wings have carvings of the cock of France being savaged by the British lion.

Inside, the gilded state rooms are rich in furniture and portraits of the Marlboroughs. Tapestries, woven in

Blenheim: steeped in the spirit of Churchill.

Brussels, celebrate the 1st Duke's victories. In the magnificent saloon, life-size *trompe l'oeil* figures, representing the peoples of the four continents and painted by Louis Laguerre in 1719–20, lean over balconies as spectators to the state banquets that still are, on occasion, held in this huge, unheated room (for the sake of symmetry, there are no fireplaces).

Despite its scale and discomforts, Blenheim also serves as a home, and the small room where Sir Winston Churchill was born in 1874 attracts as much attention as the state apartments. Like his ancestor, the 1st Duke, Sir Winston is remembered as a great war leader. Unlike the 1st Duke, who is commemorated by a monument of exaggerated proportions in the palace chapel, Sir Winston is buried in a simple grave, in the parish church of **Bladon**, on the southern periphery of the estate.

Rescued village: Some 6 miles (10 km) further north, the B4022 meets the A34, just outside Enstone, and the right turn leads to the picturesque village of **Great Tew**. Dubbed "the place where time stood still", this estate village contains scarcely a modern building, simply because the late landlord permitted no new development; indeed, as the number of labourers employed on the estate steadily declined, the stone and thatch cottages were simply left to rot. One visitor, in 1972, described the derelict houses surrounding the green as "one of the most depressing sights in the whole country".

Now, thanks to new ownership, the cottages have been fully restored to their appearance in the early 19th century, when, as part of a model farm, the village was carefully landscaped. Quite a number of the cottages were given Gothic embellishments at the time, though many date to the 16th century. Set back behind colourful gardens, they present the kind of picture that calendar and chocolate box manufacturers find irresistible.

The church of St Michael lies south of the village, just within the grounds of the park, and the churchyard is entered through a 17th-century stone gateway. Inside is a noteworthy monument to Mary Anne Boulton (died 1829) by Francis Chantrey. The Boultons, descendants of Matthew Boulton, the Birmingham engineer who made his fortune manufacturing steam engines as a partner of James Watt, acquired the estate in 1815 and gave the 17th-century house its current neo-Gothic appearance.

The B4022 continues north for just over a mile, to meet the A361. If you turn left, and then right via Swerford, a pretty village on the River Swere, you will reach **Hook Norton**. Real ale lovers will know this as the source of "Hooky", a fine beer made by traditional methods in the red-brick Victorian brewery at the west end of the village. This prominent building is surrounded by cottages built of the local orange-coloured ironstone—as is the church of St Peter, commanding the hilltop at the

Churchill's simple tombstone in Bladon churchyard.

centre of the village. The lively Norman font inside is carved with a charmingly rustic Adam, with his hammer and spade, and a flirtatious Eve, holding her apple, as well as signs of the Zodiac.

Legendary stones: Three miles (5 km) west of Hook Norton, through the village of **Great Rollright** and across the A34, you will find the remains of a prehistoric stone circle. Standing on the high ridge of the northern Cotswolds, the **Rollright Stones** form a henge of 100 ft (60 metres) in diameter and date to around 3500 BC. The stones of the circle itself are known as the King's Men, while the solitary stone on the opposite side of the road is the King and the five stones further east, once the burial chamber of a long barrow, are the Whispering Knights.

The names refer to a legend, first recorded in 1586, that the stones represent petrified men who will one day wake to rule the land. They were tricked, according to the story, by a local witch who promised their leader that he would be king of England if he could see Long Compton, the village in the valley below, from this spot. This simple task proved impossible—some say that the witch conjured up a mist—and so she transformed them with the words:

Thou and thy men hoar stones shall be And I myself an elder tree.

Other legends about the stones abound—to their detriment, since they have often been chipped away by visitors believing in their magical properties, including Civil War soldiers on their way to battle.

The Rollright Stones are too close to the busy A34 to make a good resting spot, but you will find the ideal place for a peaceful picnic by following the unclassified road back to the main road, across, and left towards the Sibfords. This high road, with fine views all round, forms the county boundary between Oxford and Warwick for much of its length, and drops, after 4 miles (7 km), down into the Stour valley at **Traitor's Ford**. Nobody seems to

The Rollright Stones: said to have magical properties.

remember now who the traitor was; but the ford, with its clear stream and woodland either side, makes a perfect spot for relaxing on a hot summer's day.

From the ford, an ancient track, **Ditchedge Lane**, leads directly to **Compton Wynyates**, accessible only to walkers—motorists have to take the longer route through Sibford Gower. Compton Wynyates, a romantic, Tudor mansion of rose-coloured brick, is no longer open to the public; but you can glimpse it, nestling into the wooded hillside, from the road to the west.

Windmill Hill, rising beyond to the north, is crowned by a stone tower mill, complete with its sails, while on **Compton Pike**, to the south, is a pyramidal structure, dating to the 16th century and built, perhaps, to support a warning beacon, to be lit in the event of invasion.

Some 5 miles west, back on the A34, is **Shipston-on-Stour**. The name (originally Sheepston) is a reminder that the town was once host to one of England's largest sheep markets, and its

Good riding country.

position astride the main road accounts for the number of handsome former coaching inns.

Odd quirk: Two miles north, **Honington Hall** (open Wednesdays and Bank Holiday Mondays in summer) is a 17th-century brick house which could pass for the ordinary domestic manor of some country squire but for the odd quirk of a series of busts all around the facades, depicting 12 Caesars. Even more extraordinary is the sumptuous plasterwork inside.

The house was built in 1685 by Sir Henry Parker who, having made a fortune as a London merchant, had the village church remodelled in a style that resembles Christopher Wren's elegant City of London churches. The monument to Parker and his son Hugh is the best of several splendid pieces of carving, in both marble and stone, to be found within.

From Honington, continue up the A34 to Newbold-on-Stour and then, if you want to avoid the main road, take the minor road left that runs parallel to the pretty, winding River Stour. At **Preston-on-Stour** you will find another stylish 18th-century church, this time in the Gothic style, and an east window made up of 17th-century glass from diverse sources, all illustrating the theme of death. The village has several ornate 16th and 17th-century timber-framed houses and even the red-brick Alscot housing estate, an early example dating to 1852, has a certain undeniable charm.

At **Clifford Chambers**, attractive cottages line the single street that leads to the manor house, restored—or, rather, rebuilt—by Sir Edwin Lutyens in 1919. Here, too, is the first of many buildings associated with Shakespeare, for the 16th-century timber-framed rectory was the home of one John Shakespeare during the 1570s. Since William's father was called John, biographers have speculated, lacking any records for the dramatist's early years, whether this might have been his childhood home.

THE SHAKESPEARE
BIRTHPLACE TRUST

MARY ARDEN'S HOUSE

ENTRANCE FOR A
VISITORS THROU
CAR PARK

STRATFORD-UPON-AVON

Stratford-upon-Avon is an extraordinary phenomenon. Visitors from all over the world, many of whom cannot quote a single line from William Shakespeare's work, consider a trip to Britain incomplete unless they visit Stratford. If any of them are puzzled, or disappointed, by what they find, they never pass the message around, for Stratford remains a top international tourist destination—comparable to Disneyland in popularity, but with only a fraction of the attractions.

Part of the problem—and perhaps part of the lure—is that so few details of Shakespeare's life can be authenticated. It is known that his father John was a successful glove-maker and wool merchant, and that his mother, Mary Arden, was the daughter of a well-to-do farmer. William went to school in Stratford, and married Anne Hathaway in 1582; they had three children. Most of his professional career in the theatre, however, was centred in London, though he spent the last five years of his life (1611–16) in Stratford. And the rest is largely speculation.

The Shakespeare industry dates to the middle of the 19th century, when a pub called the Swan and Maidenhead, in Henley Street, came on the market. This had long been considered Shakespeare's birthplace, and in 1847 a public appeal was launched to buy the building as a national monument. A trust was formed and, between 1857 and 1864, the property was restored to its "original" appearance, a process that involved virtually rebuilding the house.

Today, **Shakespeare's Birthplace** is the starting point for a tour of the town. You enter through the modern **Shakespeare Centre**, opened in 1964 as the headquarters of the Birthplace Trust. An exhibition of the costumes made for BBC television's complete cycle of Shakespeare's plays, and displays on the life and work of the dramatist, occupy visitors while they queue to enter the Birthplace itself.

Linking the two buildings is a garden planted with flowers mentioned in the plays and poems. The house itself is divided into two halves; part is furnished as a middle-class home in Elizabethan and Jacobean "style"—anyone with a knowledge of antiques will enjoy spotting the anachronisms.

The room in which Shakespeare is supposed to have been born, on 23 April 1564, is lit by a window inscribed with the signatures of illustrious visitors such as Sir Walter Scott, Thomas Carlyle and Isaac Watts. The rest of the house displays objects associated with John Shakespeare, William's father.

Just to the north of the Birthplace, in Shakespeare Street, is one of the town's several tourist attractions that have nothing to do with Shakespeare but which have accumulated here because of the captive market. The **Motor Museum** recreates the golden age of motor-

ing with its displays of luxurious vintage cars—Rolls-Royces, Bugattis and Lagondas—set against tableaux illustrating the fashions of the 1920s and 1930s.

A short distance away, at 19 Greenhill Street, old and valuable children's toys are on display in Giles Brandreth's excellent **Teddy Bear Museum**—a good place to take children when they are bored by their parents' preoccupation with stuffy old poets.

This museum faces on to the broad expanse of Rother Street, a car park for most of the week but the venue on Fridays for the town market. The **Jubilee Memorial Fountain**, at the broad end of Rother Street, is a Disneyland castle, all turrets, with a pendulum clock above and drinking troughs below, donated by George Washington Childs of Philadelphia in 1887.

Wood Street, to the left, leads to the town centre and has a sprinkling of those heavily timbered properties that we associate with the ancient heart of England, when the extensive Forest of Arden, which once covered the country north of Stratford, provided a ready supply of materials.

The **High Street** has some of the town's most ornate buildings, many of them stripped of 18th-century brick and stucco facades early in this century to reveal the original timber framing. The **Tourist Information Centre**, at the corner of High Street and Bridge Street, was originally the Cage—the town prison—and later the house of Shakespeare's daughter Judith, who married Thomas Quiney, a wine merchant.

W.H. Smith is an enjoyable 1920s building, carved with jesters' heads on its handsome shop front. Waterstone's bookshop is impeccably restored and, opposite, Dixon's has imposing 17th-century beams carved with intertwining dragons.

Further down on the right, the **Garrick Inn** and **Harvard House** make an eccentric and flamboyant pair of buildings. Both date to about 1596, having been built just after a fire destroyed much of the town. Harvard House is elaborately carved with flowers and grotesque heads, and was the home of Katherine Rogers. She married Robert Harvard of Southwark, and their son, John Harvard, died in Massachusetts in 1638, a year after he emigrated to the New World. His estate was used to found Harvard College, which now owns this house and uses it to display material relating to the Harvard family.

The far end of the High Street is closed in by the imposing **Town Hall**, a solid neo-Palladian building, completed in 1768. The statue of Shakespeare, on the Sheep Street frontage, was given by the great 18th-century Shakespearian actor David Garrick. He was greatly influential in the revival of interest in Shakespeare's dramatic works and helped to organise the first festival in his honour, in 1769. The festival was a great social occasion, patronised by royalty—hence the bold slogan "God save the King" painted in the same year

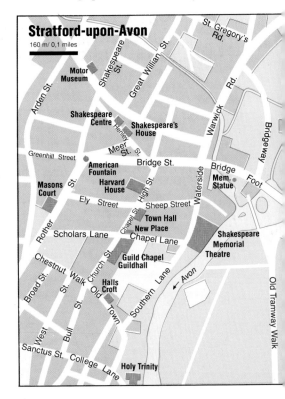

208

across the Chapel Street facade of the Town Hall.

In Sheep Street you will find numerous souvenir shops and restaurants not only flanking the street but also running up the alleys behind. The **Shrieve's House** (40 Sheep Street) is an interesting example of a 16th-century merchant's house, with a cart entrance and long, cobbled back yard, lined with buildings that would have been used as workshop and warehouse space—now converted to shops.

Chapel Street leads to **Nash's House** and New Place. The former belonged to Thomas Nash, who married Shakespeare's granddaughter, Elizabeth Hall. It is now a museum of material relating to the history of Stratford. **New Place** was one of the town's largest houses, and Shakespeare was wealthy enough to purchase it in 1597. He later retired to the house and died there on his 52nd birthday, in 1616.

Irascible cleric: A later owner, the Reverend Francis Gastrell, had little respect for the poet's memory. He was so annoyed by the constant stream of visitors wanting to see the mulberry tree in the garden, planted by Shakespeare, that he cut it down. In 1759 the irascible cleric demolished the house itself, rather than pay rates.

Sensibly, no attempt has been made to reconstruct the house. Instead, the foundations are exposed and paths thread through delightful gardens. The Knot Garden is planted with flowers known to have been grown in the 16th century, and the Great Garden beyond, originally the orchard and kitchen garden to New Place, has box and yew hedges enclosing colourful borders.

The **Guild Chapel**, opposite, served as the chapel of the Guild of the Holy Cross, a body of local worthies who regulated trade in the town, fixing prices, collecting levies and allocating funds to charitable purposes. A wealthy member, Sir Hugh Clopton, later Lord Mayor of London, paid for the rebuilding of the nave in 1496. Just visible on

New Place: where Shakespeare died.

the chancel wall is a "Doom", or Last Judgement, painting, with figures scrambling from their graves to learn their eternal fate.

Adjoining the chapel is the 15th-century former **Guild Hall**, part of which was used as the town Grammar School. It is conjectured, reasonably enough, that Shakespeare was a pupil here. The delightfully named "Pedagogue's House" in the courtyard behind was probably the schoolmaster's dwelling. Beyond, 15th-century almshouses, still used as such, stretch for a distance of 50 metres, an impressive range with massive studs and a jettied-out upper storey.

Further down Church Street the character of the buildings begins to change, as timber gives way to the brick of elegant townhouses. **Mason Croft**, an early 18th-century building, was the last home of Marie Corelli (1855-1924)—real name Mary Mackay—the prolific novelist who, despite critical derision, was as popular in her heyday as Shakespeare was in his. The house is now an international centre for Shakespearian research, owned by Birmingham University.

Turning left, into Old Town, you reach **Hall's Croft**—of all the buildings associated with Shakespeare, this one is the least altered and most atmospheric. It dates to the late 16th century and was the home of Dr John Hall, husband of Shakespeare's daughter Susanna. One room is equipped as an apothecary's dispensary, and the spacious walled garden to the rear is planted with ancient mulberry trees and perennial borders.

A little further down, an avenue of lime trees leads to **Holy Trinity Church**, idyllically sited alongside the River Avon and a fine example of a 13th-century church, embellished by the addition of a clerestory in the 16th century. You have to pay to visit the most interesting part of the church—the chancel—where Shakespeare's monument is the chief attraction.

The poet's son-in-law, Dr John Hall, took a wax impression of the poet's face at his death, and this was used by the Dutch mason Gerard Jansenni, or Johnson, as the basis for the painted alabaster bust of Shakespeare. It is thus the best likeness we have of the poet; other portraits, based on this, have tried to make him look less self-satisfied.

The nearby tomb slab, covering Shakespeare's grave, is famously inscribed:

Good Frend For Jesus Sake Forbeare
To Digg the Dust Enclosed Heare:
Blese Be Ye Man (that) Spares Thes Stones
And Curst Be He (that) Moves My Bones.

These words have often been interpreted as implying that the grave contains evidence of the "true" authorship of Shakespeare's works—for, despite very substantial evidence to the contrary, a number of people still profess to believe that Shakespeare was only a front for some other writer. All requests to investigate the tomb have, quite properly, been refused.

Burial places: Other Shakespeare family tombs are found nearby: namely, those of his wife Anne (*née* Hathaway), his daughter Susanna, and those of Thomas Nash and Dr John Hall. The 16th-century misericords should not be missed; they date from around 1500 and provide an amusing commentary on contemporary domestic life.

Just north of Holy Trinity churchyard, back in Old Town, a gate on the right leads to the **Avonbank Garden**, with its 19th-century summerhouse (now a brass-rubbing centre) and paths that follow the River Avon to the **Royal Shakespeare Theatre** complex.

The first part of the complex to come into view is the **Swan Theatre**, with its curved end and sweeping lead-covered roof, like some romantic Middle European castle. Partly used as a museum, displaying costumes, sets, props and theatrical mementoes, this incorporates all that remains of the original theatre, built in 1879 but damaged by fire in 1926. The rest of the theatre was designed by Elizabeth Scott and completed in 1932.

A radical building in its own time— not only built of, but also shaped like, a stack of bricks, and almost windowless—it now seems an embarrassing mistake. Yet it serves its purpose well, and the remodelled interior is nightly packed with visitors and school-children come to see the plays enacted that they are studying for their exams.

In front of the theatre, the **Bancroft Gardens** surround a large canal basin, marking the point where the Stratford Canal joins the River Avon. Two bridges also cross the river at this point: the first is an early 19th-century brick tramway bridge, intended to carry horse-drawn waggons, and part of an ambitious scheme that just pre-dates the earliest railway lines, intended to provide a transport link between the Midlands and London. The other bridge, a long stone causeway, was built in the late 15th century and is still in use as the main approach to Stratford.

The **Stratford Canal**, completed in 1816, runs northwards to join the Grand Union, south of Birmingham. As an alternative to travelling by car, you can follow the canal towpath for 3 miles (5 km), through the town and out, past a long flight of locks, to the hamlet of **Wilmcote**. Here, the Shakespeare Birthplace Trust has restored the 16th-century home of Mary Arden, Shakespeare's mother, as a museum of country life in Tudor Warwickshire.

For the return journey, perhaps, you can visit **Anne Hathaway's cottage**, just over a mile west of the town, in the suburb of **Shottery**. This 15th-century thatched farmhouse was once the home of Shakespeare's wife, and stands in a delightfully informal cottage garden. Furnished with Hathaway family heirlooms, pride of place is given to the famous bed that Shakespeare bequeathed to his wife—the only thing he left her in his will, fuelling speculation that their marriage might not have been a happy one.

Anne
Hathaway's
cottage.

STRATFORD TO OXFORD

Leaving Stratford by the B4086, you follow the River Avon for just over 3 miles (5 km), through cow-filled pastures, to **Charlecote Park**. Here, according to one of the many unsubstantiated stories about Shakespeare, young William is said to have been caught and prosecuted for poaching deer by the owner, Sir Thomas Lucy.

In revenge, Shakespeare based the character of his Justice Shallow (in *Henry VI, Part Two* and *The Merry Wives of Windsor*) on Sir Thomas. Shallow is described as having a coat of arms incorporating "a dozen white luces", in which he takes inordinate pride. Sir Thomas does indeed have "luces" (a pun on Lucy, and an archaic word for freshwater pike) in his coat of arms, and these can be seen inside the steepled church of St Leonard, just inside the grounds of the park.

St Leonard's was completely rebuilt in 1851–53 by Mary Elizabeth Lucy, who described its predecessor as "a wretched old church". The family monuments, however, were left alone. Shakespeare's Sir Thomas (died 1600) is the armoured figure in alabaster lying recumbent by his wife on a tomb chest. His son, also Sir Thomas (died 1605), is depicted with his widow and children. Best of all is the fine sculpture of the scholarly grandson, another Sir Thomas (died 1640), reclining beneath a pile of books.

It was the first Sir Thomas who, inheriting the Warwickshire estate in 1552, rebuilt the manor house. The result, despite 19th-century additions, is still recognisably Elizabethan, including the mellow brick gatehouse, the porch and much of the stable and brewhouse block. Before entering the house, it is a good idea to see the introductory video, shown in a room of the stable yard, which is based on the memoirs of Mary Elizabeth Lucy, the 19th-century mistress of the house who did so much to give the interior its present mid-Victorian appearance.

Red and fallow deer still roam in the park, which was landscaped by "Capability" Brown, making full use of the setting of the house, situated on the banks of the Rivers Avon and Dene.

The B4086 continues east through **Wellesbourne**, a traffic-torn village where a body of farmworkers, led by Joseph Arch, met in 1872 to form what became the National Agricultural Labourers' Union, demanding a minimum wage of sixpence a day.

Two miles (3 km) on, the road crosses a bridge over the lakes fronting **Compton Verney** mansion, built about 1714 in a wooded valley. **Kineton** comes next, a village of grey and brown lias stone cottages, with the wooded motte of a 12th-century castle by the bank of the River Dene.

Four miles (6 km) on, before the road begins to climb steeply up **Edge Hill**, you should take the minor road right to

Radway. Here it is well worth stopping and, if you have the time, leaving the car to follow a 2-mile circular walk of this historically important, and scenically beautiful, part of Warwickshire.

Radway village, with its thatched cottages of brown Hornton stone, lies on a series of terraces beneath the wooded escarpment of Edge Hill. From the road that leads northeastwards out of the village, to the right of Grafton Cottage, a steep path climbs up to woods on the brow of the hill. From the path there are views of **Radway Grange**, an Elizabethan house that was transformed by the squire and amateur architect, Sanderson Miller.

Miller was a pioneer of the Gothic Revival style, refronting the east front of the manor with ogee-arched windows around 1745—some three or four years before Horace Walpole made the style fashionable by rebuilding Strawberry Hill in Richmond.

The footpath turns right, through the woods that skirt Miller's estate, and out into the village of **Edgehill**. Here, the Edgehill Tower, adjoining the Castle Inn, is another Sanderson Miller work, built in 1746–50 and modelled on Warwick Castle. Miller built it as a place to entertain his friends, including the writer Henry Fielding whose *Tom Jones*, regarded as the first English novel, was read to Miller for his approval before it was published.

The tower is also of great historical importance, for it marks the spot where Charles I planted the Royal Standard on 23 October 1642, at the start of the first major battle of the Civil War. The actual battle site, where the king's army, led by Prince Rupert, met the Parliamentarians under the Earl of Essex—both sides suffering heavy casualties but neither able to claim victory—lies in the plain below. Owned by the Ministry of Defence, it cannot be visited, but there are clear views from the path that leads down from the Castle Inn, back to Radway. The village church contains Sanderson Miller's monument, and an

Radway Grange.

214

effigy of the Royalist Captain Kingswell, one of many who died in the inconclusive battle of Edge Hill.

Two miles south of Edgehill, by the side of the A422, is the splendid **Upton House**. Externally, the measured, stately facade dates to the reign of William and Mary, having been refronted in 1695. Internally, the house is neo-Georgian, remodelled in 1927 to house an outstanding collection of paintings accumulated by the 2nd Lord Bearstead. The collection comprises representative works by many of the best-known European Masters, including Bosch, the Breughels, Holbein, Rembrandt, Constable, Hogarth and Stubbs.

Four miles (7 km) further along the A422, just before **Wroxton**, you can detour south to **Broughton** to visit the picturesque manor house—called a "castle" on the strength of its wide defensive moat. Despite 16th-century remodelling, Broughton Castle is one of the most complete medieval houses surviving in the country, dating to

around 1300. All the Elizabethan owners did was to add the magnificent oak panelling, fireplaces and plasterwork, adding comfort and luxury to the spartan rooms, and employing craftsmen who worked in the latest Flemish, French and Italian Renaissance styles.

An important series of monuments in the next-door church commemorates the various owners, including Sir Thomas Wykeham (died 1470), a forceful figure, realistically carved, and members of the Fiennes family, ancestors of the late 17th-century traveller and writer Celia Fiennes. From Broughton, it is a short distance to the market town of **Banbury**, situated on a major road junction marked by a cross that is celebrated in the children's nursery rhyme:
Ride a cock-horse to Banbury Cross
To see a fine lady on a white horse;
With rings on her fingers and bells on her toes,
She shall have music wherever she goes.

The rhyme probably refers to a visit

made by Elizabeth I, and the present cross, erected in 1859, commemorates the marriage of Queen Victoria's daughter to the Crown Prince of Prussia. The ponderous figures of Queen Victoria, Edward VII and George V were added in 1914.

The original cross, standing on the site of the town's medieval horse fair, was destroyed by the townspeople, as was the old church—for Banbury was a hotbed of zealous Puritanism, satirised in another 17th-century rhyme:

To Banbury came I, O profane one,
And there I saw a Puritan one
Hanging of his cat on Monday
For killing a mouse on Sunday.

The church was rebuilt in a severe classical style between 1790 and 1822. Described at the time as "more like a gaol than a Christian temple", a painting of *Christ in Majesty*, imitating mosaic work, was commissioned in 1876 in an attempt to brighten the interior.

Banbury's history is told in the town's excellent small **museum**, at 8 Horsefair, opposite the cross. Another chapter will have to be written soon, for Banbury is to be at the hub of the extended M40 motorway, linking London and the West Midlands; this scheme divided the townspeople into those who welcomed the massive growth expected to result from related industrial and housing development, and those who battled to stem the tide.

Future plans include the creation of new facilities for canal cruisers, gently chugging up and down the **Oxford Canal** that passes through the eastern edge of the town. The canal was planned by the pioneering engineer, James Brindley, and completed in 1790. Faced with undulating countryside, Brindley designed a route that follows the natural contours, thus minimising the number of locks required. Consequently, the canal meanders through the Oxfordshire countryside, making hairpin bends to pass round hills, and, for the southern part of its route, following the equally contorted River Cherwell, used

Passive sport on the Thames...

to top up the water level in the canal.

The whole course of the canal, from its junction with the Grand Union at Napton, almost to the heart of Oxford, is outstandingly beautiful, and deservedly popular with narrow boat enthusiasts—most of whom hire a boat for the week but some of whom live permanently on the canal, making a living wherever they can from casual work, boat restoration or handicrafts.

The southern stretch, from Banbury to Oxford, is, arguably, the most beautiful, for the meadows between the canal and the River Cherwell often flood, and the resulting wetlands are a rich haven for rare flora and fauna. The abundance of the wildlife can only be appreciated fully by travelling the towpath on foot, or cruising by narrow boat, but almost any of the minor roads that cross the canal afford a place to stop and explore the reed-fringed banks.

Just off the canal route, there are numerous other attractions. At **Aynho**, 6 miles (10 km) south of Banbury, the church of St Michael, rebuilt in 1723–25, looks more like a country house than a place of worship. The unspoilt interior retains its 18th-century box pews, gallery and pulpit. The earlier church was the setting for a competition between two candidates for the post of Rector in 1646; each had to preach a sermon. Robert Wylde, on being told that he was the winner, wittily replied with a pun on the village name: "I got the Ay and he the No!"

Aynhoe Park (the spelling differs) bears the unmistakable stamp of "Capability" Brown's naturalistic landscaping, and the house, largely rebuilt after Royalist troops set fire to it in 1645, is the work of several idiosyncratic architects, most notably Sir John Soane.

Further south, **Upper** and **Lower Heyford** are both attractive villages, although the peace is sometimes shattered by aircraft coming and going from the huge US airbase on the hilltop above Upper Heyford. The stretch of canal between the two villages is outstanding.

..and the more active variety.

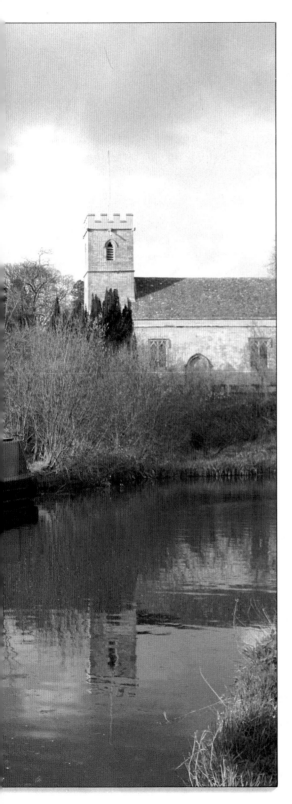

Here the canal and the **Cherwell** are separated by no more than a narrow bank. The Cherwell in summer becomes little more than a flower-filled ditch, and yet you will sometimes see huge basking perch here, so large that the water scarcely covers them. Crayfish live in the stones and brick of the canal-side wall and bridges, and the water margins are thick with reedmace, meadowsweet, water forget-me-not and yellow flag.

At Lower Heyford, the 14th-century church, old manor, farm and rectory form an attractive waterside group close to the original hay ford after which the village is named.

Less than a mile south, **Rousham Park** is, in the words of Horace Walpole, a place "to enjoy philosophic retirement". William Kent, a pioneer of the Romantic style in landscaping, transformed this naturally beautiful site, on the banks of the Cherwell, into a picturesque garden, complete with ruined follies and the cascades of Venus's Vale. Longhorn cattle, placid animals despite their ferocious-looking horns, graze in the fields beyond the sweeping lawns, and the walled gardens incorporate a 17th-century pigeon-house, complete with revolving ladder for taking the eggs from the tiers of nesting holes.

Further south, the busy roads and spreading suburbs of Oxford begin to impinge, not to mention Smokey Joe, the chimney of the cement works at **Shipton-on-Cherwell**. From the church at Shipton, known as the bargees' church, you look across the canal and river to **Hampton Gay**, once a substantial village, now no more than a church surrounded by the grassy humps of medieval house platforms, for the parish was depopulated by the Black Death of the 1340s.

At **Thrupp**, the canal widens, and the basin, with its canal workers' cottages and The Boat inn, is used as a last mooring point before the final chug into Oxford itself.

THE NORTH COTSWOLDS

The **Cotswolds** form a prominent range of hills to the west of Oxford. The limestone of the Cotswolds, formed on the bed of the shallow Midland Sea, has long provided a first-class building material, one that is soft enough to carve when newly dug, but rapidly hardens to provide a durable stone. The remarkable beauty of the Cotswolds owes much to the distinctive architecture of whole villages built of this stone and the way they nestle into the sides of gentle valleys, cut by the waters of melting glaciers at the end of the Ice Age.

The limestone lies close to the surface; the soils of the Cotswolds are shallow, not easy to cultivate but ideal pasture for grazing sheep. Until this century, wool was the Cotswolds' staple product, a source of great wealth for those who controlled the land— initially the great monastic estates of Gloucester, Tewkesbury, Evesham, Winchcombe and Malmesbury—later the landowners who acquired monastic lands after the Dissolution. In addition, a new breed of middle-class merchants accumulated great fortunes from the 14th century on by acting as middle men between the wool producers and the weaving towns of the Low Countries, Italy and Spain.

Quiet opulence: This former affluence is everywhere visible in the Cotswold landscape, characterised by opulent manor houses, cathedral-like barns and ornate parish churches built to splendid proportions by wool-rich men who counted on salvation in return for generous endowments.

Chipping Norton, 12 miles (20 km) northwest of Oxford, is a prime example: a typical Cotswold town on the northwestern limits of the limestone belt. Market Square was once the venue for an important sheep fair. Gabled almshouses—typical of Cotswold vernacular architecture, with their stone-mullioned windows and drip mouldings to channel rain away from the face of the buildings—line the path to St Mary's Church. This has an unusual hexagonal porch, with leering devils carved on the bosses inside, and the soaring nave was rebuilt around 1485 by the wool merchant, John Ashfield. To the north of the church are the extensive remains of a Norman motte and bailey castle.

Chipping Norton also has an imposing tweed mill, visible on the right as you leave the town on the A44 Evesham road. Bliss Valley Mill, with its domed tower, was designed in 1872 by the Lancashire mill architect, George Woodhouse, to look like a country house—which is what it has ended up as, for after the mill closed in 1980 it was converted into luxury apartments.

Four miles (7 km) on, to the left, a minor road leads to **Chastleton House**, built around 1605 by another wool merchant, Walter Jones. Shortly afterwards, the family fortunes declined and the house escaped later improvements,

surviving as a pure example of Jacobean domestic architecture. At the top of the house, a long gallery runs the length of the building, originally intended for indoor games, such as bowls, and this, like many of the rooms, is lavishly plastered with bold Flemish-style friezes and ceilings.

Moreton-in-Marsh comes next, a busy town on the junction of the Roman Foss Way and the later Oxford to Worcester road. Numerous former coaching inns still do a brisk trade serving cream teas to passing motorists, but there is a cluster of characterful shops at the northern end of the High Street. Where the Oxford road joins the High Street there is a 16th-century curfew tower; the bell in the tower continued to be rung until 1860, reminding householders to "cover their fires" (the derivation of "curfew") before retiring to bed—for many a town (most notably London in 1666) was destroyed when stray sparks triggered a conflagration.

Two miles (3 km) out of Moreton, the A44 climbs steeply up the Cotswold scarp, through the pretty but traffic-torn village of **Bourton-on-the-Hill**, and towards the summit a left turn leads to **Sezincote**. Here you will find one of the most curious and delightful houses ever built in the English countryside: an Indian palace built in golden limestone, tucked into the valley of the River Evenlode, which is channelled into a series of canals representing, in Moghul fashion, the rivers of life.

Begun in 1805, Sezincote was built for Charles Cockerell who, on retiring from service with the East India Company, built himself a rajah's palace, complete with onion domes and peacock-tail windows. The Prince Regent, on seeing it in 1807, loved it so much that he ordered existing plans for Brighton Pavilion to be scrapped, and new ones drawn up "more like Sezincote". External appearances, though, are deceptive, for guided tours reveal that the interior is elegantly European in the classical tradition.

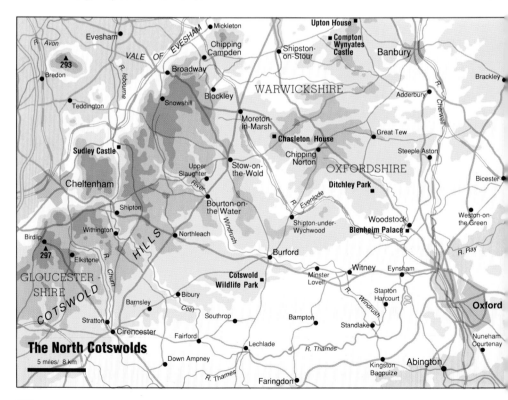

The North Cotswolds
5 miles/ 8 km

Oriental influence: Another expatriate returning home created **Batsford Arboretum**, on the opposite side of the A44. Lord Redesdale, a retired Tokyo diplomat, built his manor house in neo-Elizabethan style, beginning in 1888, but he planted the surrounding path with oriental species and decorated it with Japanese temples and statues of the Buddha. The arboretum is especially colourful in springtime, when the cherry trees bear their dense clouds of blossom, or in autumn, when the Japanese maples turn a fiery crimson.

The village of **Blockley**, 2 miles west, brings us back to the traditional Cotswolds. Formerly an estate belonging to the bishops of Worcester, the surrounding hillsides once supported vast flocks of sheep, and flourishing villages round about were deliberately destroyed to create further grazing.

Blockley survived, and today's village consists of elegant townhouses occupying the heights and smaller rows of cottages squeezed into narrow terraces all the way down the valley side. In the valley bottom only one mill survives (now a private house) of the six that produced silk to supply the ribbon makers of Coventry.

Blockley's church contains several imposing Renaissance and Baroque monuments to the owners of **Northwick Park**. This 17th-century mansion, now converted to apartments, lies just north of Blockley, and the road that skirts the western perimeter of the estate provides a splendid view of nearby **Chipping Campden**.

Campden is arguably the Cotswold's most beautiful market town. Certainly, it is the best preserved, thanks to the work of the Campden Trust, established in 1929 to restore and maintain town properties using traditional materials. One of the founders of the Trust, F.L. Griggs, designed many of the attractive wrought-iron signs that hang from shops in the High Street, where the buildings read like a history of Cotswold vernacular architecture in micro-

cosm, spanning every period from the 13th century to the 19th.

Early in the 20th century Campden was "invaded" by craftsmen from the Mile End Road in East London, where C.R. Ashbee, inspired by the example of William Morris, had founded his Guild of Handicrafts, devoted to reviving skills lost to industrial processes. Descendants of George Hart, one of the original 50 craftsmen who came with Ashbee in 1902, still make handcrafted silverware in the Old Silk Mill in Sheep Street.

Two other men have left a lasting mark on Campden. The fine Market Hall, jutting out into the High Street, was given by the local squire, Sir Baptist Hicks, in 1627. Further north, opposite Church Street, is Campden's oldest house, built around 1380, with an ornate two-storeyed bay window, by William Grevel.

Needless to say, both men made their money from wool, Sir Baptist at a time when the Cotswolds cloth trade was

beginning to decline, faced by competition from abroad. Even so, he was able to endow the almshouses in Church Street, built in 1612 in the shape of the letter I to honour James I, and also to build a mansion alongside the church. This was destroyed in the Civil War—some say by Hicks himself, to prevent it from falling into Parliamentary hands, others say by drunken Cromwellian troops. Enough survives, though, including the gate houses and two garden pavilions, to indicate what a fanciful building the manor had been.

The church itself is attributed to the earlier man, William Grevel, described on his memorial brass as "the flower of the wool merchants of all England". He left money for the church to be rebuilt and the work, completed some 100 years after his death, is a splendid example of the Perpendicular style at its best.

A mile northwest of Campden, over the summit of Dover's Hill, is a natural amphitheatre on the Cotswold scarp. Worth visiting for the panoramic views over the **Vale of Evesham**, this is also the venue for the "**Cotswold Olympicks**", held every Friday following the Spring Bank Holiday, followed by the Scuttlebrook Wake Fair on the next day. The "Olympicks", which feature shin kicking and stick fighting amongst the bizarre events, were founded by the eccentric local lawyer Robert Dover in 1612, and, after crowds of "beer-swilling Birmingham yahoos" got the games prohibited in 1852, they were revived in 1951.

Two miles north of Campden are two of England's finest gardens, standing on opposite sides of the same road above **Mickleton**.

Hidcote Manor Garden, for all its maturity, was begun only in 1948; all that existed before was a few walls and 11 acres (4.5 hectares) of windswept Cotswold upland. Major Lawrence Johnson transformed this into one of the most influential gardens of our age, "a cottage garden on the most glorified

The folly perched on Broadway Hill.

scale", according to the writer Vita Sackville-West. The structure of the garden is relatively formal, based on the concept of a series of garden rooms, walled with yew and planted thematically—yet the underlying discipline is scarcely evident as climbers tumble from one room to the next, and happy combinations of self-seeded flowers are left to do as they will.

Kiftsgate Court is equally renowned in gardening circles for its prolific rambling rose, *Rosa filipes* "Kiftsgatc". Having colonised several trees, it must surely be England's largest climbing rose, and is delightful in early summer, cascading down in great showers of white blooms. The rest of the garden is full of unusual plants, and the views from the swimming-pool terrace look over wooded slopes down to the Vale of Evesham.

From Mickleton, the A46 southwestwards follows the Vale, with the steep-faced Cotswold scarp rising to the left, all the way into **Broadway**. Packed with tourists throughout the summer, this town of ancient golden houses nevertheless merits a visit. Those who cannot afford lunch at the Lygon Arms, renowned for its cuisine, can at least admire its handsome Renaissance doorway, dated 1620, and the cordon-trained fruit trees growing the full height of the facade.

Many another ancient and wisteria-clad town house now serves as a tea-shop, boutique or art gallery, and the world-renowned furniture maker, Gordon Russell, has his showroom and factory at the bottom end of the High Street.

If you want to escape the crowds, you can follow the Cotswold Way long-distance footpath from the centre of the town, up the steep sides of **Broadway Hill**, to the **Tower** at the summit. This folly was built in 1800 and stands 65 ft (20 metres) tall on top of a 1,024-ft (412-metre) hill, giving extensive views which, on a clear day, extend to the cities of Worcester and Warwick.

Thatchers are seldom short of work in the Cotswolds.

William Morris used to use the tower as a holiday retreat, and there are displays in the tower about his life and work, and about the Cotswold wool industry. Less than a mile to the northeast, along the ridge of the hill, is another picturesque folly, built in the 18th century as a "gaze-about house", now part of the pub called The Fish Inn.

At the western end of Broadway, a narrow road signposted to Snowshill Manor passes the Norman **church of St Eadburga**, standing next door to the Court House whose ancient topiary yews spill from the garden into the churchyard.

Two miles on is **Snowshill Manor**, a popular National Trust property best avoided at weekends because of the sheer volume of visitors. The former owner, Charles Paget Wade, led a solitary life here between 1919 and 1951, carefully restoring the Tudor house that had once belonged to Catherine Parr, the last of Henry VIII's six wives. Wade filled his house to the rafters with a magpie collection of extraordinary diversity: everything from bicycles to Samurai armour. Perhaps his best achievement was the terraced garden, created by clearing away unsightly 19th-century buildings, brimming with colourful flowers.

From Snowshill, a high, narrow lane crosses the heights of the Cotswold uplands, attractive in summer, but bleak and chill in winter, through Taddington and down into the beautiful, wooded Windrush valley. **Temple Guiting** (pronounced *Guyting*) was once a property of the crusading Knights Templar, and the Windrush, much diminished in size since the stream has been tapped to provide drinking water, used to drive the hammers of fulling mills, used in wool processing.

This industry continued into the 18th century: the tomb of John Mowse (died 1787) in St Mary's Church records that he was a wool dyer, who employed a great number of the poor of the parish in the various parts of his trade. He may

Leading a merry dance at Cotswold Farm Park.

also have contributed to the rebuilding of the church, with its fine wooden furnishings and George II coat of arms, unusually made out of plaster.

Two miles southwest, at **Cotswold Farm Park**, headquarters of the Rare Breeds Survival Trust, the Henson family keeps a flock of the traditional breed of Cotswold sheep upon which the medieval prosperity of the region was based. Nicknamed "Cotswold lions" for their distinctive long, curly fleece, these big-limbed animals are descended from sheep introduced by the Romans. The foundation of the Cotswold Sheep Society by another local farmer, in 1892, saved the breed from extinction, but even now they are regarded as a rare breed—like the Gloucester Old Spot pigs and Old Gloucester cows that are also protected and displayed at the Farm Park.

Six miles (10 km) downstream, the River Windrush flows through the centre of **Bourton-on-the-Water**, crossed by a series of elegant 18th-century stone bridges. Bourton is a village to avoid if you do not like people, for the combined attractions of the Model Village—a one-ninth scale replica of Bourton itself, made in 1937—a Motor Museum, Model Railway and Birdland all make this one of the most-visited tourist attractions of the region.

The Slaughters: This same fate has overtaken the nearby hamlets of **Lower** and **Upper Slaughter**, so named because of the sloughs, or marshes, that once bordered the little River Eye as it flows through and between the two villages. Simple clapper bridges, made of massive planks of limestone, cross the stream as it flows between carefully tended banks and in front of the mill in Lower Slaughter, a much-photographed building.

Similar in character, but far more peaceful, is the little hamlet of **Upper Swell**, with its 18th-century bridge, water mill and mill pool fed by the River Dikler. Occasionally in summer, the **Abbotswood** estate, south of Swell, is open under the National Gardens Scheme. Well worth visiting, Abbotswood is one of the finest works of Sir Edwin Lutyens, who designed the garden, with its pools and water channels, as well as the striking house, in 1902.

Stow-on-the-Wold, a mile east, sits on the summit of an 800-ft (240-metre) hill and has the reputation for being a chilly place: "Stow-on-the-Wold, where the wind blows cold" is an ancient taunt.

Array of antiques: The great Stow horse fair is now held at **Andoversford** (near Cheltenham), moved because of the nuisance caused by gypsy horse breeders converging on the town three times a year (the Fair is held in mid-May, mid-July and mid-October). Stow prefers more genteel visitors and caters for them with numerous antique shops, tea rooms and a museum of antique dolls in Sheep Street.

Stow's church, to the west of the grassed-over Market Square, was so ill-treated by Royalist prisoners, captured in the Battle of Stow, one of the fiercest of the Civil War in the 1640s, that it had to be repaired extensively. From this time dates the curious Gothic north porch, flanked by two twisted and ancient yews.

The A436 west of Stow meets the A44, and from there it is a short drive back to Oxford. Lovers of literature might like to make a final stop at **Adlestrop** for two reasons. First, Jane Austen was a frequent visitor to Adlestrop House, formerly the rectory, where her uncle was the incumbent. The house private but visible from the churchyard—has an 18th-century Gothic facade and was the model for her descriptions of Northanger Abbey.

The other reason is the station; it is now closed but the original sign fills the village bus shelter. Below it, a bench bears a brass plate inscribed with the words of Edward Thomas's brief poem, evoking all the pleasures of a summer Cotswold day: "Yes, I remember Adlestrop".

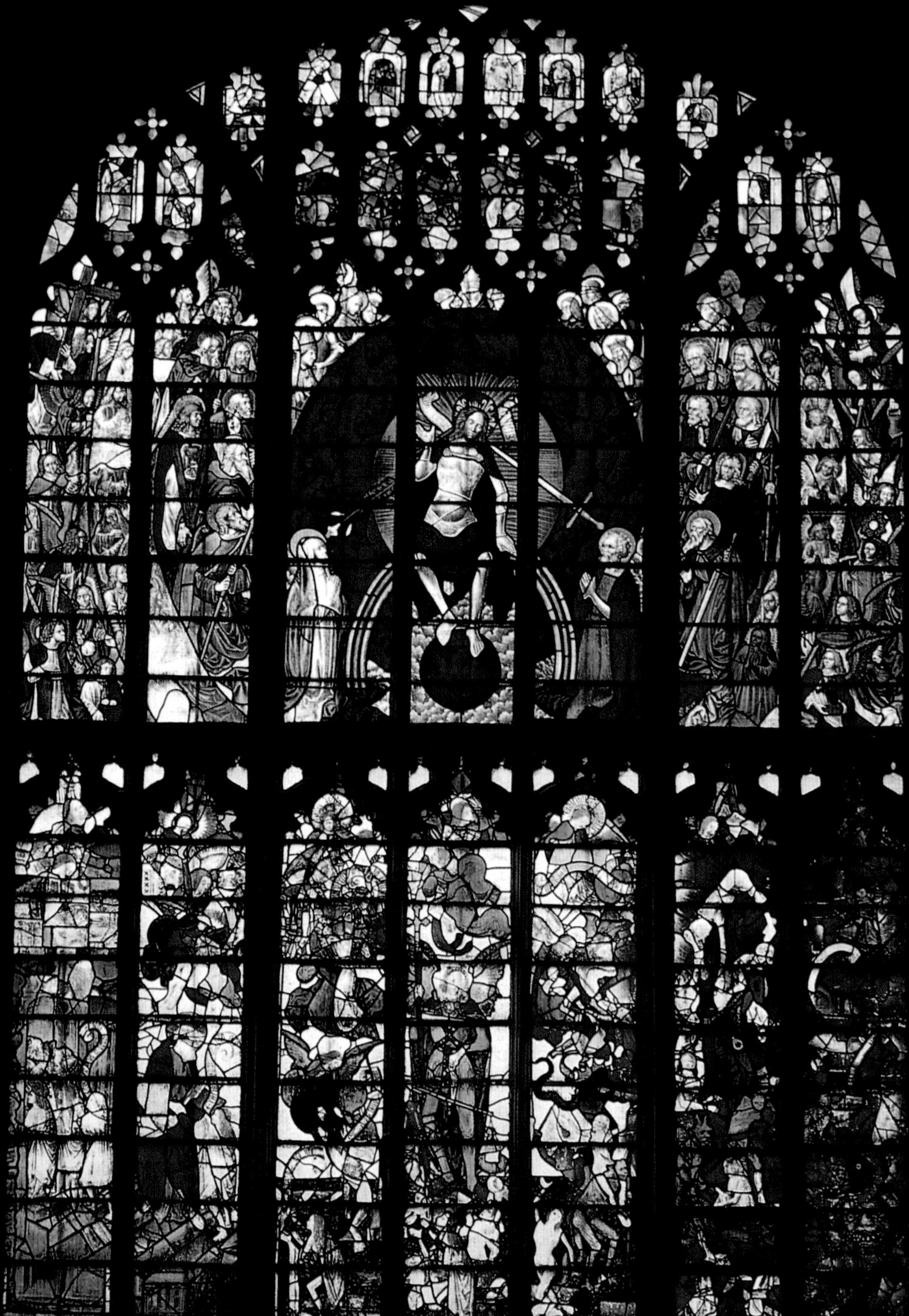

THE UPPER THAMES

Walkers can follow the River Thames from Oxford all the way to its source near Cirencester along the newly designated **Thames Long Distance Footpath**. You can also hire a motor cruiser and take to the water, at least as far as Lechlade, the river's highest navigable point. By car you will miss out on some of the river's tranquillity but you can easily divert to see the attractive villages, houses and churches that lie within a few miles of the river.

Heading out of Oxford on the B4044, you cross the river 6 miles (10 km) west at **Swinford Toll Bridge**, an elegant stone bridge built in 1769 to replace a dangerous ford. In Eynsham, turn south on the B4449 to **Stanton Harcourt**. Here you will find a fascinating medieval manor house complex surrounding the parish church. The gate house was built in 1540 and enlarged in 1953 to form the house of the present owners. Much of the original manor house was demolished in 1735 and the stone reused to build a new Harcourt family seat at Nuneham Courtenay.

Pope's Tower, however, remains. This was originally the manorial chapel, and is named after the poet Alexander Pope who resided here in 1717 and 1718 while working on his translation of Homer's *Iliad*. A window pane records his stay and is scratched with the words "In the year 1718 I Alexander Pope finished here the fifth volume of Homer".

The Great Kitchen also survives, built in 1380 and reroofed in 1485. The octagonal timber roof is very beautiful—"like the web of a giant spider" according to one architectural historian—yet Pope recorded that local people felt differently: "They believe witches keep their Sabbath here, and that once a year the Devil treats them with an infernal vision, *viz.* a toasted tiger stuffed with tenpenny nails."

It is difficult to imagine such horrors taking place here now, since the old walls and fish ponds of the manor have been transformed into a pleasing formal garden, and the nearby church of St Michael contains many fine monuments to the Harcourt family.

Three miles (5 km) south, through Standlake, the B4449 meets the A415, which crosses the confluence of the River Windrush with the Thames by means of a 15th-century bridge—replacing one of the first bridges to be built across the Thames in 1280.

At **Kingston Bagpuize** (pronounced *Bagpews*), 2 miles (3 km) south, Lady Tweedsmuir often conducts visitors personally around her home, Kingston House, built in the reign of Charles II, and—unusually in this region of stone—out of the then fashionable red brick. The house has a magnificent cantilevered staircase and the Georgian summerhouse, in the beautiful gardens, stands above an Elizabethan cockpit.

At **Pusey House**, 4 miles (6 km) west,

the garden is considered one of England's finest. Designed in 1934, long herbaceous borders, packed with plants, lead to a lake where water-loving plants surround a Chinese Chippendale-style bridge. Great banks of shrubs and mature trees frame distant views of the Berkshire Downs.

At **Faringdon**, 5 miles (8 km) west, the 17th-century Town Hall, supported on stout limestone columns to provide a market below, stands on an island in the centre of the Market Place surrounded by Georgian inns and town houses.

Just to the southwest, **Great Coxwell** barn is one of England's earliest and finest medieval barns. William Morris called it "as noble as a cathedral" and the great timber roof, supported on stone columns, dates to the late 13th century when Cistercian monks built it to store their tithes.

William Morris knew this corner of Oxfordshire intimately. He purchased the Thames-side manor at **Kelmscott**, 3 miles northwest of Faringdon, in 1871 and lived there until his death in 1896. The manor, furnished with his own textiles, wallpapers and portrait of his wife Jane, painted by Rossetti, is open on the first Wednesday of each month in summer. Morris is buried in St George's churchyard nearby.

Buscot House, on the other side of the river, also has Pre-Raphaelite connections for the walls of the parlour are used to display Burne-Jones's rich series of paintings based on the story of Sleeping Beauty, executed in 1890. The same artist designed the Good Shepherd window in the village church, some 2 miles west of Buscot House itself.

From the nearby Buscot Lock, you can walk along the Thames to **Lechlade**, just over a mile away. Walking is by far the best way to approach the town for, as you reach St John's Bridge, there is a splendid view of the elegant church and spire, rising above the surrounding water meadows.

St John's Lock marks the highest navigable point of the river and the

The Thames, languid at Lechlade.

nearby marina is always busy in summer with holidaymakers. By the side of the lock is a friendly reclining stone figure known affectionately as "Old Father Thames"—though he in fact represents Neptune, and was carved by the Italian artist Rafaelle Monti for the 1851 Great Exhibition. He resided at Crystal Palace until 1958, when he was moved to the source of the Thames near Coates, and then transferred to this more public spot in 1974 because of repeated vandalism.

As you cross the meadows to Lechlade church, you follow in the footsteps of the poet Shelley who, in 1815, stayed here after rowing up river from Windsor. He composed his *Stanzas in a Summer Evening Churchyard* while sitting beside the church, having dined well on "three well-peppered mutton chops" at the New Inn.

Beautiful as it is though, the church is scarcely a rival to the magnificent building at nearby **Fairford**, built by the wool merchant Tames, father and son, from 1490. The magnificent and near-complete set of 15th-century stained glass was produced in the workshops of Barnard Flower, Master Glass Painter to Henry VII and also responsible for the windows of King's College Chapel, Cambridge. Based on woodcuts in the *Biblia Pauperum* (Poor Man's Bible), one of the earliest printed books, the windows provide a wonderful vision of pre-Reformation religious beliefs; in particular, the enthralling west window depicts in vivid detail the torments of the Damned in Hell.

The richly carved choir screen, featuring the pomegranate emblem of Katherine of Aragon, widow of Prince Arthur and then wife of his brother, Henry VIII, dates to around 1501, like the choir stalls, carved with scenes from fable and popular sermons. Outside, jesters and grotesque beasts tumble around the parapet.

East and south of Fairford, the River Thames gets lost, almost, among acres of gravel workings and the water-

Hanging around in the High Street.

parks—providing facilities for fishermen and weekend sailors—created out of the flooded pits left after the gravel has been extracted.

Four miles (7 km) southwest of Fairford, the church at **Down Ampney** has a display of Vaughan Williams' memorabilia; the composer was born in 1872 in the nearby Old Vicarage. The other **Ampneys**, strung out along the Ampney Brook to the north, all have Saxon churches: best of all is the little church of **Ampney St Mary**, standing alone in fields south of the A417, for the original village was abandoned in 1348 because of the Black Death.

Three miles west is **Cirencester**, dubbed the "Capital of the Cotswolds". In Roman times it was Britain's second biggest city, and the award-winning **Corinium Museum**, in Park Street, shows the wealth of material that has been uncovered in the town, including accomplished mosaics and tableaux illustrating daily life in the Roman city.

The wide Market Place, lined with pastel-painted Regency and Victorian shops, is fronted with one of the Cotswolds' largest and finest wool churches—graced by a richly embellished 15th-century tower, and entered through an imposing fan-vaulted porch whose upper room once served as the town hall. From the tower there are panoramic views over the town and over the chestnut-lined avenues of **Cirencester Park**, laid out by the 1st Earl Bathurst with the help of his friend, the poet Alexander Pope. Most of the park's 30,000 acres (12,000 hectares) is open to the public.

Beginnings: To find the **source of the Thames**, you have to leave Cirencester on the A433 Foss Way and look for a layby after the Coates turning and before the railway bridge. About 100 metres back from the layby, towards Cirencester, a path to the north leads across fields to the source, at the edge of the woods surrounding Trewsbury House. Such detailed directions are necessary because the spring is elu-

Cirencester, "Capital of the Cotswolds".

sive—and often totally dry in summer.

There is a rival "source" of the Thames, and a more spectacular one than this muddy patch, at **Seven Springs**, 12 miles (20 km) north of Cirencester, just off the A436 to the left of the junction with the A435. Local people unsuccessfully petitioned Parliament in 1937 for this to be recognised as the true source. It does, however, mark the beginning of the Churn, a pretty river that makes the drive to Seven Springs along the A435 especially attractive.

Almost every village along the route will demand your attention and delay you—for all of them have Saxon or early Norman churches; if you only have time to visit one, it should be St John's at **Elkstone**, the most complete 12th-century Romanesque church in the region, and covered in bold carvings of dragons and beakheads—barbaric figures that seem to suggest an older, perhaps Scandinavian, tradition of art.

From Seven Springs the A435 drops over the Cotswold scarp to **Cheltenham** in the Vale below. This town, with its elegant Regency and neo-Grecian buildings, was no more than a village until medicinal springs were discovered in the 18th century and, after George III's visit in 1788, it was adopted as a summer resort by the wealthy.

Later, Cheltenham was a place of retirement for colonial civil servants and army officers (contemptuously described by William Cobbett as "East India plunderers, West India floggers and English tax dodgers"). Today it is noted for its smart shops, annual arts festival and horse racing. In March, during Gold Cup week, the top event of the National Hunt calendar, the town is transformed into an outpost of Ireland.

To avoid the busy main road back to Oxford, take the A40, but turn right 3 miles east of Cheltenham at Dowdeswell and follow the road to **Withington**. This pretty village has one of the Cotswolds' most characterful pubs, The Mill, and the road westward, with

Left, Cheltenham. Right, Thames lock-keeper.

views of the beautifully wooded Coln valley leads to Chedworth Roman villa. The villa enjoys an idyllic setting, in a sheltered combe, and dates originally to around AD 180. Centrally heated dining rooms and sauna baths were provided as a retreat from the cold English winters. One lively mosaic floor depicting the four seasons portrays winter as a shepherd in woollen cloak and hood.

At **Northleach**, you can hear tape recordings of more recent shepherds, talking in the rich Cotswold accent about their work—just one of the features that makes the **Cotswold Countryside Collection**, housed in an 18th-century prison, a rewarding museum.

Northleach parish church continues the rural theme, for wool merchants paid for its construction, and many of those who donated funds are commemorated by an outstanding series of memorial brasses: look particularly for the Scors-Fortey brass of 1450, for the border is engraved with charming vignettes, including a snail, a pig, a hedge-

hog and a crab. Note, too, that the inscription gives the year of Thomas Fortey's death as MCCCC47, the last two figures being an early example of the use of Arabic, rather than Roman, numerals; this indicates that Cotswold wool merchants had contacts with their Moorish counterparts in Spain.

A detour south to **Bibury** will again avoid the congested A40, and Bibury is certainly worth a visit, despite the crowds of coach-borne tourists who come to see the village dubbed the most beautiful in England. From the Saxon church at the east end of the village you can follow the trout-filled River Coln, past Arlington Row, a group of 17th-century weavers' cottages, to Arlington Mill, a museum that contains a representative collection of furniture made by members of the Cotswold Arts and Crafts movement in the early 1900s.

At **Barnsley**, 3 miles southwest, Rosemary Verey's outstanding and influential garden, created in the grounds of the former rectory, has become al-

Bibury: the most beautiful village in England?

most a pilgrimage centre for those who know and love her gardening books.

East of Bibury you can either take the high road to **Coln St Aldwyns**, not neglecting to look back for a view of the many-gabled Bibury Court, built in 1633, or you can take the valley footpath, following the banks of the gentle **River Coln**. This unspoiled river, fringed by meadowsweet and reedmace, makes Coln St Aldwyns, with its 16th-century manor house, barn and dovecote, a village of almost unreal beauty, like a living Constable painting.

The village is almost continuous with **Hatherop**, where the "castle", built in the 1850s in French Gothic style, is now a girls' school, and **Quenington**, where the little Norman church has two tympanums, one carved with the Harrowing of Hell, the other with the Coronation of the Virgin.

Three miles east, **Eastleach Turville** and **Martin** stand on opposite banks of the River Leach, linked by an ancient clapper bridge made of massive limestone slabs. In spring, visitors come for miles to admire the river banks, smothered in wild daffodils.

At **Southrop**, a mile downstream, the church contains a unique and intriguing Norman font, carved with armoured figures representing the Virtues, trampling and stabbing beasts that represent the Vices. The names of the Vices are carved in mirror writing, as if to stress they represent the opposite of Good.

At **Filkins**, off the A361 west of Southrop, the Cotswold Woollen Weavers make handwoven cloth in a converted barn, amid displays explaining the history of wool in the Cotswolds.

The **Cotswold Wild Life Park**, 2 miles north, is an open-air zoo where African and tropical animals graze incongruously in an English park around a neo-Gothic manor.

More quintessentially English is the market town of **Burford** to the north, with its broad High Street, lined with trees and wool merchants' houses, falling steeply away to the River Windrush.

Ploughing competition at Filkins using steam traction. Overpage: Burford.

The stately church, with its 180-ft (55-metre) spire, stands right by the river. The font has the words "Anthony Sedley prisoner 1649" scratched into its lead lining. Sedley was one of three Levellers, members of a breakaway religious sect, who took part in a mutiny against Cromwell's army during the Civil War. The three men were trapped in the church, executed and buried in the churchyard.

Another monument to dissent is the curiously named hamlet of **Charterville Allotments**, 5 miles (8 km) east along the A415. The hamlet was created by the wealthy socialist Feargus O'Connor around 1847 as a means of providing rural homes and small holdings for poor families from industrial towns—the scheme failed when O'Connor went bankrupt soon after.

Immediately north is the romantic ruined manor house of **Minster Lovell**, standing among willow trees by the side of the River Windrush. The manor was built in 1432 by William, the 7th Lord Lovell. His grandson, Francis Lovell, was a prominent supporter of the Yorkist cause during the Wars of the Roses, and, according to local legend, he took refuge in the house after defeat in battle, hiding in a secret room where he starved to death. In 1728, workmen found a skeleton which they assumed to be his, and John Buchan vividly retold the tale in his novel *The Blanket of the Dark*.

And so to bed: The last stop before Oxford is the town of **Witney**, famous the world over for the production of soft, woollen Witney blankets, an industry that dates to the 13th century. Blanket Hall, in the High Street, was built in 1721 for the weighing and measuring of blankets, and 18th-century mills and weavers' cottages ring the town.

Just to the southeast, off the B4022, **Cogges Manor Farm Museum** recreates rural life at the turn of the century with cooking, washing and dairying demonstrations every day, and theme weeks during the year covering every subject from lambing to lacemaking.

THE LOWER THAMES

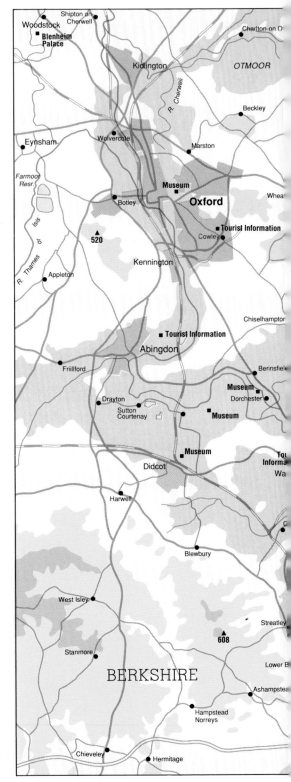

Abingdon lies 8 miles (13 km) south of Oxford, and if you choose to walk there, along the western bank of the Thames, or take the river cruiser from Folly Bridge in Oxford, you will enjoy views of **Nuneham Park**. This huge neo-Palladian mansion was built in the late 1700s in a natural amphitheatre landscaped by "Capability" Brown. Walpole called it "the most beautiful place in the world", but the poet Oliver Goldsmith thought differently.

To create the park, the old village of Nuneham was cleared and a new estate village built to the north. Goldsmith's poem *Deserted Village* lamented the power of "the man of wealth and pride" to uproot his tenants and destroy their centuries-old way of life.

Abingdon, once the county town of Berkshire until the rapid growth of Reading, has a splendid Town Hall, fitting to its former status. This magnificent Renaissance stone building was built in 1678 by Christopher Kempster, a master mason who had worked for Christopher Wren, and clearly shows Wren's influence. There is a museum upstairs in the former Assize Court, and the open area below is used as a market.

Of Abingdon's once powerful Benedictine Abbey, little now remains, apart from some mock ruins, built in the 19th century from the few remaining stones, and the 15th-century gateway attached to St Nicholas' Church.

From the Market Square, the graceful spire of St Helen's Church, 150 ft high (46 metres), draws the eye. The street leading to it is lined with characterful houses—a mixture of 16th-century timber framing and Georgian brick.

St Helen's splendid churchyard is surrounded by almhouses; Christ's Hospital, founded in 1446, is fronted by a long timber cloister, while to the right, Twitty's Almshouses of 1707, and, to the left, Brick Alley Almshouses of

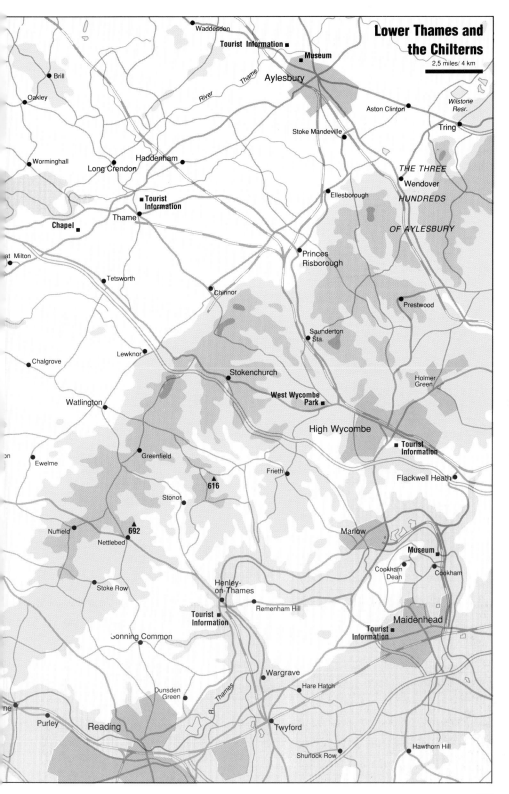

Lower Thames and the Chilterns

2.5 miles/ 4 km

Waddesdon

Tourist Information ■

■ **Museum**

Aylesbury

River _Thame_

Aston Clinton

Wilstone Resr.

Tring

Brill

Oakley

Stoke Mandeville

THE THREE

Worminghall

Haddenham

Long Crendon

Ellesborough

Wendover

HUNDREDS

■ **Tourist Information**

Thame

OF AYLESBURY

Chapel ■

at Milton

Princes Risborough

Tetsworth

Chinnor

Prestwood

Lewknor

Saunderton Sta.

Chalgrove

Holmer Green

Stokenchurch

Watlington

West Wycombe Park ■

High Wycombe

■ **Tourist Information**

Greenfield

Frieth

Ewelme

▲ 616

Flackwell Heath

Stonor

Nuffield

▲ 692

Nettlebed

Marlow

Museum ■

Cookham Dean

Cookham

Stoke Row

Henley-on-Thames

Tourist ■ Information

Maidenhead

Gonning Common

Remenham Hill

Tourist ■ Information

Wargrave

Hare Hatch

Dunsden Green

R. Thames

ne

Purley

Reading

Twyford

Shurlock Row

Hawthorn Hill

1718, are both extraordinarily ornate, with chequered brick, balconies and roof-top belvederes.

St Helen's is remarkably wide and has no fewer than five aisles, representing 15th and 16th-century additions to the 13th-century church. The roof of the inner north aisle is covered with a rare series of panels painted around 1390 with a Tree of Jesse.

Didcot, 5 miles (8 km) south of Abingdon, is visible from afar, since the six great cooling towers of the coal-fired power station, built in the 1960s, dominate the skyline. The railway station marks the point where the Great Western Railway (known to enthusiasts as God's Wonderful Railway) meets the line from Worcester and the Midlands. No-one with a passion for steam should miss the **Didcot Railway Centre** alongside, with the engine sheds filled with lovingly restored locomotives.

Northeast by 5 miles is the historic town of **Dorchester**, with its beautiful abbey built on the spot where St Birinus,

sent by Pope Honorius to convert the West Saxons, founded a church in AD 635. The former abbey Guest House, later the town school, contains a museum explaining the history of the town, and the abbey, now the parish church, is packed with treasures: a rare Norman lead font, an east window of flowing tracery filled with 14th-century glass, and a Jesse window whose stonework is carved with figures of kings and prophets showing the lineage of Christ.

Ewelme, 4 miles southwest, is one of Oxfordshire's showplace villages, lying beneath the Chilterns. Rainwater filtered through the chalk emerges here, and the pure water used to be diverted to watercress beds, dotted about the village. At the west end of Ewelme, the church, almshouses and school all date from between 1430 and 1450, when they were endowed by the Duke of Suffolk and his wife Alice, grand-daughter of the poet Geoffrey Chaucer.

Alice, dressed as simply as a nun but wearing a coronet and the Order of the

Left, Didcot Railway Centre. **Right**, once more with feeling at Mapledurham manor house.

Garter, lies under a magnificent tomb canopy in the church. In St John's Chapel is the brass of her father, Thomas, Chaucer's son; he donated the splendid carved wooden font cover. Jerome K. Jerome, author of that great celebration of the pleasures of the Thames, *Three Men in a Boat*, is also buried in the churchyard.

The history of **Wallingford**, 3 miles southwest by the Thames, is well summed up by its name. An important Roman town because of its position by a relatively safe ford across the Thames, it was walled by King Alfred in the 9th century, and further fortified by the Normans, who built the castle whose remains lie to the north of the town. The town's defences remained strong enough up to the 17th century for this to be the last Royalist stronghold in the county to surrender to Cromwell; he ordered the destruction of the castle that had proved so useful to his enemies.

The town has long since outgrown its walls, but the grid pattern of streets in the town centre reflects its Saxon origins, and the graceful stone bridge, 300 ft long (90 metres) with 17 arches and last rebuilt in 1809, still forms a major through route for traffic.

Below Wallingford the character of the riverside towns begins to change. The closer to London, the more you find of large Victorian and Edwardian villas, and railway stations, dotted every 4 miles or so along the Thames valley, carry train loads of commuters to and from London daily. The names read like lines from a Betjeman poem: Tilehurst, Pangbourne, Goring and Streatley.

The last two, **Goring** and **Streatley**, are manicured villages facing each other across the Thames where it cuts through a narrow gap in the chalk hills, dividing the Chilterns from the Berkshire Downs. Below Streatley, on the west bank of the river, is **Basildon House**, built in 1776 for Sir Francis Sykes who had made a fortune in India. The house is a severe neo-Palladian pile, but beautifully furnished and posi-

Dorchester: its cobbled high street follows the line of the old Roman road to Silchester.

tioned to enjoy extensive views of the river and the wooded cliffs of the Chilterns beyond.

On the opposite bank, reached by narrow, tree-shaded country lanes from Goring, is the more ancient and more endearing **Mapledurham manor house**. Apart from the lovely Elizabethan house, with its great chimneys, oak staircases and portraits of the beautiful sisters, Martha and Teresa Blount—celebrated by leading poets of the day—you can also visit the fully restored water mill in the grounds, the last survivor of the many mills that once harnessed the river's power.

Reading, a sprawling town which has grown and grown ever since the railway arrived, is best avoided—although the town has three excellent museums, devoted to archaeology (Town Museum), industry (Blake's Lock) and rural life (University).

Instead, thread through the country lanes north of the town via Sonning Common to **Greys Court**, a jumble of medieval, Tudor and Jacobean buildings with a maze in the garden, and a mighty wheel house, driven by donkey power, and used until 1914 to draw water from the 200-ft (60-metre) well.

From here, you drop over the hill and down into **Henley-on-Thames**, host since 1839 of the world-famous river regatta, held annually in the first week of July. Because the regatta is considered an important event in the London social season, the glittering balls and riverside parties—where eligible young ladies are introduced to the "right sort" of young men, and companies lavish entertainment on their clients— are every bit as important as the racing.

The town, too, is very "upper crust", with houses, especially those with riverside views, costing a considerable fortune, and shops selling *haute couture* and delicatessen provisions suitable for long, lazy summer picnics; for chillier days, Henley has several excellent pubs selling the products of the local Brakspear's brewery.

Henley-on-Thames, to which rowing crews flock each summer.

Eight miles (13 km) east, the picturesque village of **Cookham** is protected from the suburban sprawl that spreads out from London by beautiful woodlands owned by the National Trust. The eccentric artist Stanley Spencer spent much of his life here, wheeling the perambulator which he used to carry his canvases, easels and paints, and stopping to incorporate the local river scenes and buildings into his pictures. The town has a gallery devoted to his work, and his painting of the Last Supper hangs in the church.

Grand hotel: On the opposite bank from Cookham is **Cliveden**, the huge classical house built by Lord Astor in 1851. As the home of Lady Astor, Britain's first woman Member of Parliament, between the wars it was the glittering centre of the nation's social and political life. The National Trust now owns the property and leases it as an hotel, but the spectacular terraced gardens are open to the public, and these form the venue for a popular open-air theatre festival at the end of June and the beginning of July.

From Cliveden, we leave the Thames and head north through the uninviting commuter suburbs of Beaconsfield and High Wycombe. West of the long, straight road through Wycombe, where the Oxford and Aylesbury road divides, this sprawl suddenly ends, halted by the rising hills of the Chilterns and the estates of Sir Francis Dashwood.

The present Sir Francis still lives in **West Wycombe Park**, though the grounds are open to the public and used as the setting for spectacular theatricals, with firework displays, in summer. The earlier Sir Francis, who built the house in the mid-18th century, was a leading light of the Hell-Fire Club; this group of high-spirited young aristocrats mocked the religious piety of their day by holding Black Masses in honour of the Devil, and their motto was *Fay ce que voudras* ("Do as you please").

The eccentric Sir Francis also helped to relieve unemployment by hiring local

Houseboat at Cookham.

men to dig a series of tunnels and caves into the soft chalk of the hillside above his home. The caves descend to an artificial river called the Styx and may have been used for Hell-Fire rituals. After visiting them, it is worth climbing the hill to see the parish church. The golden globe on top of the tower was used by Dashwood to entertain his friends (one of whom called it the "Globe Tavern").

Higher still, and east of the church, is a strange hexagonal mausoleum, built both as an eye-catcher, crowning the hill's summit and visible from the road below, and as a memorial to members of the Dashwood family.

Just north of Wycombe, off the A4128, is another celebrated house, **Hughenden Manor**. This 18th-century house, bought by Benjamin Disraeli in 1847 and converted to his tastes, is furnished with memorabilia and the possessions of Queen Victoria's favourite Prime Minister.

From Wycombe, the A40—once one of England's busiest roads but now almost a rural lane, since the building of the M40 alongside—crosses the beech-covered heights of the Chilterns and then drops spectacularly over the edge at **Beacon Hill**, descending into the Vale of Aylesbury. The town of **Thame** has a broad High Street, almost a mile in length and lined with 18th-century brick houses.

Fowl versus fumes: Beyond, to the northwest, lies some of Oxfordshire's least populated countryside. At **Brill**, with its hilltop windmill, you look down into the great bowl of Otmoor, a 4,000-acre (1,600-hectare) region of formerly waterlogged common land, much of it designated as a Site of Special Scientific Interest. A public campaign to prevent the M40 motorway crossing the moor succeeded in having it diverted to the north, preserving this spot for the water birds who migrate in great numbers between their feeding grounds on the Wash and the River Severn.

At **Boarstall**, 2 miles west, you can see a 17th-century duck decoy, originally used for capturing the resident fowl for sale in local markets, and still used to catch ducks for ringing.

From here you can make a circular tour round the rim of the fens, visiting the "seven towns" of Otmoor. Best of them all is **Charlton**, with its landmark church, the "cathedral" of Otmoor. This contains a very rare pre-Reformation rood screen, decorated every May Day with a large cross of flowers which remains until September.

Charlton—meaning "free man's village"—was built by generations of moormen, who fought attempts to enclose the land so fiercely, destroying fences and hedges, that in 1829 the Oxford Militia was called in to arrest the leaders. They were taken to Oxford, only to be released by sympathetic townspeople with cries of "Otmoor for ever". Though enclosure did eventually take place, Otmoor still remains a marshy wilderness, and a complete contrast to the busy city of Oxford, just 5 miles away.

Left and right: quiet times by the Thames.

COTSWOLD WILD LIFE PARK

Narrow Gauge Railway • Adventure Playground • Picnic Areas • Restaurant & Bar • Brass Rubbing • Gift Shop

OPEN THROUGHOUT THE YEAR EXCEPT CHRISTMAS DAY FROM 10am
(Last admission 6 pm or dusk which ever is the earlier) Free car parking
Costwold Wildife Park Ltd., Burford, Oxford OX8 4JW. Telephone: (099 382) 3006

20 miles west of Oxford on A361, 2 miles south of the A40 at Burford

TRAVEL TIPS

GETTING THERE

NOTE: *Unless a separate exchange code is shown, all telephone numbers are for Oxford (UK trunk dialling code 0865, international 44-865).*

BY AIR

The nearest airport is Heathrow (40 miles/ 64 km), the second nearest, Gatwick (70 miles/112 km). Both are linked to Oxford by an express coach service, CityLink X70; this departs every half-hour from Heathrow 7 a.m.–7 p.m. during the summer and less in winter. A period return from Heathrow is £9, a day return £7.50, a single, £6. There are eight journeys a day from Gatwick. Recorded timetable information giving times and fares first to Heathrow then Gatwick can be obtained on tel: 0865-722270 (24hrs).

BY SEA

Oxford is one of the the UK's most inland towns. The nearest port offering a cross-Channel service is Portsmouth (80 miles/ 128 km). A National Express bus service links Oxford to the south coast every hour daily.

BY TRAIN

British Rail's Network Southeast provides an hourly service beteeen London's Paddington station and Oxford. The journey takes about an hour. Oxford station is a 10-minute walk from the centre of the city.

Other direct lines from London Paddington stopping at Oxford are the services to Bicester (infrequent), Worcester, Birmingham via Coventry and Birmingham International for the National Exhibition Centre and Birmingham airport, with a Saver return fare (daily) of £10 or £15.50 for an ordinary return.

Trains to London depart hourly, on the hour, between 10 a.m. and 5 p.m., with a less frequent service later.

Return fares from Oxford to London vary from just over £8 to almost £20, depending on when you travel. An off-peak day return is the best value.

Fare enquiries and general information, tel: 722333.

Recorded timetable information, tel: 249055.

BY BUS

Two rival companies, Oxford Tube and the Oxford Bus Company (CityLink), run between Oxford and London and have proved so cheap, convenient and comfortable that even *The Times* published an article analysing how the competition keeps fares so low.

From London, the Oxford Tube coach leaves from Grosvenor Gardens (to the left on leaving the main Victoria British Rail and Underground stations). All coaches stop on request at Marble Arch (10 minutes after departing Victoria), Notting Hill Gate (15 minutes) and the Kensington Hilton at Shepherds Bush. The Tube runs from 7.50 a.m.–12.15 a.m., with a service every 20 minutes between 10 a.m. and 7 p.m. The single fare is £6 from London; £6.50 day return; £6.95 period return. Students and Senior Citizens: £4.50 single; £4.95 day and period return.

CityLink coaches leave from London's Victoria Coach Station every 30 minutes and stop at Grosvenor Gardens and Marble Arch.

Most journeys take 80 minutes but during peak periods you should allow more time due to traffic congestion in London. For travel information, telephone 727000 (Oxford Tube) or 772250 (CityLink).

The Oxford Bus Company also runs frequent local bus and coach services serving many places of local interest—Abingdon, Blenheim Palace, Henley-on-Thames, High Wycombe, Stratford-upon-Avon and Windsor.

BY CAR

Oxford is well served by main roads in all directions, though by few motorways. It is 56 miles (90 km) from London by the A40 and M40; the journey takes about an hour. The approach roads into Oxford, especially from London, are heavily congested during the morning and evening rush hours and on Saturday.

TRAVEL ESSENTIALS

VISAS & PASSPORTS

Visitors need a valid passport to enter the UK. Passports are stamped on arrival and usually allow a stay of six months. Enquiries about passports and visas should be made to the relevant embassy in London.

CUSTOMS

Visitors to the UK face few restrictions on the items they import for personal use, but there are limits to the quantity of alcoholic drinks, tobacco and perfume that can be imported duty-free.

Duty-free allowances fall into two categories: one rate for goods bought in a European Community country on which duty has already been paid (i.e. *not* in a duty-free shop); and another rate for the rest.

The allowances for the first category are: 1½ litres of spirits, or 3 litres of fortified or sparkling wine, or 5 litres of table wine; plus 300 cigarettes or cigarillos, or 75 cigars, or 400g of tobacco; plus 90cc of perfume, 375cc toilet water; and other goods to a maximum value of £250.

The allowances for the second category are: 1 litre of spirits, or 2 litres of fortified or sparkling wine, or 3 litres of table wine; plus 200 cigarettes or 100 cigarillos, or 30 cigars, or 250g of tobacco; plus 60cc perfume, 250cc toilet water; plus gifts or other goods up to an ungenerous value of £32.

Any queries may be addressed to HM Customs and Excise, Wingate House, Shaftesbury Avenue, London W1, tel: 071-437 9800.

ANIMAL QUARANTINE

Birds and mammals will normally be quarantined for six months. Details of the regulations about bringing animals into and out of the UK may be obtained from the Ministry of Agriculture, Fisheries and Food, Marston Road, Oxford OX3 OTP, tel: 244891. One of the nearest quarantine kennels is Spire Ridge Ltd, Bath Road, Midgham, Reading RG7 5XE, tel: 0734-712187. There are no quarantine kennels in Oxfordshire.

WHAT TO WEAR

In youthful, cosmopolitan Oxford, you can wear just about anything and not be considered out of place. Students wear very casual clothes—either jeans and sweaters of doubtful age and condition—or the fashions of the day. Older people tend to wear plain, country clothes and "sensible" shoes. Even in summer, the weather is variable so visitors need some warm clothing and comfortable footwear for the notably uneven flagstones. Formal dress is encouraged in some hotels and restaurants and for evening entertainment, particularly in university circles.

GETTING ACQUAINTED

GEOGRAPHY & POPULATION

In no other part of Britain has geology so influenced the landscape and architecture. The underlying rock in the area is oolite limestone, formed under pressure millions of years ago from the crushed shells of primitive sea organisms. Its small spherical grains vary in colour and texture depending on their location and depth. Wind and rain has moulded the limestone into a rolling countryside and the rock favours the growth of beech trees.

The stone has always delighted builders, from the creators of prehistoric burial mounds to the architects of Oxford's cathedrals to learning. When mellow, it alters dramatically in colour, often from one moment to the next as a cloud formation shifts. Buildings made from this stone, wrote the novelist J.B. Priestley, can keep "the lost sunlight of centuries glimmering about them".

For centuries, agriculture and the wool industry provided Oxford with an economic base as a thriving market town. Car manufacturing fuelled its growth in the 20th century, taking its population from 57,000 in 1920 to more than 80,000 in 1930. Since World War II, the city's population has remained relatively static. Out of term, it is something over 90,000; when students are in residence it increases to more than 116,000.

CLIMATE

The English are justly famous for their preoccupation with the weather—not surprisingly, since it remains utterly unpredictable. In Oxford, winters are mild and summers are dull and wet or sunny and airlessly hot, depending on which week you visit. Most of the summer is cool enough for a jacket. Bring wet weather clothes whatever the season.

TIME ZONES

Oxford, like the rest of the UK, follows Greenwich Mean Time (GMT). In late March the clocks go forward one hour for British summer time and in late October are moved back to GMT.

CULTURE & CUSTOMS

Oxford's cultural development is inseparable from the men and women who have, over the centuries, attended the University, then gone on to change the course of history in the world at large. And part of the fun of exploring Oxford lies in the realisation that so many of the world's most illustrious people have walked the same streets. Oxford graduates include 24 British prime ministers; 24 Nobel Prize winners; seven current holders of the Order of Merit (an honour in the gift of the Sovereign and limited to 24 holders at any one time); numerous writers, poets, founders of religions, scientists, artists, philosophers—some living, many dead.

The poet **John Donne** (1572–1631), for example, attended Hart Hall; he later became Dean of St Paul's. **John Wesley** (1703–91) and his brother **Charles** (1707–88) were both at Christ Church. John became an English evangelist and founder of "method in religion" (Methodism). **John Henry Newman** (1801–90), best remembered for his *Apologia pro Vita Sua*, in which he decribed the development of his religious thought, graduated from Trinity in 1816.

Philosophers include **Thomas Hobbes** (Magdalen Hall, 1603), who published *The Leviathan* in 1651, **John Locke** (Christ Church, circa 1654) and **Jeremy Bentham** (Queen's, 1760).

John Ruskin (1819–1900) who was at Christ Church until 1836, became a renowned art critic and author. **Percy Bysshe Shelley** (1792–1822), a master of language and of literary form, was sent down from Oxford for his pamphlet *The Necessity of Atheism*. Other literary luminaries include the lexographer **Dr Samuel Johnson** (Pembroke 1728), **Oscar Wilde** (Magdalen 1874), **Robert Browning** (1812–89) Balliol, and **Lewis Carroll** (Charles Dodgson), a mathematical don at Christ Church and author of *Alice in Wonderland* and *Through the Looking-Glass*. More recent names include **J. R. R. Tolkien**, **W. H. Auden**, **Robert Graves**, **Graham Greene**, **Evelyn Waugh** and **T. S. Eliot.**

Well-known women graduates are mostly writers or politicians: **Dorothy Sayers** (Somerville 1920), **Indira Gandhi** and **Dame Iris Murdoch** (both from Somerville in 1938) and **Benazir Bhutto** (Lady Margaret Hall, 1973).

Hugh Walpole, generally regarded as the first "Prime Minister", was an Oxford man, and 24 British prime ministers have followed in his footsteps. They are: **Spencer Compton, Earl of Wilmington** (PM 1742–43) Trinity; **Henry Pelham** (PM

1743–54) Hart Hall; **George Grenville** (PM 1763–65) Christ Church; **William Pitt** the Elder, **Earl of Chatham** (PM 1766–68) Trinity; **Frederick, Lord North** (PM 1770–82) Trinity; **William Petty, Earl of Shelburne** (PM 1782–83) Christ Church; **William Henry Cavendish Bentinck, Duke of Portland** (PM 1783 and 1807–09) Christ Church; **Henry Addington, Viscount Sidmouth** (PM 1801–04) Brasenose; **William Wyndham, Lord Grenville** (PM 1806–07) Christ Church; **Robert Banks Jenkinson, Earl of Liverpool** (PM 1812–27) Christ Church; **George Canning** (PM 1827) Christ Church; **Sir Robert Peel** (PM 1834–35 and 1841–46) Christ Church; **Edward Stanley, Earl of Derby** (PM 1852, 1858–59 and 1866–68) Christ Church; **William Ewart Gladstone** (PM 1868–74, 1880–85, 1886 and 1892–94) Christ Church; **Robert Cecil, Marquess of Salisbury** (PM 1885–86, 1886–92 and 1895–1902) Christ Church; **Archibald Philip Primrose, Earl of Rosebery** (PM 1894–95) Christ Church; **Herbert Henry Asquith, Earl of Oxford and Asquith** (PM 1908–16) Balliol; **Clement Attlee, Earl Attlee** (PM 1945–51) University; **Sir Anthony Eden, Earl of Avon** (PM 1955–57) Christ Church; **Harold Macmillan, Earl of Stockton** (PM 1957–63) Balliol; **Sir Alec Douglas-Home, Lord Home of the Hirsel** (PM 1963–64) Christ Church; **Harold Wilson, Lord Wilson of Rievaulx** (PM 1964–70 and 1974–76) Jesus; **Edward Heath** (PM 1970–74) Balliol; and **Margaret Thatcher** (PM from 1979) Somerville.

Among scientists, **Roger Bacon** first studied arts at Oxford in 1231, then devoted himself to experimental science, especially alchemy and optics. Founder of English philosophy, he became a Franciscan friar in 1257. **Robert Boyle** (in Oxford 1654–68) with **Robert Hooke** (1635–1708) laid the foundation of the modern sciences chemistry and physics. The Astronomer Royal, **Edmund Halley**, (1656–1742) was at Queen's, 1673; he was the first to predict the return of a comet and his meteorological observations led to his publication of the first map of the winds of the globe (1686).

The Oxford scientists **Howard Walter Florey** and **E. B. Chain** shared the Nobel Prize with **Alexander Fleming** for the clinical development of penicillin. The most widely used antibiotic today, cephalosporin, was discovered in 1955 by **Edward Abraham**, working in a University laboratory.

Famous musicians from Christ Church are **Sir William Walton** and **Sir Adrian Boult,** while **Sir Thomas Beecham** was at Wadham.

Some students just couldn't wait to attend Oxford. **Edward Gibbon** (Magdalen) matriculated at 14 after staying up only a year and **Jeremy Bentham** (Queen's) when he was only 12. The latest child prodigy is **Ruth Lawrence**, born in 1971; she came up when she was nine and matriculated with First-class Honours in mathematics three years later.

WEIGHTS & MEASURES

Britain's shelves are filled with goods which state both imperial and metric weights, but the imperial system is still preferred. Milk and beer come in pints and half-pints; fruit, vegetables, cheese etc. continue to be sold in pounds and ounces, though resistance to metrication is starting to weaken. Road signs give distances in miles.

ELECTRICITY

240 volts is standard. Hotels will usually have dual 110/240 volts sockets for razors.

BUSINESS HOURS

Most of the larger shops in the city centre are open six days a week, the normal hours being 9 a.m.–5.30 p.m., although many remain open until 8.30 p.m. on Thursdays.

BANKS

Oxford is well supplied with banks. Major branches of **Barclays** are open Monday–Friday 9.30 a.m.–4.30 p.m. Its main branches, with cash-card machines, are at: Old Bank, High Street; 54 Cornmarket Street (also open Saturday 9.30 a.m.–12 noon); 105 London Road, Headington; Gibbs Building, Oxford Polytechnic, Gipsy Lane, Headington; and 211 Banbury Road, Summertown (also open Saturday 9.30 a.m.–12 noon).

Lloyds has its main branch at Carfax, open 9.30 a.m.–4.30 p.m. Monday–Friday and on Saturday from 9.30 a.m.–12 noon.

National Westminster has its main branch at 121 High Street, open 9.30 a.m.–3.30 p.m. Monday–Friday. **The Royal Bank of Scotland**, 106a High Street, and the **Midland Bank**, 65 Cornmarket Street, and the **Co-operative Bank**, 12 New Road all have the same opening hours as NatWest. Some city centre banks offer bureau de change facilities on weekdays and Saturday mornings, as do some travel agents. **Deak International** at the railway station offers a foreign exchange service 7 days a week.

LIBRARIES & BOOKSHOPS

Central Library: Westgate, tel: 815549. Open: Monday, Tuesday, Thursday and Friday 9.15 a.m.–7 p.m; Wednesday and Saturday 9.15 a.m.–5 p.m. Periodicals room and large local history section.

Bookshops: Oxford is the home of bookshops. Famous booksellers include Blackwell's in Broad Street and Oxford University Press at 116 High Street. Book Bargains of Oxford is at 2 St Ebbes, and Motor and Railway Books is at 8 The Roundway, Headington.

Thornton's, 11 Broad Street, has English and foreign-language books, plus a large secondhand and rare books department. At 72 Cowley Road, **Worldwise** is a Third World community bookshop; a few doors away, at 54, **The Private Shop** sells magazines and books that respectable newsagents won't stock even on their highest shelves. **W. H. Smith** is at 22 Cornmarket and in the newly luxurious Square in Cowley while **Dillons** is in William Baker House, Broad Street. There are a number of religious bookshops: **St Aldate's Church bookshop** is at No 94 and the **Newman-Mowbray Bookshop** at 87 St Aldgate's, while the **Christian Book Centre** is at 57c St Clement's.

LANGUAGE SCHOOLS

Many people visit Oxford to learn English and there is a wide choice of language schools:

Swan School of English, 111 Banbury Road, Oxford OX2 6JX, tel: 53201.

Godmer House, 90 Banbury Road, Oxford OX2 6JT, tel: 515566.

Isis Private School, 30 Warnborough Road, Oxford OX2 6JA, tel: 510369.

The Eckersley School of English, 14 Friars Entry, Oxford OX1 2BZ, tel: 721268.

Lake School of English, PO Box 97, 14b Park End Street, Oxford OX1 1HW, tel: 724312.

G & J Student Services Ltd, 2 Gloucester Street, Oxford OX1 2BN, tel: 726745/250565.

PRIVATE COLLEGES

There are also colleges not associated with the University: secretarial colleges, tutorial colleges and "crammers"—places for concentrated courses to re-sit entrance examinations or improve results of examinations held. The leading "crammer" is Greene's Tutorial Establishment in Pembroke Street. The more general colleges include:

The Marlborough Secretarial College, 110A High Street, Oxford OX1 4HU, tel: 249484.

Oxford and County Business College, 34 St Giles', Oxford, tel: 511404.

St Joseph's Hall, Tutorial College, Junction Road, Oxford OX4 2UJ, tel: 711829.

Warnborough College, American Liberal Arts College, Boars Hill, Oxford OX1 5ED, tel: 730901.

TOWN TWINNING

Oxford is twinned with Leiden in Holland, Bonn in Germany and Leon in Nicaragua. Exchange visits are arranged on a regular basis and celebrations and yearly events are organised by Twinning Committees and the Lord Mayor's office. Details and literature are available at the Town Hall.

RELIGIOUS SERVICES

Public services are held at Oxford Cathedral, Christ Church, on weekdays at 7.15 a.m., 7.35 a.m., 6 p.m and on Sundays at 8 a.m., 10 a.m., 11.15 a.m. and 6 p.m. throughout the year. There are also services generally open to the public in the college chapels of Magdalen, New College, Mansfield (United Reformed) and Manchester (Unitarian) during the University terms (Michaelmas, 1 October–17 December; Hilary, 7 January–25 March or the Saturday before

Palm Sunday, whichever is the earlier; and Trinity (20 April or the Wednesday after Easter, whichever is the later, until 6 July).

ANGLICAN CHURCHES

St Michael-at-the-Northgate, Ship Street (City Church): Sunday 8 a.m., 9.45 a.m., 11 a.m., 12 noon, 6.30 p.m; Wednesday 1.15 p.m; Friday 12.15 p.m.

St Mary-the-Virgin, High Street (University Church): Sunday 8 a.m., 10 a.m., 11 a.m. (winter 11.15 a.m.), 6 p.m.

St Aldate's Church, St Aldate's: Sunday 8 a.m., 10.30 a.m., 6.30 p.m; Wednesday 7.30 a.m. (term), 11 a.m., 1.10 p.m.

St Barnabas, Cardigan Street: Sunday 8 a.m., 10.30 a.m., 6.30 p.m.

St Cross, St Cross Road: Sunday 10 a.m.

St Ebbe's, St Ebbe's Street: Sunday 11 a.m., 6 p.m.

St Giles', Banbury Road: Sunday 8 a.m., 10.30 a.m., 6.30 p.m; Wednesday 10 a.m.

St Mary Magdalen, Magdalen Street: Sunday 8 a.m., 10.30 a.m., 6 p.m; weekdays 11.15 a.m., 6 p.m., 6.15 p.m.

St Thomas the Martyr, Becket Street, off Hollybush Row: first Sunday in month 10.15 a.m; other Sundays 9.45 a.m.

ROMAN CATHOLIC CHURCHES

St Aloysius, Woodstock Road: Sunday 9.30 a.m., 11 a.m., 6 p.m; Monday, Thursday, Saturday 10 a.m; Tuesday 7.30 a.m; Tuesday, Wednesday, Friday, Saturday 6.30 p.m.

Blackfriars, St Giles': Sunday 8 a.m., 9.30 a.m., 11 a.m. Polish Mass 6.15 p.m; weekdays 7.45 a.m., 1.05 p.m., 6.15 p.m.

University Catholic Chaplaincy, The Old Palace, Rose Place: during term: Sunday 9 a.m., 11. a.m., 6.15 p.m., 8 p.m; weekdays 7.45 a.m., 12.15 p.m., 6.15 p.m.

OTHER PLACES OF WORSHIP

Baptist Church, Bonn Square: Sunday 10.30 a.m. Christaldelphian, Tyndale Road.

First Church of Christ Scientist, 36 St Giles': Sunday 11 a.m; Wednesday 8 a.m. Elim Pentecostal, Botley Road.

Jewish Synagogue, Richmond Road: Friday 7.30 p.m., Saturday 10.30 a.m.

Lutheran, a service fortnightly at St Mary-the-Virgin, High Street.

Mandal: Hindu Mandal, tel: 248839.

Wesley Memorial Church: Methodist, New Inn Hall Street: Sunday 10.30 a.m., 6.30 p.m.

Muslim: Mosque, 10 Bath Street, St Clement's; also Stanley Road.

Orthodox Greek and Russian: 1 Canterbury Road.

Oxford Spiritualist Church, 39B Oxford Road, Cowley.

Quaker Meetings: Friends' Meeting House, 43 St Giles': Sunday 9.30 a.m., 11 a.m; Wednesday 11.45 a.m.

Salvation Army Citadel, Albion Square: Sunday 11 a.m., 6.45 p.m.

Seventh Day Adventists, Chester Street.

United Reformed, St Columba, Alfred Street: Sunday 10.45 a.m.

Asian Christian services are held in South Oxford Baptist Church, Wytham Street.

COMMUNICATIONS

MEDIA

Newspapers and magazines: The *Oxford Mail* is the city's leading Monday to Saturday evening newspaper. The *Oxford Times*, published on Saturday, carries the week's news and the biggest coverage of property for sale. The *Star*, the Courier and the *Oxford Journal* are free papers delivered to houses within a 20-mile radius.

Oxford and County Newspapers (*Oxford Mail, Times and Star*), Newspaper House, Osney Mead, Oxford, tel: 244988.

Oxford City Courier, 2–4 Ock Street, Abingdon, tel: 35555.

Oxford Journal, Witney Road, Eynsham, Oxford, tel: 724761.

Radio and television: BBC Radio Oxford, 269 Banbury Road, Oxford OX2 7DW, tel: 311444. (FM 95.2 MW 1485KHz/ 202m) broadcasts local news and talk programmes, Monday–Friday 6 a.m.–10 p.m., Saturday 7 a.m.–6 p.m. and Sunday 8 a.m.–5.30 p.m. When Radio Oxford is not broadcasting, the channel reverts to BBC Radio 2.

Fox FM, Brush House, Pony Road, Cowley, Oxford, OX4 2XR, tel: 748787. (Oxford FM 102.6, Banbury 97.4) is an Oxfordshire advertising service with music and chat programmes 24 hours a day.

Central Independent Television, Albion House, St Ebbes, tel: 250100, broadcasts local TV news in the Oxfordshire area, tel: Abingdon 0235-554123 .

POSTAL SERVICES

The main post office in St Aldate's is open Monday–Friday 9 a.m.–5.30 p.m. (open until 9.30 p.m. Wednesday), Saturday 9 a.m.–12.30 p.m. A currency exchange service is also available there. The main sorting office is in Becket Street, a side-street opposite the railway station entrance, where the last collection is at 7 p.m. for next-day delivery, or 5 a.m. for local, same-day mail. Most post offices close at 5.30 p.m. but those in shops may close for lunch and on Wednesday afternoons. Advice on letter post may be obtained by telephoning Freefone Royal Mail. The parcels office is tel: 747586 (no deliveries in Oxford on Tuesday). For details of using Datapost for a guaranteed overnight parcel delivery, tel: 0800-884422 free of charge. Oxford postcodes start with OX1 in the city; OX2, Summertown, OX3 Headington and OX4 Cowley.

TELEPHONES

Most of Oxford's traditional red phone boxes have now been replaced by the new open-hood type. The majority take £1, 50p, 20p and 10p coins. Those with a green sign accept only Phonecards, which can be purchased from newsagents and post offices; they cost £10, £5 and £2. Phone booths are located at Carfax, Queen's Street, St Aldate's post office, the railway station, Gloucester Green and in many pubs and restaurants. To call the operator, tel: 100; Directory Enquiries, tel: 192; the Talking Clock, tel: 8081. The National Code for Oxford is 0865.

TELEX & FAX

To dictate a telex message for delivery by British Telecom International Services, tel: London 071-492 7111.

Local telex services are:

Air Wave Services, 58 Between Towns Road, Cowley, tel: 775373 (Telex 83201 Bizcom G).

Enterprise Business Services, 24–25 Walton Crescent, tel: 515345 (Telex and Fax).

Faxes can be sent from:

Faxodec, 5 Cambridge Terrace, Oxford, tel: 244455; Fax 249847; Telex: 83147 Plan P Via or G.

S & S Stationery, 9–13 Hollow Way, Cowley, is one of the cheapest fax bureaux, tel: 777412.

MEDICAL SERVICES

Oxford's Health 2000 campaign aims at making the city the healthiest in the country. There are no obvious health hazards, though road accidents involving pedestrians and cyclists are all too common. EC countries have a reciprocal agreement for free medical care, but medical insurance is advisable. Emergency treatment is given free at the John Radcliffe Hospital.

HOSPITALS

John Radcliffe (including accident and maternity units), Headley Way, Headington, Oxford, tel: 64711.

Churchill Hospital, Headington, Oxford, tel: 64841.

Eye Hospital, Walton Street, Oxford, tel: 249891.

Abingdon Hospital, tel: Abingdon 0235-22717.

DENTISTS

Dental surgeons who offer NHS and private treatment and an emergency service are:

The Dental Surgery, 22 Beaumont Street, Oxford, tel: 243702.

Hewes & Evans, 279 Banbury Road, Oxford, tel: 58822.

GETTING AROUND

MAPS

The Ordnance Survey City Map, scale 1:10,000 is an essential publication and costs less than £2. It has an inset of the city centre at 1:7000 scale, naming all the colleges clearly. Street route restrictions, tourist information, services and abbreviations are printed in English, French and German.

The Oxford Information Centre sells a map for 20p, with the main sites numbered and listed on the back. The address and opening times of places of interest are given.

Blackwell's Bookshop in Broad Street gives out a free *Guide to Oxford* with a clear map, a key to the main places to visit and an index of colleges.

BY BUS

Oxford and the surrounding area is served by local double-decker buses (with smoking allowed upstairs), mini-bus services and direct buses from car parks on the Park and Ride scheme into the centre. The local services are covered by Oxford Bus Company, 395 Cowley Road, Oxford OX4 2DJ, tel: 711312. The Oxford Mini-Bus Company, tel: 772250 also operates in the city.

Park and Ride: Park and Ride buses provide a frequent service at a cheap fare between the city centre and the peripheral car parks. Parking in central Oxford is extremely difficult, especially on Saturdays, and you will often save time by using this service. Peripheral car parks operating Park and Ride buses are clearly signposted as you enter the Oxford area.

BY CAR

Car Rental: Conditions for car rental state that the driver must be over 21 and have held a full driving licence for more than a year. Most hire charges include unlimited mileage, VAT, insurance and a 24-hour breakdown service. Payment may usually be by cash, cheque or credit card.

Europcar, c/o Hartford Motors, Seacourt Tower, West Way, Oxford, tel: 246373. Cars, vans and Ford Cargo trucks. £27.50 a day minimum. AA breakdown service. One-way hire.

Swan National, Dawson Street, (St Clement's, between Cowley and Headington Roads) tel: 240471. £30 a day for smallest models. National breakdown service, payment by cash, cheque or credit card. £30 petrol deposit. One-way hire from Oxford to anywhere in the country. Also rents vans and mini-buses.

Fiat Rental, J D Barclay, Barclay House, Botley Road, Oxford OX2 0HQ, tel: 722444. No one-way hire. No petrol deposit. £50 damage deposit aged 21–25. £21 a day minimum (Fiat Panda).

Petrol Stations: Most petrol stations are self-service and are open 8 a.m.–8 p.m. 24-hour petrol stations can be found at Oxford Travel Lodge at the Peartree Roundabout on the A34 and at the Shotover Arms, Headington Roundabout, on the A40.

Car Parking: Finding a space in Oxford is like finding gold dust and you are likely to discover that all the car parks are full by 9 a.m. on weekdays and Saturdays. All car parks, including the multi-storey car parks at Westgate and St Ebbe's, are clearly signposted. The charges vary according to the length of stay. Tickets are purchased from machines when you arrive and must be displayed on the windscreen; wardens are unforgiving if you exceed your time limit. At Westgate, you pay as you leave.

Street parking is deliberately restricted, and traffic wardens, who can impose heavy fines for illegal parking, are very vigilant. In many of the central streets, parking is restricted to residents, who have to purchase and display a special licence.

If you want to avoid the problem of parking, take the Park and Ride service. You can park your car free of charge at the Pear Tree car park in the north, coming in on the A34 from Chipping Norton, the A423 or the A43; the Redbridge car park in the south on the A34 from Abingdon or the A423 from Reading; Seacourt in the west, convenient for A40 and A420 traffic, or Thornhill in the east on the A40 from London. You can then take a bus to the centre. Bus fares are reasonable and services are frequent during the daytime, but not Sundays. Secure your car properly and, if possible, remove the radio, as thieves operate in all car parks in Oxford.

In the evening (after 6 p.m.) city centre parking is much easier; you can park for a small fee in the Westgate multi-storey car park and without payment in some streets.

TAXIS & CHAUFFEURS

There are taxi ranks at the railway station, St Giles' and St Aldate's. Owing to the one-way traffic system there is no short way across the city to the railway station, so fares tend to be high. Short journeys start at £2.50. Both ABC Taxis, tel: 770681 and 001 Cars tel: 60600/63356 give a 24-hour service.

For chauffeured car hire, Whites of Oxford, 53 Stanway Road, Risinghurst, tel: 61295 give a good personal service. They also run luxury minibuses and coaches.

CYCLING

Cycling is popular in Oxford and visitors can hire bicycles from Rent-a-bike (Denton's Cycles), 294 Banbury Road, tel: 53859, or from Pennyfarthing, 5 George Street, tel: 249368. Cycles are normally three-speed and with lights, basket and lock. Charges: £5 a day; £9 a week; £30 a student term.

BUS TOURS

South Midland Open Top Buses tour the city of Oxford and also go to Blenheim Palace and Woodstock daily during the summer season. The buses are also available for hire, as are mini-buses (49 seats) and executive coaches, tel: Witney 0993-76679.
Percivals Coaches: Lamarsh Road, Botley Oxford, OX2 0LE, tel: 246509. This local coach operator runs holiday tours, day excursions and an express coach network.
National Express: operates nationwide coach network from Oxford to places as far apart as Aberdeen and Newquay. A timetable is available from National Express at Gloucester Green Bus Station or National Travelworld, 138 High Street, tel ephone enquiries and credit card bookings tel: 0865-

791579. For a reservation fee of £1.20 a ticket you can book an assured reservation and travel at the journey time of your choice. This is particularly recommended for busy times, overnight journeys and suburban boarding points.

COACH TRAVEL

National Express, tel: 791579. London Express coaches run twice daily, No 882, from Burford via Witney and Oxford to London, leaving Burford (Cotswold Arms) at 7.50 a.m. and 3.50 p.m; Witney at 8.10 a.m. and 4.10 p.m; Oxford at 8.45 a.m. and 4.45 p.m., arriving at London (Victoria Coach Station) at 10.20 a.m. and 6.20 p.m. Tickets may be purchased from any National Express agent.

WHERE TO STAY

HOTELS

The Tourist Information Centre has compiled a complete list of all hotels, guest houses and inns in the Oxford area (30p). The centre also operates a reservations service. Not all establishments take young children, so it is worth checking in advance.

IN THE CITY

- **Expensive**

Bath House Hotel: 4–5 Bath Place, tel: 791812, fax: 790760. Newly-established family-run hotel in an elegant cluster of restored 17th-century cottages. Some of the en-suite bedrooms have four-posters. £70 single/£65 per person double.
Cotswold Lodge Hotel: 66a Banbury Road, tel: 512121/30. 52 rooms, all with private bathroom, colour TV. Fully licensed restaurant and lounge bar. Conference and banquet facilities. £67.50 single/£87.50

double.

Eastgate Hotel: High Street, Oxford. tel: 248244. Hotel and licensed restaurant. £70 single/£85 double.

Linton Lodge Hotel: Linton Road, off Banbury Road, tel: 53461, fax: 310365. Restaurant, conference facilities, dinner-dances for 150, private functions. TV, radio, telephone, en-suite. Poor service/uninspiring food at high prices. £75 single/£90 double, room only.

The Randolph (Trusthouse Forte Group): Beaumont Street, tel: 247481. Restaurant, coffee shop, Fellows' lounge, Chapters Bar all with a Victorian theme. £69 single/£89 double, room only.

The Royal Oxford Hotel (Embassy Hotels): Park End Street, tel: 248432. 25 rooms, each with colour TV and own telephone. A lively buffet lunch bar; restaurant open 7 p.m.–9.30 p.m. Monday–Saturday. £60 double B & B.

● **Moderate**

The Old Black Horse: 102 St Clement's, tel: 244691. Attractive building in up-and-coming area just over Magdalen Bridge. £38 single B & B.

The Old Parsonage Hotel: 3 Banbury Road, tel: 310210. An old 13th-century hospital called "Bethleen" or "House of Bread". Renovated in the early 17th century and still retaining many of its original features. Quiet garden. Restaurant, TV lounge, parking. £28 single/£45 double B & B/£58 double en-suite/no TV in rooms.

Parklands Hotel: 100 Banbury Road, tel: 54374. This privately run hotel was originally an Oxford dons' residence built in the Victorian era. It is surrounded by a walled garden and is situated on the main Banbury Road into Oxford. 17 bedrooms, 11 en-suite. Restaurant and bar. £27/£34.50 single; £38/£51.50 double B & B.

Victoria Hotel: 180 Abingdon Road (near Folly Bridge), tel: 724536. £38.50 single B & B.

Westgate Hotel: 1 Botley Road, tel: 726721. Very convenient for the station. £30 single B & B.

Willow Reaches Hotel: 1 Wytham Street (off the Abingdon Road, along Norrey's Avenue), tel: 721545. A comfortable private hotel, south of the city centre in a quiet

corner away from traffic. All bedrooms en-suite, centrally heated with colour TV, radio, tea/coffee makers and telephone. Residents' bar. Lounge with teletext TV; garden; ample parking. English and Indian meals. £39 single/£48 double B & B.

● **Budget**

Courtfield Private Hotel: 367 Iffley Road, tel: 242991. £20 single B & B.

Isis Guest House: 45–53 Iffley Road, tel: 242466/248894. Owned by St Edmund Hall, it is open for B & B in July, August and September. Private car park. £20 a person en suite/£17 a person, including a good breakfast.

OUT THE OUTSKIRTS OF OXFORD

Foxcombe Lodge Hotel: Fox Lane, Boars Hill, tel: 730746. Restaurant and conference facilities. All rooms with colour TV, radio, direct-dial telephone. Friendly atmosphere. £50 single/£60 double.

The Priory Hotel: Church Way, Iffley, tel: 774449. Large house set in quiet garden. Cheaper rooms in an annexe. Dances and jazz sessions held regularly. Restaurant/bar. Single, £40 no bath/£65 with; doubles £50/£70.

The Tree Hotel: Iffley Village, tel: 775974, fax: 747554. Comfortable hotel in attractive setting, 1½ miles from the city centre. £40 single/£65 double.

The Westwood Country Hotel: Hinksey Hill Top, tel: 735408. Rooms for wheelchair users. £40 single/£55 double B & B.

IN THE COUNTRY

The Abingdon Lodge Hotel: Marcham Road, Abingdon, tel: 0235-553456. Has 63 bedrooms, en-suite, radio, TV, in house movies, trouser press, direct dial telephones and hospitality tray. Restaurant, bar, conference facilities. £62 single/£66 double, including continental breakfast; weekends £45 single/£50 double also weekend breaks, half board £40.50 single/£65 double inclusive English breakfast and lunch or dinner.

Bay Tree Hotel: Sheep Street, Burford OX8 4LW, tel: 099382-2791. Once the home of Sir Lawrence Tanfield, Elizabeth I's Lord Chief Baron of the Exchequer, this

16th-century house has 23 en-suite rooms, some oak-panelled and with four-poster beds. There's also a walled garden and terraced lawns. £55 single/£85 double.

The Bear Hotel and Restaurant: Woodstock, tel: 0993-811511. Renowned for its luxurious accommodation and magnificent cuisine. An historic coaching inn which boasts modern conference facilities. £75 single/£100 double, room only.

The Belfry Hotel: Milton Common, near Exit 7 off M40, tel: 0844-279381. 60 bedrooms en-suite all with colour TV, radio, telephone. Specialises in conferences. £57.50 single/£70 double, including continental breakfast.

The Bell at Charlbury, OX7 3AP, tel: 0608-810278. A quiet hotel that offers Getaway breaks for two-night stays including breakfast and evening meal for £43 a person per night. Gliding, fishing and horse riding can be arranged. £45 single/£65 double.

The Coach and Horses: Chislehampton, tel: Stadhampton 0865-890255. On B480, 7 miles (11 km) from Oxford and 5 miles (8 km) from Exit 7 on the M40, adjacent to farmland in rural Oxfordshire. Nine tastefully decorated and furnished bedrooms, all with private facilities and shower, some also with bath. Excellent accommodation for the tourist or business person. £41.40 single/£56 double B & B.

The Feathers Hotel: Market Street, Woodstock, tel: 0993-812291. Famous restaurant but impersonal service. Rooms en-suite and with TV. From £50 single/£75–£105 double including English breakfast.

Fox Hotel, Market Place, Chipping Norton OX7 5DD, tel: 0608-642658. Historic hotel newly refurbished. £20 single/£35 double with shared bathroom/£40 double en-suite.

King's Arms Hotel, Horton-cum-Studley, Oxon, tel: Stanton St John 086735-235. En-suite rooms from £35 with TV and English breakfast. Dinner dances held on Saturdays.

The Maytime: Asthall, between Burford and Witney, tel: Burford 099782-2068. Comfortable accommodation, all on the ground floor, with private bathroom, shower, TV, radio and tea/coffee making facilities; restaurant with traditional country fare with extensive seasonal menu and vege-

tarian dishes at very reasonable prices. £35 single/£48 double B & B.

Punch Bowl Inn, 12 Oxford Street, Woodstock, OX7 1TR, tel: 0993-811218. Early 16th-century house with traditional atmosphere. Small restaurant with good food and real ale. £22–£28 single/£32–£35 double including English breakfast.

The Well House Restaurant and Hotel, 34–40 High Street, Watlington OX9 5PY, tel: 049161-3333. A 15th-century house in a village 12 miles (19 km) east of Oxford. Good international cuisine. £19 single/£39 double B & B.

YOUTH HOSTELS

Oxford's **Youth Hostel** is nearly 2 miles (3 km) west of the city at Jack Straw's Lane, Headington, Oxford, tel: 62997. Accommodation for members only £4.30 a night. Non-members may join on arrival (£7 a year for adults).

CAMPING

International Touring Camping Site and Sport and Outdoor Life Centre, Touchwood Sports, 426 Abingdon Road, Oxford, tel: 246551.

Cotswold View Caravan and Camping Site, Enstone Road, Charlbury, OX7 3JH, tel: 0608-810314.

FOOD DIGEST

WHERE TO EAT

Restaurants abound in Oxford and everyone has a favourite. These are some suggestions but you may easily discover others:

- **At the top end of the market**

Gee's, 61 Banbury Road, tel: 53540. In a beautiful Victorian conservatory; excellent seafood specialities; attentive service.

La Sorbonne Restaurant, 130a High Street, tel: 241320/242883. In a beautifully preserved 16th-century Oxford house. La Casse Croute shares its kitchen but prices are more affordable. Desserts are fabulous.

• **Different**

Baededers Restaurant, 43a Cornmarket, tel: 242063. The cocktail bar is the up-market place to be at the moment; eating extends the stay.

The Blue Coyote, 37–38 St Clement's, tel: 241431 is undoubtedly original. You might try crab cakes or buffalo chicken wings. American brunch served Saturday and Sunday 10 a.m.–2 p.m. Smart rather than cheap.

Brown's, Woodstock Road, tel: 511995. Hot and noisy, queues at weekends and steep bar prices, but the food is consistently good, plentiful and reasonably priced. The in-place for young people.

The Carlton Blue, 179 Cowley Road (just past Tesco's), tel: 251511. An experience. Great food at good prices. Caribbean and vegetarian menu.

Go Dutch, Park End Street, tel: 240686. Excellent pancakes and desserts. The food is very filling, served in a friendly fashion in homely surroundings.

The Greek Taverna, 272 Banbury Road, Summertown, tel: 511472. No plate throwing but pleasant, brightly lit and clinically clean. Animated chatter and exquisite cuisine.

Hi-Lo Jamaican Eating House, 70 Cowley Road, tel: 725984. Some love it, others hate it. You're treated to the best reggae record collection this side of Kingston; the Jamaican rum drinks are magic and the food, which takes hours to arrive, is tasty and unusual.

Munchy-Munchy, 6 Park End Street, tel: 245710. Inspired Malaysian-Indonesian food with exquisite ice cream. Tables close together and long waits at weekends. Most enjoyable during the week. Closed: Sunday and Monday.

The Nosebag, 6–8 St Michael's Street, tel: 721033. An upstairs, split-level restaurant with an oak-beamed ceiling and bright, homely decor that has a special charm of its own. Serves a wide range of healthy food, all

home-made. Delicious home-made cakes, for which The Noesbag is famous—a must with freshly ground coffee or a pot of tea, hot chocolate with cream and cinnamon, chilled milk or fruit juice. Licensed for cider and house wine with meals. Not as cheap as might be expected.

Rendezvous Restaurant, Gloucester Green, tel: 793146. New grill, restaurant, brasserie. Open: 7 days a week for lunch and dinner, business or pleasure.

ITALIAN

Fasta Pasta, 3 Little Clarendon St, tel: 57394. Delicious, daily changing pasta dishes, but the service is certainly not fasta.

Pasta Galore, 103 Cowley Road, tel: 722955. A two-tiered dining area, candlelight and good service. Jazz recordings and bands at weekends. Varied menu.

Pizza Express in the Golden Cross, Cornmarket, tel: 790442. This is not the usual run-of-the-mill pizza house but an up-market, champagne bar and good service venue to be enjoyed. Superb toppings on the pizzas and delicious garlic bread.

Rimini's, 97 St Clements Road, tel: 241158. Wide selection and reasonably priced. Attractive interior with a cosy, warm atmosphere. Large helpings of English-styled Italian food.

CHINESE

The Bandung, Walton Street, tel: 511668. Excellent service and romantic ambience. The Indonesian-Chinese set menu includes eight dishes and a bottle of wine; probably the best value in Oxford.

The Dear Friends, 4 Woodstock Road, tel: 54996. Will definitely abuse your wallet but you could enjoy the same food by ordering a take-away.

The Liaison, 29 Castle Street, tel: 242944. Lovely interior and marvellous food with a diversity of set menus.

The Opium Den, 79 George Street, tel: 248680. Good food, chopstick authenticity and high degree of image-consciousness. Be prepared to queue.

The Pak Fook, 100 Cowley Road, tel: 247958. Popular eating place but the great atmosphere has gone now that the restaurant is licensed and customers are no longer allowed to bring their own carrier bags full of cheap wine.

INDIAN

The India Garden Tandoori Restaurant, 129 High Street (first floor), tel: 252250. Unexciting. Take-away service.

Jamals Tandoori, 108 Walton Street, tel: 54905. Most curry connoisseurs consider this to be about the best in Oxford. Book.

The Moonlight Tandoori, 58 Cowley Road, tel: 240275. A deservedly high reputation, especially for vegetarian curry fans.

Polash Tandoori, 25 Park End Street, tel: 254244. A mixture of Indian and European food–venison and trout, for example. Worth a visit if you can afford it.

The Taj Mahal, 116 Turl Street, tel: 243783. For those who love a traditional Indian curry with "authentic" cosiness. If the waiters seem too superior for your tastes, you can always order a take-away.

CAFES & SNACK BARS

The Carfax Take-Away, 135 High Street. The Oxford chip shop. Cheap, friendly, huge portions and a wide choice of menu.

Heroes, 8 Ship Street. Really good sandwiches, so lunch early or late to avoid queues.

The Oxford Sandwich Company in the Covered Market is just as good but avoid lunchtime when queues are enormous.

Queen's Lane Coffee House, 40 High Street, is cheaper and what it lacks in style is made up for by the chocolate brownies and student atmosphere.

Rosie Lee's, 5 High Street. The place for delicious cream teas and conveniently situated near the Bodleian.

St Aldate's Church Coffee House, 94 St Aldate's. Opposite Christ Church College on the corner of Pembroke Street, tel: 245952. Open: Monday–Saturday 10 a.m.–5 p.m. A peaceful oasis in the heart of the city providing the best in home cooking from coffee and cakes to a three-course meal.

St Giles' Café, St Giles'. Large plates of chips, sausages and beans are guaranteed to fill you up for the rest of the day. Oxford's truest English-style café.

KEBAB VANS

Between late evening and the early hours of the morning, vans selling inexpensive kebabs are dotted all over the centre of Oxford—much to some residents' dismay. A large doner kebab costs about £1.70—a price fixed by all the van owners, so there's no point in shopping around. Approved by Oxford City Council, whose Health Inspectors keep an eye on the hygiene, but the myth persists that kebab-eaters live dangerously. Try St Giles', where several vans are located, if you want to take the risk.

RESTAURANTS IN THE COUNTY

The Ark, A338 to Wantage Road, Frilford, near Abingdon, tel: 391911. Conservatory restaurant with a country menu; the Corinthian Room specialises in game, such as venison and guinea fowl.

The Bear, North Morton, Didcot, Oxon, tel: 0235-813236. Revamped free-house pub with log fireplace. Steak, duck and salmon regularly on the menu.

Le Manoir Aux Quat'Saisons, Great Milton, tel: 08446-8881. Internationally renowned chef Raymond Blanc cooks up meals which are gastronomically stunning but financially debilitating in his 14th-century manor set in 27 acres (11 hectares) of garden and parkland.

Tiffany's Restaurant, Market Place, Deddington, Oxon, tel: 0869-38813. English country cooking with French provincial flair and imaginative vegetarian dishes.

THINGS TO DO

WATERWAYS

No visit to Oxford is complete without a trip on the water. For those who like to take it easy, Thames excursions by public cruiser are arranged by Salters Bros of Folly Bridge, tel: 243421/2. For the more energetic, punts, canoes, rowing boats and private cruisers can be hired for use on the Thames, Cherwell or the Oxford Canal from the firms below.

Boats:

College Cruisers: Combe Road Wharf, tel: 54343.

Medley Boat Station: Port Meadow, tel: 511660.

Orchard Cruisers: Castle Mill Boatyard, Cardigan Street, tel: 54043.

Punts:

Cherwell Boathouse: at the bottom of Bardwell Road, tel: 515978. Punts £5 an hour, £25 deposit.

C. Howard & Son: Magdalen Bridge, tel: 61586. Punts and rowing boats £5 an hour, £10 deposit.

W.T. Hubbucks: Folly Bridge, tel: 244235. Punts, skiffs and canoes £4 an hour, £20 deposit.

WALKS

Oxford is best seen on foot and guided walking tours leave the Information Centre daily throughout the summer season and on Saturdays during the rest of the year. Tel: 726871. The centre also also sells a leaflet detailing walks through Oxford. Particularly recommended are the towpath walks from Folly Bridge to Iffley along the Thames, and from Binsey village to the famous Trout Inn at Godstow.

Within the city of Oxford are many areas of attractive countryside. A network of public footpaths make much of this countryside accessible to the general public.

Shotover Country Park is managed by Oxford City Council for public recreation. Shotover Plain and adjoining land to the south, together with Brasenose and Magdalen Woods, is an area of some 410 acres (164 hectares). The upper slopes of Shotover Hill are a mixture of grassland, heath, scrub and open woodland and have extensive views over the Thames Valley to Wittenham Clumps, Didcot Power station and to the escarpment of the Berkshire Downs. Magdalen Woods has a 20-station fitness trail suitable for use by all the family.

Port Meadow is an urban common which is open to the public as long as the grazing animals are respected. There are a number of entrances but the best known are from the car

park at the end of Walton Well Road and from the car park at the Wolvercote Bathing Place on the Godstow Road. Port Meadow is a flat, low area of extensive grassland near the River Thames, which has remained unchanged for centuries. Cattle, horses and geese are grazed by those with common grazing rights.

Lye Valley Local Nature Reserve is a place to enjoy a pleasant walk. Close to the stream are reed beds which are inhabited by sedge warblers, and there are interesting patches of fen vegetation with rare and attractive plants. The path leads from Girdlestone Road, Headington, to Southfield Golf Course with a spur which leads alongside the Church Hospital to Hill Top Road.

The **Chilswell Valley** is otherwise known as Happy Valley. To the west of the A34 in South Hinksey, turning off to the Garden Centre, this extremely attractive valley provides magnificent views of Oxford and contains many pleasant picnic sites. The highest part of Chilswell Valley is a steep-sided, flowery gulley which teems with butterflies and other insect life in summer. A circular walk enables visitors to explore the whole of this interesting valley.

The **Oxfordshire Way** is a countywide path running from Bourton-on-the-Water in Gloucestershire to Henley-on-Thames. The distance is 62 miles (100 kms). A booklet giving accommodation en route is available from the English Tourist Board, 8 Market Place, Abingdon, Oxon OX14 3UD.

SIGHTS TO SEE

This is a check-list of the main places to see or visit in Oxford:

Bodleian Library: Broad Street. Developed by Sir Thomas Bodley between 1598 and 1613, and now world-famous, with more than four and a half million volumes. Hours: Monday–Friday 9 a.m.–4.45 p.m., Saturday 9 a.m.–12.30 p.m. Closed: Sunday and 24 December–1 January and the week commencing late summer Bank Holiday. The Library is not open to the public, but regular guided tours are run.

Carfax Tower: all that remains of the 14th-century St Martin's Church. Notable for the quarter boys that strike the chimes. There is an excellent view of Oxford from the top of the tower. Open: 20 March–25 October, Monday–Saturday 10 a.m.–6 p.m; Sunday 2–6 p.m (4. p.m. 26 October–23 November).

Divinity School: 15th-century perpendicular Gothic building with vaulted ceiling, described by some as the most beautiful room in Europe.

Examination Schools, High Street. The first building of Clipsham stone, with carvings of the viva voce exam and degree ceremony over the main entrance. No entry to the public.

Golden Cross: one of Oxford's oldest inns in Cornmarket Street. It still has the yard where Shakespeare's plays are thought to have been performed and leads to an attractive shopping arcade.

Martyrs' Memorial: erected in St Giles' in 1841–43 as a memorial to Bishops Latimer and Ridley who were burned at the stake for their faith in 1555 and Bishop Cranmer who suffered the same fate in 1556. A cross in the roadway in Broad Street marks the spot where Latimer and Ridley died.

Oxford Castle: St George's Tower in Paradise Street and the Mound, overlooking Nuffield College in New Road, are all that remain of the castle built about 1071. They can only be seen from the road.

The Painted Room: formerly a room in the old Crown Tavern at 3 Cornmarket Street where Shakespeare reputedly stayed on his journeys between London and Stratford. Contains some Elizabethan wall paintings. For access, enquire at the Information Centre.

Radcliffe Camera: built in Catte Street between 1737 and 1749 with money left by Dr John Radcliffe, an eminent physician. Now a reading room for the Bodleian Library. Not open to the public.

St Michael at the Northgate Church: the City Church in Cornmarket Street. The Saxon tower, once part of the northern fortifications of the city, is the oldest building in Oxford and offers views over the spires.

St Mary the Virgin: The University Church in High Street. Once used for university meetings, degree ceremonies and trials (Latimer, Ridley and Cranmer stood trial here). Nave and chancel date from the late 13th century. Good views of Oxford from the tower. In summer a Brass Rubbing Centre and a short film on Oxford, *The*

Oxford Experience, are based here. Open: mid-March–30 September, daily 10 a.m.–6 p.m.

The Shark: New High Street, Headington, opposite the can-can girl's legs that jut out prominently from the Not The Moulin Rouge cinema. The cinemas's Canadian owner, Bill Heine, erected a huge metal "sculpture" of a shark diving into the roof of his house to demonstrate, after the Chernobyl disaster, that people are not safe in their own homes. Some neighbours thought it added to the gaiety of life; but most did not and, because Mr Heine did not seek prior planning permission from the local council before importing his shark, a series of court actions have tried to make him remove it. How long it remains in his roof, therefore, depends on Mr Heine's agility in discovering legal loopholes.

Sheldonian Theatre, Broad Street: designed by Christopher Wren and built between 1663 and 1669, it is used mainly for university ceremonies, including the annual Encaenia, at which people of distinction receive honorary degrees. The ceiling, painted by Robert Streater, is meant to suggest an open-air theatre. Note the 13 emperors' heads outside. Good views of Oxford from the top. Open: Monday–Saturday 10 a.m.–1 p.m., 2–4.45 p.m. (3.45 p.m. mid-November–mid-February).

Town Hall: Headquarters of Oxford City Council, built in St Aldate's in 1895–97. The City Plate can be seen by arrangement between 10 a.m. and 5 p.m. on weekdays, tel: 249811, the Lord Mayor's Secretary.

University Botanic Garden: Rose Lane. In summer open Monday–Saturday 8.30 a.m.–5 p.m; Sunday 10 a.m.–12 noon, 2–4.30 p.m. Glasshouses open daily 2–4 p.m.

COLLEGES

All Souls College and Codrington Library, High Street (founded 1438), tel: 279379. The twin towers were designed by Hawksmoor. The college also has a sundial by Wren. Open: daily 2–5 p.m.

Balliol College, Broad Street (1263), tel: 277777. Open: daily 10 a.m.–6 p.m.

Brasenose College, Radcliffe Square (1509), tel: 277830. Open: daily 10 a.m.–6 p.m.

Christ Church, St Aldate's, tel: 276150. Projected by Cardinal Wolsey in 1525 and established by King Henry VIII in 1546. Main features are Tom Tower dominating St Aldate's, Tom Quad, the largest quadrangle in Oxford and the college chapel which is also the Oxford Cathedral. Tom Tower houses the six-ton Great Tom bell which tolls 101 times at five minutes past nine every evening to signify the closing of the gates to the original 101 scholars. Open: Cathedral: Monday–Saturday 9 a.m.–5 p.m., Sunday 12.30 p.m.–5 p.m. Chapter House: Monday–Saturday 9 a.m.–6 p.m., Sunday 12 noon–6 p.m; October–March closes at 5 p.m. Hall: Monday–Saturday 9.30 a.m.–12 noon, 2–6 p.m; October–March, closes at 4.30 p.m.

Corpus Christi College, Merton Street (1512), tel: 276700. Open: daily 1.30–4.30. p.m.

Exeter College, Turl Street (1314), tel: 279600. Open: during term daily 2–5 p.m; during vacation daily 10 a.m.–dusk.

Green College, Woodstock Road, tel: 274770.

Hertford College, Catte Street (1874), tel: 279400. Open: daily 9.30 a.m.–dusk.

Jesus College, Turl Street (1571), tel: 279700. Open: during term daily 2–4.30 p.m.

Keble College, Parks Road, tel: 272727. Founded in 1868 as a memorial to John Keble, a prominent 19th-century churchman. Holman Hunt's famous painting, *The Light of the World*, hangs in the chapel. Open: daily 10 a.m.–dusk.

Lady Margaret Hall, Norham Gardens (1878), tel: 274300.

Linacre College, St Cross Road (1962), tel: 271650. Open: daily 9 a.m.–5 p.m.

Lincoln College, Turl Street (1427), tel: 279800. Open: Monday–Saturday 2–5 p.m., Sunday 11 a.m.–5 p.m.

Magdalen College, High Street, tel: 276000. Dates from 1458. The tower, at the eastern entrance to the city at Magdalen Bridge, was completed in about 1509. The college choir sings from the top of the tower at 6 a.m. on 1 May. The college also has a deer park. There is a good view from Addison's Walk. Open: daily 2–6.15 p.m.

Manchester College, Mansfield Road (1786), tel: 241514. Open: during term 9 a.m.–4 p.m.

Merton College, Merton Street, tel: 276310. Probably Oxford's oldest college, dating from 1264. Stands with Corpus Christi College in Oxford's last remaining cobbled street. Its library is one of the oldest in England—there are even some chained books—and the 14th-century Mob quad is the oldest complete quadrangle in Oxford. Open: Monday–Friday 9 a.m.–5 p.m. Saturday/Sunday 10 a.m.–5 p.m; October–March closes at 4 p.m. The library is open Monday–Friday 2–4 p.m. and admission costs 30p.

New College, New College Lane, tel: 248451. Founded by William of Wykeham in 1379, it contains some of the best remaining parts of the ancient city wall. In the college chapel can be seen the founder's crozier, a fine example of medieval craftsmanship, and Epstein's sculpture, *Lazarus*. Open: during term 2–5 p.m; during vacation daily 11 a.m.–5 p.m.

Nuffield College, New Road (1937), tel: 248451. Open: daily 9 a.m.–5 p.m.

Oriel College, Oriel Square (1326), tel: 276555. Open: 2–5 p.m.

Pembroke College, Pembroke Square (1624), tel: 276444. Apply at the Lodge.

The Queen's College, High Street (1341), tel: 279120. Open: daily 2–5 p.m.

St Anne's College, Woodstock Road (1952), tel: 274800.

St Anthony's College, Woodstock Road (1948), tel: 59651.

St Catherine's College, Manor Road (1963), tel: 271700. Open: daily 9 a.m.–5 p.m.

St Edmund Hall, Queen's Lane (1957), tel: 279000. Look for the "gargoyles" of the Rev. Midgley with his dog Fred. Open: daylight hours.

St Hilda's College, Cowley Place (1893), tel: 276884. Open: daily 2–5 p.m.

St Hugh's College, St Margaret's Road (1886), tel: 274900.

St John's College, St Giles' (1555), tel: 277300. Includes the Canterbury Quadrangle, a masterpiece of 17th-century architecture, and a fine garden. Open: daily 1–5 p.m.

St Peter's College, New Inn Hall Street (1929), tel: 278900. Open: daylight hours.

Somerville College, Woodstock Road (1879), tel: 270600. Open: daily 2–5.30 p.m.

Trinity College, Broad Street (1555), tel:

279900. Open: daily 2–5 p.m.

University College, High Street (1249), tel: 276602. Open: afternoons when conferences are not in residence.

Wadham College, Parks Road (1610), tel: 277900.

Wolfson College, Linton Road (1966), tel: 274100.

Worcester College, Worcester Street (1283), tel: 278300. Noted for its park-like garden and lake.

PERMANENT PRIVATE HALLS

Self-governing, non-profit making academic halls who were conferred with a licence to accept academic students in a statue of 1918. An Oxford University degree may be gained at these halls:

Campion Hall (1896), Brewer Street, OX1 1QS, tel: 240861.

Greyfriars (1957), Iffley Road, OX4 1SB, tel: 243694.

Mansfield College (1886), Mansfield Road, OX1 3TF, tel: 270999. Open: daily 9 a.m.–5 p.m.

Regent's Park College (1810), Pusey Street, OX1 2LB, tel: 59887.

St Benet's Hall (1897), 38 St Giles', OX1 3LN, tel: 515006.

ANNUAL EVENTS

The Oxford Information Centre, St Aldate's, tel: 726871, will be able to give actual dates and times of all events.

Degree Days: Days on which degrees are conferred by the University are listed in the University diary.

FEBRUARY

Torpids: College rowing races held on the Isis. Usually held in the 6th week of Hilary Term. One of the great rowing events in the University calendar. In February or early March a competition is held to introduce freshmen (first year undergraduates) to the University rowing course between Iffley Lock and Folly Bridge. The crews race in lanes and a win is known as a bump.

MAY

May Morning (1 May): 6 a.m. Magdalen College choir sings from Magdalen Tower. Morris dancing in Radcliffe Square and Broad Street. A not-to-be-missed event. Take up position half-way across Magdalen Bridge about 5.30 a.m. and after the chorus wander around town having a boozy breakfast and watching the revellers making merry in all manner of fancy or formal dress.

Lord Mayor's parade: Held on Spring Bank Holiday Monday. A parade of decorated floats starting at St Giles' and finishing at South Park.

Eights Week: held in late May or early June, this is a series of inter-collegiate rowing races. College crews move up and down a league table depending on each day's racing. The race is in a single line and each crew attempts to "bump" or touch the boat in front. Once this has been achieved the race is won or lost.

Beating the Bounds (Ascension Day): starts at the Church of St Michael at the Northgate at 10.30 a.m.

Artweek: A time when more than 300 artists and craftspeople of all ages open their workshops and homes so that the public can meet them and discover their methods and motivations. From end of May to beginning of June.

Whitsun: The Headington Quarry Morris Dancers occupy a unique position in Oxford's history and in the story of Morris dancing. A chance meeting between the folk song collector Cecil Sharp and the Headington Quarry Morris Dancers, led by their musician William Kimber, on Boxing Day 1899 led eventually to the national revival of interest in Morris dancing. William Kimber was to lead the Headington Morris to world fame. He inherited his skills from his father, who in turn had learned his Morris from an earlier generation of Quarry dancers. The tradition continues with a young team which remains famous in the folk world.

JUNE

Encaenia: the ceremony takes place at 12 noon on the first Wednesday in the week following full Trinity term. Honorary degrees are conferred by the University at the Sheldonian Theatre.

JULY

Sheriff's Races: held on Wolvercote Common. Amateur horse races, side shows and stalls.

AUGUST

Oxford Regatta: details from the City of Oxford Rowing Club, tel: 511720.

SEPTEMBER

St Giles' Fair: Held in early September. A once-famous annual enjoyment for town, gown and surrounding countryfolk. It can still be fun, but some see it as an expensive, tacky fair with a dubious safety record and knee-deep litter.

OCTOBER

Oxford Round Table Firework Display: Britain's firework displays traditionally take place on Guy Fawkes' Night (5 November). This one is held in late October in South Park, and is a worthwhile spectacular.

NOVEMBER

Christ Church Regatta: generally held the 7th week of Michaelmas term. All enquiries (written) to Boat Captain, c/o Christ Church, St Aldate's, Oxford.

DECEMBER

Lord Mayor's Carols: held in the Town Hall. Date announced in the autumn.

Christmas Music: At Christmas the chapel choirs of Christ Church, Magdalen and New College combine their regular liturgical duties with carol concerts that sometimes feature major orchestras and internationally famous soloists. The public may apply for tickets in advance.

Christ Church: 23 December: Nine Lessons and Carols. Tickets from the Chapter Secretary no later than 16 November; enclose a stamped, addressed envelope.

Magdalen College: Mid December: Carols by Candlelight (Tickets may be purchased in advance from the College Office).

New College: End November: Advent Carol Service. Early December: Carol Service (Tickets in advance from the Precentor).

The Headington Quarry Morris Dancers' Mummers Play and sword dance: Boxing Day.

PLACES TO VISIT

ON THE UPPER THAMES

Lechlade: **St John's Lock** is the first and highest lock on the River Thames, guarding a Victorian statue of Old Father Thames. Originally carved for the Crystal Palace he was rescued from the ruins and placed by the source of the Thames at Coates, near Cirencester, but vandalism prompted this latest move.

From the bridge and the famous Trout pub, the A417 leads to **Buscot House**. Built in 1780 the Adam-style house is set on high ground at the centre of a landscaped park with a formal Italianate water garden linking the house and a 22-acre lake. The house forms an ideal setting for the important Faringdon Collection of works of art. For the river user, a stroll from Buscot Lock makes an excellent outing. Open 28 March–30 September, Wednesday–Friday second and fourth Saturday and immediately following Sunday 2–6 p.m. Open Good Friday but closed Bank Holiday Mondays.

Filkins: **Cotswold Woollen Weavers**, tel: 036786-491. A small country woollen mill run by an enterprising couple. Genuine Cotswold tweeds and flannel fabrics, garments and rugs are all designed and woven on the premises; shop; coffee shop. Open: Monday–Saturday 10 a.m.–6 p.m., Sunday 2–6 p.m. Also at Filkins is **The Swinford Museum**, open by appointment only, April–October, Friday–Sunday 10 a.m.–6 p.m, tel: Filkins (036786) 365.

Kelmscott: on the north bank, is a hideaway village where William Morris lived from 1871 until his death in 1896. The 16th-century manor house, his "heaven on earth", has been carefully restored to show the work of Morris the craftsman, artist, writer, decorator, designer and printer. He is buried in the churchyard. **Kelmscott Manor** is open April–September, first Wednesday in each month 11 a.m.–1 p.m., 2–5 p.m.

Near **Clanfield** the river flows under the Radcot Bridges, the oldest on the river, dating back to the 12th century. Cotswold stone was barged from here for the building of the Oxford colleges. During the Civil War the bridge was held by the Royalists defending Faringdon when Prince Rupert met the Parliamentary cavalry in what is now called Garrison Field.

Bampton: further along the A4095, is famous for Morris Dancing, and a festival of dance and song takes place each Spring Bank Holiday.

Near Abingdon: Oxon (A415/A420). **Kingston Bagpuize House and Gardens** tel: 820259. The garden contains fine trees, flowering shrubs and bulbs. The Charles II manor house is an early example of neoclassical architecture and is thought to have been designed by Sir Roger Pratt, a disciple of Inigo Jones. The house has a cantilevered staircase, well-proportioned panelled rooms and some good furniture. It is the home of Lord and Lady Tweedsmuir and is shown to visitors by the owners and their family. Open: 2.30–5.30 p.m. Wednesdays and Sundays in May, June and September, also May and August Bank Holidays. Groups by appointment. Home-made teas, small gift shop and plant stall.

Through **Eynsham** the river passes under the **Swinford Toll Bridge**, built in 1769 for the fourth Earl of Abingdon.

The river loops around **Wytham Great Wood** and **Wolvercote** with its ruined **Godstow Nunnery** bearing the legend of Fair Rosamund. Here the river enters **Port Meadow** with a view of Oxford's famous skyline of towers and spires.

THE WINDRUSH VALLEY

Burford: Delightful Cotswold town built on the wealth of the wool industry 400 years ago. In the heart of the town is The Tolsey, used by the Corporation of Burford from 1351 to 1859, and now the local museum. Open: Easter–October, daily 2.30–5.30 p.m. Visit Sheep Street; The Priory, Symon Wisdom's four-gabled 16th-century house; **Falkland Hall** and **The Great House**; enjoy the riverside, the inns and cottages. Burford church is the second largest in Oxfordshire. Below the north transept is the tomb of Speaker Lenthall who as Speaker of the House of Commons, resisted Charles I's storming of Parliament to seize five Members of Parliament on a charge of treason.

Lenthall, Sir Lawrence Tanfield, Chief Baron of the Exchequer under James I, and Christopher Kempster, Wren's clerk of works during the building of St Paul's Cathedral, were famous men of Burford in an age when more than 30 coaches a day came into the courtyards of the town's inns.

Cotswold Wildlife Park is south of Burford on the A361 and mid-way between Oxford and Cheltenham, tel: Burford (099382) 3006. Has 200 acres (80 hectares) of gardens and woodland; aviary and aquarium, reptile house and butterfly house—with giant spiders and leaf-cutting ants—and a wide variety of animals—leopard, white rhino, zebra, ostrich, camel, gazelle, puma, otter and red panda, amongst others; picnic areas; brass rubbing centre; adventure playground; narrow-gauge railway; bar and restaurant; reduced rates for parties. Facilities for the disabled. Open: daily 10 a.m.–6 p.m.

Burford Garden and Leisure Centre and Craft Workshops, Shilton Road (off A40), Burford, tel: 099382-3117. Everything for the English country garden. Coffee shop, children's playground, mini putting green, craft workshops. Range of house plants, garden plants, bonsai trees, gift section, pet products etc.

Minster Lovell: On the banks of the Windrush, west of Witney, stand the remains of the 15th-century **Minster Lovell Hall**. The fine dovecot, village church and ruins are set in a quiet corner of a very beautiful village. Open: 15 March–15 October, Monday–Saturday 9.30 a.m.–6.30 p.m., Sunday 2–6.30 p.m. Rest of the year closes at 4 p.m.

Witney: In 1677 there were 150 looms in the town and today the firm of Charles Early and Marriott can trace a direct line back from their president, Mr Richard Early, to the original Mr Early who began his apprenticeship in Mill Street in 1669. **Church Green** is surrounded by the great church of St Mary, a row of almshouses, 16th and 17th-century houses and the 17th-century Buttercross. The **Town Hall**, restored **Corn Exchange** and unusual **Blanket Hall** are worth seeing. On the A415 is the **ancient bridge of Newbridge** dating from 1250. With The Maybush inn on one side and the cosy Rose Revived hotel on the other, the bridge spans both Thames and Windrush and they join at Standlake.

Standlake and **Stanton Harcourt** offer good walks and thatched houses and inns. Alexander Pope worked on his translation of the Iliad at Stanton Harcourt in a small study in what has become known as Pope's Tower, near to the **Manor House**, most of which was demolished in the 18th century. The Manor has some fine porcelain, silver and furniture and a medieval kitchen. There is a fine chancel screen in the nearby church. Open: May–July, Thursday and Sunday 2 p.m.–6 p.m. tel: 086731-881928.

THE LOWER THAMES

Abingdon: A pleasant town with the remains of a once-powerful abbey. The imposing Napoleonic prison has been imaginatively converted into a riverside leisure centre. Visit the 17th-century County Hall standing guard over an attractive market place, the Roysse Room, the churches of St Nicholas and St Helen and the rows of delightful almshouses. Good moorings, boat hire and daily summer boat trips to Oxford and return. **Abbey Buildings**, Thames Street. Open: daily 2–6 p.m. Closed: Good Friday and Monday and October–March; County Hall and Museum: Open: daily 2–5 p.m. Closed: Bank holidays and Monday; Guildhall, Abbey Close: by appointment, tel: 0235-20202. **Long Alley Almshouses**, St Helen's churchyard: exterior daily; the Governors' Hall may be seen by appointment. **Upper Reaches Hotel Watermill**, Thames Street: may be seen from the hotel restaurant.

Dorchester: Once an important Roman town, with a magnificent medieval abbey and museum.

Wallingford: Remains of the castle and a traditional town square. A walk along the Thames towpath lined with houseboats in the summer, is most enjoyable.

Goring: Bridges and wiers and keen anglers spaced out along one bank of the river, while the other is lined with expensive homes and immaculate lawns.

OUT OF OXFORD

From Oxford to Stratford: Just off the A34 before Woodstock is the village of **Bladon** where Sir Winston Churchill chose to be buried next to his parents in the graveyard on the hill by the little parish church.

A mile from Bladon and 8 miles (13 km) north of Oxford, is **Blenheim Palace, Woodstock**, the country's largest house, set in 2,200 acres (880 hectares) of parkland landscaped by "Capability" Brown. The quiet and tree-lined Park Street leads to Blenheim Park and to one of the most spectacular views in England. The home of the 11th Duke of Marlborough, the palace was a gift from Queen Anne on behalf of a "grateful nation" for the victory over the French and Bavarians at Blenheim in 1704 by John Churchill, the first Duke of Marlborough. From the Great Hall with the magnificent ceiling painted by James Thornhill, visitors tour the great palace that Sir John Vanbrugh created between 1705 and 1722. The Churchill Exhibition includes perhaps the plainest room in the palace where Churchill was born on 30 November 1874. He loved Blenheim. It was here he proposed to Clementine Hozier. The Palace collection includes tapestries, paintings, sculpture and fine furniture set in magnificent gilded staterooms. There is an interesting display of antique greeting cards.

Open: Palace: daily mid-March–31 October 10.30 a.m.–5.30 p.m. (last admission 4.45 p.m.). Park: daily throughout the year 9 a.m.–5 p.m. Butterfly House and Garden Centre: daily mid-March–October 10 a.m.–6 p.m. (last admission 5.30). Garden Centre only: daily November–mid March 10.30 a.m.–4.30 p.m. Open Top Bus Tours to Blenheim Palace leave Oxford Information Centre daily during the summer season.

Woodstock is a charming Cotswold country town with tea shops and lovely old inns and cottages. The splendid **County Museum** with the town stocks outside complete with a little roof covered with Stonesfield slates is housed in the 16th-century Fletcher's House. Crafts, industries and the domestic life of Oxfordshire combine to illustrate the history of the county (*see Museums section*). To the south of the town is the world-famous Bear Hotel, reputed to have been first licensed in 1232. Frequent local buses go to Woodstock from Oxford and Witney (South Midland) and Stratford and Banbury (Midland Red). For more information telephone the Thames and Chilterns Tourist Board, Woodstock 811038.

Take time to visit the **Glyme Valley** and

the lovely villages of **Wootton**, **Glympton** and **Kiddington**. **Enstone** offers the opportunity to explore the **Wychwoods** or **Great Tew**, a picturesque village of thatched cottages.

Further on the A34, **Chipping Norton** is the highest town in Oxfordshire and St Mary's Parish Church its oldest building, dating back to the 12th century. Nearby is a row of almshouses bequeathed to the town in 1646 by Henry Cornish. At one end of the broad Market Place is the Town Hall, with its imposing stone columns and at the other the Guildhall, headquarters of the medieval Guild. In the busy grey stone town of Morton-in-Marsh the Tourist Information Centre is based in the main street in a craft shop.

Approaching Stratford on the A422, you pass **Upton House**—a National Trust William and Mary house set in extensive lawns with colourful terraced herbaceous borders and pools in a deep valley garden. Inside are outstanding collections of porcelain, tapestry and fine furniture, as well as numerous Old Masters. Open: April–October, Saturday and Sunday 2–6 p.m; May–September, Saturday–Wednesday 2–4 p.m. For further information contact The Administrator, Edge Hill (029587) 266.

STRATFORD-UPON-AVON

From London there is a fast InterCity train service between London Euston, Watford Junction and Coventry which connects with a special express motorcoach to and from Stratford. From Oxford (Gloucester Green) there are two-hourly coach services operated by National Express.

Stratford-upon-Avon received its first market charter in 1196 and still holds two town markets and one major cattle market each week. Among its historic buildings is **Harvard House**, the home of Katherine Rogers, mother of John Harvard, founder of the American University; the **Guild Hall**— the old grammar school where Shakespeare was a pupil—and, next door, some fine almshouses. In the **Bancroft Gardens**, adjoining the **Royal Shakespeare Theatre**, are attractive floral displays and acres of river meadow parkland. Major events include the Shakespeare Birthday celebrations in April, the Stratford Festival in July and the historic Mop Fair in October.

Shakespeare's Birthplace, Henley Street: Shakespeare was born and spent his early years in this half-timbered building of a type common in Elizabethan Stratford. One half of the property includes the living-room, kitchen and bedrooms and has period furnishings to re-create the atmosphere of a middle-class home of the period. The other half contains an exhibition illustrating the life and work of the dramatist, as well as the history of the property itself.

New Place/Nash's House: The site and foundations of New Place, the house in which Shakespeare spent his retirement, are preserved in an Elizabethan garden setting occupying the corner of Chapel Street and Chapel Lane. The entrance to the site is through the adjoining Nash's House, which belonged to Thomas Nash, the first husband of Shakespeare's grand-daughter, Elizabeth Hall. The house is furnished in period style and houses a museum of local history.

Hall's Croft: In the Old Town, Hall's Croft was the home of Shakespeare's daughter, Susanna, and her husband, Dr John Hall. It contains some exceptional Elizabethan and Jacobean furniture. Dr Hall's medical dispensary is particularly interesting and there is a beautiful walled garden.

Anne Hathaway's Cottage at Shottery village, 1 mile from the town centre: The picturesque thatched home of Shakespeare's wife, before her marriage. The home was a 12-roomed farmhouse in the time of the Hathaways, a yeoman farming family. The kitchen has an open fireplace and bakeoven still intact.

Mary Arden's House and the **Shakespeare Countryside Museum**, at Wilmcote, 3 miles (5 km) northwest of Stratford: This Tudor farmstead, with its old stone dovecote and various outbuildings, was the girlhood home of Shakespeare's mother. The house contains rare pieces of country furniture and domestic utensils. The barns, stable, cowshed and farmyard are used to display an extensive collection of farming implements and other bygones illustrating life and work in the local countryside from Shakespeare's time.

Opening times:
Shakespeare's Birthplace* and Anne Hathaway's Cottage: 24 March–31 October, Monday–Saturday 9 a.m.–6 p.m.**,

Sunday 10 a.m.–6 p.m.**; November–March Monday–Saturday 9 a.m.–4.30 p.m., Sunday 1.30–4.30 p.m.

Mary Arden's House and Countryside Museum; New Place/Nash's House; and Hall's Croft: 24 March–31 October, Monday–Saturday 9 a.m.–6 p.m.**, Sunday 10 a.m.–6 p.m; November–March, Monday–Saturday 9 a.m.–4.30 p.m. Closed: Sunday.

* Includes the BBC Television Shakespeare Costume Exhibition.

** Until 5 p.m. in October.

Last admissions are normally 20 minutes before closing time. The properties are closed on Good Friday morning, Christmas Eve, Christmas Day, Boxing Day and the morning of 1 January.

CULTURE PLUS

MUSEUMS

Ashmolean Museum of Art and Archaeology: Beaumont Street, tel: 278000 (Education Service, tel: 278015). Britain's oldest public museum, founded in 1683, is now housed in C.R. Cockerell's neo-classical building of the 1840s. On display are superb collections of relics of past civilisations—from Ancient Egypt through to 19th and early 20th-century European Art; silver, bronzes, ceramics, pottery, sculpture, coins and other objects ranging from the 9th-century King Alfred's Jewel to Guy Fawkes's lantern and Stradivari's violin, Le Messie. The bookstall stocks a comprehensive range of Christmas cards, postcards, calendars, illustrated booklets and giftware. Open: Tuesday–Saturday 10 a.m.–4 p.m., Sunday 2–4 p.m. and Bank Holiday Mondays 2–5 p.m. Closed: 1 January, Good Friday, Easter Sunday, St Giles' Fair and at Christmas. Admission free.

Museum of the History of Science: Old Ashmolean building, Broad Street, tel: 277280. The museum is housed in the oldest public museum building in the country, opened in 1683 as the original Ashmolean Museum. The displays include fine collections of early scientific instruments, sundials, mathematical instruments, clocks, cameras, the original penicillin apparatus and Einstein's blackboard. Open: Monday–Friday 10.30 a.m.–1 p.m., 2.30–4 p.m. Closed: Bank Holidays, Christmas week and Easter week. Admission free.

Pitt Rivers Museum of Ethnology: Parks Road, (entrance through University Museum) tel: 270927. One million objects collected by 18th and 19th-century explorers, among them Captain Cook. Open: Monday–Saturday 2–4 p.m. Admission free.

New Extension to Pitt Rivers Museum: Balfour Building, 60 Banbury Road, (music gallery) tel: 274726. Exhibition of musical instruments which can both be heard on earphones as well as seen. Open: Monday–Saturday 2–4 p.m. or by appointment. Admission free.

The University Museum: Parks Road, tel: 272950. The museum is housed in a splendidly imposing Victorian Gothic structure, with rich naturalistic carving and a huge glass-roofed gallery. Exhibits include the University's important geological and mineral collections, and the giant skeletons of prehistoric animals. Open: Monday–Saturday 12 noon–5 p.m. Admission free.

The Museum of Oxford: St Aldate's/Blue Boar Street, tel: 815559. The museum tells the story of Oxford from the earliest times, and covers the development of the University and the change from a county town to a modern industrial city. The museum, which includes a shop, is unsuitable for the disabled. Open: Tuesday–Saturday 10 a.m.–5 p.m. Admission free.

The Oxford Story: 6 Broad Street. The history of the town and the University, as conceived by Heritage Projects (Oxford) Ltd; strong emphasis on waxwork tableaux and taped commentary, tel: 728822. Open: daily except Christmas Day. 24 March–30 September 9.30 a.m.–5 p.m; 1 October–23 March 10 a.m.–4 p.m. (last admission half an hour before closing). £3 adults, £1.50 children.

The Regimental Museum of the Ox-

fordshire and Buckinghamshire Light Infantry: Slade Park, off the ring road between Headington and Cowley. The militaria of the county regiment of Oxfordshire and Buckinghamshire, now incorporated in the Royal Green Jackets. Includes a fine medal collection, uniforms, badges, pictures and regimental silver. Open: Monday–Friday 10 a.m.–12.30 p.m. and 2–4 p.m. but visitors should check in advance with the Curator, tel: 716060 ext. 141 as there are plans to close for some time.

The Rotunda Museum of Antique Dolls' Houses: Grove House, Iffley Turn, Oxford OX4 4DU, tel: 777935. A fine private collection of over 40 historic dolls' houses (1700–1900) with their period furniture, carpets, dinner services, silver, miniature books and inhabitants. Open: from the first Sunday in May–mid-September, Sundays only, 2.15–5.15 p.m. At other times, and for groups, by written appointment only. Admission £1.50. No children under 16.

Christ Church Picture Gallery: Christ Church, St Aldate's, tel: 276172. Permanent collection of European Old Master paintings and changing displays of Old Master drawings, mainly Italian, from the 14th to 18th centuries. Open: Monday–Saturday 10.30 a.m.–1 p.m. and 2–5.30 p.m., Sunday 2–5.30 p.m. (October–March closes at 4.30 p.m.). Admission: Children, members of the University and Polytechnic free; students, OAPs and unemployed 20p and adults 40p. Guided Tours: Thursday, 2.15 p.m. and 3 p.m.

The Museum of Modern Art: 30 Pembroke Street, Oxford OX1 1BP, tel: 722733. Recorded information: tel: 728608. A museum with an international reputation that caters for contemporary art enthusiasts. A changing programme of exhibitions of paintings, sculpture, photography, architecture, drawing, print making and design; films, lectures, workshops and performances. Coffee shop and access for the disabled. Open: Tuesday–Saturday 10 a.m.–6 p.m., Sunday 2–6 p.m. Closed: Monday, Christmas Day, Boxing Day, New Year's Day and Good Friday. Minimum exhibition charge £1.50; concessions, members free.

Bate Collection of Historical Instruments: Faculty of Music, Floyds Row, St Aldate's, tel: 276125. A comprehensive collection of more than 900 items, including woodwind, brass, percussion and Javanese Gamelan instruments; a large collection of keyboards and a unique display of bowmaker's tools and equipment. Shop. Guided tours available. Open: Monday–Friday 2–5 p.m. Museum closed occasionally during curator's absence; visitors should check in advance.

The British Telecom Museum: 35 Speedwell Street, tel: 246601. A selection of telephone and telegraph equipment tracing the history and evolution of telecommunications. Open: by appointment. Admission free.

COUNTY MUSEUMS

The Oxfordshire County Museum: Fletcher's House, Park Street, Woodstock, tel: (0993) 811456. Numerous galleries illustrating the development of the county and the way of life of its people from prehistoric times. There is a bookshop and coffee room leading out into pleasant gardens. Temporary exhibitions are held regularly. Open: May–September: Monday–Friday 10 a.m.–5 p.m., Saturday 10 a.m.–5 p.m., Sunday 2–6 p.m; October–April Tuesday–Friday 10 a.m.–4 p.m., Saturday 10 a.m.–5 p.m., Sunday 2–5 p.m. Not suitable for disabled people. Admission free.

Cogges Manor Farm Museum: Church Lane, Cogges, near Witney, tel: Witney (0993) 772602. An Edwardian farm with working kitchens and dairy, livestock, agricultural vehicles and implements, river walk, picnic gardens, orchard and a large visitors' centre with bookstall and cafeteria. There are many weekend demonstrations and events. Large park for cars and coaches. The disabled are welcome. Open: from early April–early November, Tuesday–Sunday and bank Holiday Mondays, 10.30 a.m.–5.30 p.m. (4.30 p.m. from October). Admission: Adults £1.60, Children, OAPs and students 80p.

Tolsey Museum: High Street, Burford, tel: (Secretary) Clanfield (036781) 294. The social and industrial history of this splendid Cotswold town, with varied material including the Royal Charters and town maces housed in the 16th-century Council Chambers. Open: from Easter–end of October 2.30–5.30 p.m. daily. Admission: Adults 25p, students and OAPs 10p, children 5p.

Abingdon Museum: County Hall, Market Place, tel: Abingdon (0235) 23703. The museum is in the Old County Hall, built in 1677 (possibly to designs by Sir Christopher Wren) when Abingdon was the county town of Berkshire. There are local history and archaeological displays, with relics of the abbey and some of the borough plate. Open: Tuesday–Sunday, 1–5 p.m. Admission: Adults 10p, children 5p.

Banbury Museum: 8 Horsefair, tel: Banbury (0295) 59855. Overlooking Banbury Cross, the museum has permanent displays which tell the story of the town and the surrounding area. Local artists' work is displayed in the coffee bar and there is a changing programme of exhibits in the Photographers' Gallery. Open: April–September Monday–Saturday 10 a.m.–5 p.m; October–March Tuesday–Saturday 10 a.m.–4.30 p.m. Admission free.

Bloxham Village Museum: The Court House, Bloxham, tel: Banbury (029589) 720283. The museum is housed in the Old Court House which still belongs to the Bloxham Feoffees, trustees of the ancient Bloxham charities. The collection reflects past life in this ancient and beautiful village, one of the largest in the ironstone area of north Oxfordshire. Disabled visitor access; shop. Open: Easter–September, Sundays and Bank Holidays, 2.30–5.30 p.m; October Sundays 2.30–4.30 p.m; November–Easter, second Sunday each month 2.30–4.30 p.m. Admission: Adults 20p children 10p.

Granary Museum: Butlin Farm, Claydon, Banbury, tel: Farnborough 258. Housed in a former granary and cowshed, the displays show 19th and early 20th-century material from the homes, farms, offices and craftsmen's workshops of north Oxfordshire. Also a 1912 Aveling and Porter Steam Roller. Open: Monday–Saturday 10 a.m.–dusk; Sunday 10.30 a.m.–5.30 p.m. Admission: Donations suggested of 40p adult, 20p children.

Didcot Railway Centre: Tel: Didcot (0235) 817200. Recreating the golden age of the Great Western Railway: regular programme of steaming days. Meals served in a dining car. Open: Daily 1 April–29 October, weekends in winter, Tuesday–Sunday and Bank Holiday Mondays from April. Contact centre for steaming programme.

Pendon Museum of Miniature Land- scapes and Transport: Long Wittenham, tel: Clifton Hampden (086730) 7365. Delightfully detailed miniature landscapes, including working trains of the 1930s set in the wilds of Dartmoor and farms and cottages grouped in a typical village from the Vale of the White Horse. Also railway relics. Open: 2–5 p.m. Saturday and Sunday all year round and from 11 a.m.–5 p.m. on Bank Holiday weekends from Easter–August. Closed: 11 December–5 January. Admission: Adults £1.50, children and OAPs £1.

Vale and Downland Museum Centre: The Old Surgery, Church Street, Wantage, tel: Wantage (02357) 66838. Set in a converted 16th/17th-century cloth merchant's house with modern extensions and a reconstructed barn, the museum has permanent displays showing the geology, local history and archaeology of Wantage and the Vale of the White Horse. There is a programme of temporary exhibitions. Open: Tuesday–Saturday 10.30 a.m.–4.40 p.m., Sunday 2.30–5.30 p.m.

Uffington Tom Brown's School Museum: Broad Street, Uffington, tel: Uffington (036782) 635. The life and works of Thomas Hughes, author of *Tom Brown's Schooldays*, with other historical material from the area. Open: Easter–end of September, weekends and bank Holidays only 2–5 p.m. Admission: Adults 20p, OAPs and accompanied children free. Open at other times by arrangement.

Fawley Court Historic House and Museum: Marian Fathers, Fawley Court, Henley-on-Thames, tel: Henley (0491) 574917. Splendid collection of historic Polish material—paintings, books, documents, arms and armour—housed in a fine late 17th-century house and in part of a 12th-century manor house. Open: October, November and from 1 March Wednesday, Thursday and Sunday 2–5 p.m; December–February open to groups by appointment only. Admission: Adults £2, OAP £1.50, Children £1.

Wallingford Museum: Flint House, High Street, Wallingford, tel: Wallingford (0491) 35065. A permanent exhibition depicting 1,000 years of Wallingford's history, from Saxon town to present day, with a special display on the castle. Open: Tuesday–Saturday, Bank Holiday Mondays 2–5 p.m., Saturday 10.30 a.m.–12.30 p.m., Sunday (June, July, August) 2–5 p.m. Closed: December, January, February. Admission: Adults 50p, children free.

THEATRES

The Apollo Theatre: George Street, Oxford OX1 2AG. Postal bookings are welcome. Box Office: tel: 0865-244544/5; Party bookings: tel: 0865-723834. There is a varied programme of opera and ballet, plays, musicals, pop and classical concerts, a Christmas pantomime, comedy and shows for young theatregoers. Prices range from £3.50 to £7.50 for regular events, with special concessions, to a £6 to £20 price range for top star entertainment. The theatre and bars have been redecorated: the Carousel Bar has a tented ceiling, drums and horses for the fun of the fair, while in the Billy Budd Bar everything is ship-shape.

The Burton-Taylor Theatre: behind the Playhouse, Gloucester Street. Box Office: tel: 793797. Built in 1973 after a generous donation to the University by Richard Burton and Elizabeth Taylor, and recently refurbished with a new theatre foyer and dressing rooms. Specialises in student and fringe productions with new plays and Edinburgh Festival comedies all year round.

Holywell Music Room: Holywell Street, the oldest music room in Europe. Many famous musicians, including Haydn, have played there since it opened in 1748. The resident professional orchestra is the Oxford Pro Musica.

The Newman Rooms: recently opened in Rose Place, St Aldates, tel: 722651. The venue for a variety of plays and musicals at reasonable prices from £2.50.

The Old Fire Station Arts Centre: contains a fully-equipped studio theatre and rehearsal space in a completely new complex of bars, restaurants and galleries.

Oxford Playhouse: George Street. Gradually reopening by producing occasional performances.

Pegasus Theatre: Magdalen Road, off Iffley Road, tel: 722851. Youth theatre activities, Tuesday 8 p.m. Performances on Saturdays.

Details and tickets for live entertainment in Oxford, London and Stratford are available from the Oxford Information Centre, St Aldate's, tel: 727855.

CINEMAS

Three mainstream cinemas show recently released films:

Phoenix 1 and **2** in Walton Street, tel: 54909.

Cannon Cinemas: George Street, with three studios, tel: 244607.

Cannon Cinema: Magdalen Street, tel: 723067.

Two other cinemas offer more adventurous screenings for film buffs:

Penultimate Picture Palace: Jeune Street, off Cowley Road, tel: 723837.

Not the Moulin Rouge: New High Street, Headington, tel: 63666.

NIGHTLIFE

NIGHTCLUBS

All "nightclubs" and discos in Oxford are geared to young people. Anyone nudging 30 will probably wish they were somewhere else.

Downtown Manhattan: George Street (Below Apollo Theatre), tel: 721101. Full every night, hot and sweaty. Student nights are Mondays (The Playpen) and Wednesdays (The Mudd Club). Attracts mainly Poly and foreign students.

Bogart's: 15a St Clement's, (The Plain), tel: 241047. Women admitted free on Thursday and other nights if they smile nicely. Friday and Saturday are "No jeans or trainers" nights. Decor is tacky. The dance floor is on the lowest level; the bar in the middle and a "talking room" on the top.

Boodles: 35 Westgate Centre, tel: 245136. Tuesday is the big night. Patronised by Sloanes and Yuppies. Bouncers keep out anyone they don't like the look of, so there may be a problem getting in.

The Coven: Oxpens Road, tel: 242770. The place to go on a Saturday night to meet Oxford non-student youth. A most impressive nightclub—lights, lasers, smoke and a video screen. The management is erratic, so you never know quite what to expect.

PUBS

Oxfordshire still has many long-established breweries, but their markets are contracting as a result of drink/driving campaigns and the popularity of lagers, low-alcohol beers and wines. Morrell's, the Oxford brewery founded in 1782, is the latest to admit to financial problems; sales have been falling at the 138 tied houses which sell their beers. Hook Norton Brewery has 34 tied houses and a free trade business in the Midlands while the Henley Brewery, W. H. Brakspear and Sons, founded in 1779, supplies many traditional pubs tucked away in the Oxfordshire countryside. Morland & Co of Abingdon can claim to be one of the oldest surviving breweries in England. In 1711 John Morland started brewing in the village of West Ilsley on the Berkshire Downs. Although Whitbread has a large shareholding in Morland, the company has remained independent. Another Oxford brewery, part of the national Allied-Lyons group, has revived its local name—Halls Oxford and West Brewery Co Ltd—and now owns 370 pubs.

There are an enormous number of pubs in Oxford. Many serve real ale and bar food and attractions might include fruit machines, video machines, darts, pool, table football, bar billiards, pinball, piano, cribbage and dominoes and live music—mostly jazz.

The Bear, Alfred Street, tel: 244680. Full of Christ Church students. The Bear is one of Oxford's oldest pubs (there has been a pub on its site since 1242) and has genuine charm. Enclosed in its tiny, panelled rooms, with their smoke-kippered ceilings, are over 7,000 ties displayed in cabinets on the walls and rafters—from the Cheltenham College Mind Games Society to the East of Suez Golfing Club. There is excellent pub grub, and in summer you can eat out in the adjoining yard. In winter the Bear comes into its own; when the fire is lit and dusk gathers, there is no cosier drinking place in Oxford.

The Crown, 49a Cornmarket, tel: 242-784. Very near to being a family pub. A quiz night is held most Wednesday evenings.

Eagle and Child, 49 St Giles', tel: 58085. Plenty of history. J. R. R. Tolkien, C. S. Lewis and others visited the pub every morning between 1939 and 1962. Mixed clientele and very popular.

The Grapes, 7 George Street, tel: 247372. A narrow, one-bar Victorian pub with mahogany panelling and old prints on the walls, conveniently situated opposite the Apollo Theatre and are therefore very busy before and after performances. Bar food, hot and cold meals but no atmosphere.

The Head of the River, Folly Bridge, tel: 721600. Halls brewery had the bright idea of turning this former warehouse and boatyard into a pub. The result is a massive drinking complex with a huge paved couryard, bars on three levels (the top two are for cocktails and wine), a restaurant and salad bar and, at the back, a sandwich place called Upper Crusts. The design theme of Thames memorabilia has been somewhat overdone, but nothing can detract from its superb riverside location by Folly Bridge. This guarantees a capacity crowd in summer—mostly tourists and Town. In winter it can be "quiet as a grave", according to the barman.

Horse and Jockey, 69 Woodstock Road, tel: 52719. A superbly restored pub close to the Radcliffe Hospital. Outside dining in summer. Cold table and hot pots, casseroles, grills and real ales. Two centuries ago it was full of jockeys who raced in nearby Port Meadow—now the young horsey set drink G & T and talk about expensive cars.

The Jericho Tavern, 56 Walton Street, tel: 54502. Live jazz music most nights but the nearby residents are doing their best to stop it. Full range of pub food and good beer.

King's Arms, Holywell Street, tel: 242369. A pub with a certain amount of class that calls itself a coffee shop and public house. Full of students in cliques. In the evenings there is standing room only and a deafening hubbub. Lunchtimes are more sedate as dons, students, visiting scholars, Bodleian librarians, and eccentrics parade. The range of real ales, food, and facilities is broad. The Coffee Room offers the best espresso and fresh sandwiches in town, the hot dishes are generous and inexpensive and the cold platters genuinely tempting. A surprise is the tuckshop and a table of newspapers and magazines in the small back room (once, but no longer, for men only). Irritations include the Tannoy system blaring out food orders, clattering fruit machines and a slow coffee queue—but the KA is still, and probably always will be, the Gown pub of Oxford.

Lamb and Flag, 12 St Giles', tel: 513787. A 500-year-old pub with original beams over fire. Good place for cosy chat in the back bar or a blast on the six video machines.

The Royal Oak, 42–44 Woodstock Road, tel: 54230. Numerous interesting small rooms. Well-stocked games room.

The Turf, 4 Bath Place, Holywell Street, tel: 243235. Reached by narrow winding passages, the Turf is a famous Oxford hostelry with origins in the 13th century. Its history, plus the fact that it is the only central Oxford pub with a respectable beer garden (nudging against the last remaining section of the old City Wall), ensure that tourists and students with visiting parents flock here. Ye Olde English flavour is also reflected in the country wines and cider on offer plus a good range of real ales and delicious mulled wine. There is a food bar in the Back Garden and a hot potato bar.

The Welsh Pony, 48 George St, tel: 242998. More like a European café than a town pub. Customers come in for coffee as much as for alcohol, and food is served from 8 a.m. until 8 p.m. Pleasant decor of 1950s film posters.

The Wheatsheaf, Wheatsheaf Yard, 129 High Street, tel: 243276. A 300-year-old character pub with its own thoroughfare named after it, off the south side of The High, 100 yards from Carfax. Home-cooked food, grills and casseroles. Pints are still hand-drawn from traditional beer engines. A famous student pub.

OUT OF THE CENTRE

The Boat at Thrupp, tel: Kidlington (08675) 4279. A watering hole for houseboat owners whose colourful craft line the canal alongside.

The Golden Ball, Littlemore, tel: 779370. This old stone-built, cottage-style pub with its low ceilings and oak beams has a splendid collection of stamped mugs and serves a wide range of hot and cold bar food. A jukebox is obtrusive in the Cardinal Study bar, which takes its name from Cardinal Newman, namesake of the college opposite.

Morris dancers perform outisde in the summer.

The Isis, Iffley Lock, Iffley, tel: 247008. The only way to reach this beautifully located pub beside the river is by foot, boat or bike from Iffley Lock. Huge garden. Plenty of rowing and memorabilia inside as well as an old-English nine-pin bowling alley.

The Perch, Binsey Village, tel: 240386. Lives off its name. Good food (if it doesn't run out) but can you take the bolshie bar staff and masses of stuffed fish?

The Trout, Godstow Road, Wolvercote, tel: 54485. The magic of the Trout, like an old but still potent piece of music, always surprises. The glistening weir, the resplendent peacocks and the view across Port Meadow to the spires is an idyllic setting in which to sip a Pimms, nibble a smoked salmon sandwich and watch the river flow down to Oxford. Interesting literary and historical associations lend their charm—from Fair Rosamond, Henry II's mistress, whose ring (now in the Ashmolean) was found on the island opposite, to Alice in Wonderland.

The Victoria Arms, Mill Lane, Old Marston, tel: 722652. Punt up the Cherwell past the Parks and Parson's Pleasure, then under the Marston Ferry Road Bridge before finally pulling in for a well-deserved drink at the "Vicky". Walk up the meadow to an ample terrace and a good range of beers and lagers, friendly staff and a restaurant. The pub has been redecorated and, despite local suspicions that it was being "tarted up", a genuinely agreeable ambience has been created.

White Hart, Wytham, tel: 244372. Wonderful selection of home-cooked dishes and varied salad bar. Cotswold stone, beams and cosy corners on different levels. Garden open all the year. Lovely for lunch.

PUBS IN THE COUNTY

The Barley Mow: Clifton Hampden, near Abingdon, tel: Clifton Hampden (086730) 347. A riverside pub with attractive gardens and pleasant view from the restaurant. Uncomfortably crowded in winter in bars designed centuries ago for short people. Good food and ambience.

The Bell: Long Hanborough, tel: Freeland (0993) 881324. A traditional village pub renowned for its jovial country inn atmosphere and excellent food at reasonable prices.

The Clanfield Tavern: Bampton Road, Clanfield Tel: 036781-223. Delightful 16th-century listed building situated in a pretty Cotswold village. A la Carte restaurant open every day for lunch and dinner. A recent winner of the Oxfordshire Pub Garden of the Year award.

The King's Head and Bell: East Saint Helen's Street, Abingdon, tel: 0235-20157. Said to have been used by Charles I for council meetings during the Civil War and by Handel while he composed his Water Music. Delicious home-cooked food is served in the bar and the 40-seat bistro restaurant. A charming old courtyard where you can enjoy a drink. Popular with residents and visitors alike.

The Plough at Noke (off the B4027), tel: Kidlington 08675-3251. On the edge of the Otmoor countryside this friendly pub with superb home cooking has live country music every Tuesday evening.

The Trout: by St John's Bridge, Lechlade on Thames, tel: Lechlade (0367) 52313. Fishing, by rights granted by Royal Charter, is one of the many attractions at this superb ancient pub. Several beamed bars with cosy log fires in winter; a garden lawn set with tables stretching to the edge of the Weir Trout Pool for summer barbecues; a pretty candlelit restaurant with excellent food; welcoming and friendly staff. Seems to be on every visitor's itinerary.

The White Hart at Fyfield, off the A420, 8 miles (13 km) from Oxford. Tel: Frilford Heath (0865) 390585. A 15th-century Chantry House with an original beamed ceiling and gallery. A free house with a wide range of real ales. Restaurant, specialising in Old English game dishes and bar food catering for all tastes—from frogs legs to chicken and chips.

SHOPPING

CITY STORES

Oxford shops offer an intriguing mixture of the traditional and the modern and the city has three modern shopping precincts as well as its full share of fashion boutiques. The main shopping area is compact and easy to explore on foot.

To the north of Oxford's central cross-roads, known as Carfax, runs **Cornmarket Street,** which contains Boots, Littlewoods, W. H. Smith and many other shops. The courtyard of the Golden Cross inn on Cornmarket now leads, via an attractive arcade of shops, to the Covered Market. At 2 & 3 Golden Cross is The Oxford Collection—one of the most atmospheric shops in town selling Town v Gown chess sets, tiny boxes with enamelled miniature views of the 1877 Boat Race; playing cards backed with 18th-century caricatures of University personalities and a wide range of other nostalgia products.

The **Clarendon Centre**, etched in bright blue, is a new arcade of shops; most of them (or so it seems) sell shoes.

Broad Street, running east from the northern end of Cornmarket Street, is Oxford's book street, with no fewer than six separate book shops, including Blackwell's.

West from Carfax runs **Queen Street**, also a pedestrian area but open to buses. It includes a large Marks and Spencer store, Lewis's and many smaller shops. At the end of Queen Street is the fully enclosed **Westgate Centre** with numerous stores including the central food supermarket, Sainsbury's. The fine public Central Library, with a large local history section and a periodicals reading room, is at the Westgate entrance. The Westgate is also easily accessible from the multi-storey car park to which it is linked. Opposite the library is **New Inn Hall Street** with the

Photo Shop Ltd at No. 3, tel: 728200, where film processing only takes an hour. The *Oxford Mail* and *Times* newspaper offices are on the other side of the road.

The **High Street** joins Carfax from the east and curves down to Magdalen Bridge; the college buildings which line it are interspersed with small traditional businesses, including antique and print dealers. Transworld Travel at No 19, tel: 726875, is open 9 a.m.–4.30 p.m. and Saturday 9 a.m.–12.30 p.m. and tucked away down **Wheatsheaf Passage** a few yards further down is Gill & Co Ltd, Britain's oldest ironmongers. Established since 1530, they stock over 7,000 lines. W. P. Hine & Co, 52 High Street, tel: 242663, are the main agents for Burberry Raincoats—a favourite for tourists.

At 84 High Street is the Frank Cooper Shop and Museum, telling the story of the famous Oxford marmalade business. In 1874 Sarah Cooper used an old family recipe to make 76lbs of marmalade on her kitchen range. This quantity was rather too much for the family, but the flavour was so agreeable and Frank Cooper so proud of his young wife's skill, he decided to sell the surplus in his grocery shop. Open: Tuesday–Saturday 10 a.m.–6 p.m. Closed: 1–2 p.m. for lunch, tel: 245125. At No 90 Betjeman and Barton have opened a branch of their famous teashop chain.

On the other side of High Street, with three entrances, is the **Covered Market**, built in 1774 to provide a permanent home for the many stallholders who had earlier cluttered the city streets. It is a gourmet's paradise for fresh and cooked meat, game, fish, cheeses, fruit, vegetables and flowers, bread and cakes. Unfortunately the service falls behind the standard of the products on sale and you may more likely get the rudeness of youth behind the counter rather than the politeness of a traditional expert. Clothing, jewellery and leather goods are also available at bargain prices and there are some good, reasonably-priced cafés.

The fourth arm of Carfax is **St Aldate's**, which leads south, with the Information Centre on the right (the Information Centre may move to Gloucester Green). Further on down, is the main Post Office at 102 St Aldate's, Oxford OX1 1AA. The Philatelic Counter is open Monday–Friday 10 a.m.–1

p.m. and 2–5 p.m; Saturday 10 a.m.–12.30 p.m At 83 St Aldate's, opposite Christ Church, is Alice's shop, the little 15th-century "Sheep Shop" said in Lewis Carroll's *Through the Looking Glass* to be "full of all manner of curious things". The real-life Alice, daughter of the Dean of Christ Church, to whom Lewis Carroll told his tales, used to buy her Barley Sugar sweets there. Carroll wove the shop into his story, transforming the old lady who kept it into a sheep who sat at the counter knitting with a multitude of needles. It now sells the largest selection of "Alice" memorabilia in the country, together with Oxford gifts and souvenirs, Oxford University T-shirts and sweatshirts in the University colours.

Oxford also has a fine tradition of menswear and tailoring. Castell's in Broad Street, Walters of The Turl, and Hall, Shepherd and Woodward are all local specialists in this field.

Women in search of clothes are well catered for by the department stores C & A and Lewis's in the Westgate Centre and by Debenhams in Magdalen Street and chains such as Benetton in the Westgate Centre, Fenwick at 28 St Ebbes, and Next at 7 Queen Street, though the sizes and fashions are mostly suitable for young people. Boutiques open and close with rapidity, and soaring business property taxes, on a par with London's, will no doubt cause more small retail shops to disappear. Campus Clothes, 44 High Street is the in place for ball gowns.

George Street, with a variety of newly opened shops links Cornmarket Street to Gloucester Green and the city's open market, held every Wednesday. Stalls sell food produce and wide range of other goods.

Visitors looking for gifts and souvenirs will enjoy a walk along Little Clarendon Street, which leads off the northwest corner of St Giles'. The street, which includes a number of unusual craft and gift shops, is worth the short detour from the city centre.

AUCTIONS & ANTIQUES

Oxford has numerous antique shops and several auction houses. The local press has details of current auctions and sales. A good place to start is the Oxford Antiques Centre, The Jam Factory, Park End Street, tel: 251075, opposite the railway station. Open:

Tuesday–Saturday 10 a.m.–5 p.m. (also open the first Sunday in the month, 11.30 a.m.–5 p.m.).

SPORTS

SPECTATOR

Association Football: Oxford United play at the Manor Ground, Osler Road, Headington, tel: 61503.

Rugby Football: Oxford University play at Iffley Road, tel: 241064 and the Oxford Rugby Club plays at the Southern Bypass, tel: 243984.

Athletics: Regular meetings are held at the Iffley Road running ground and at the city-owned track at Horspath.

Cricket: Oxford University cricket club plays first-class games against county sides in the University Parks, Parks Road, tel: 54050.

Greyhound Racing: Tuesday, Thursday and Saturday at 7.45 p.m. at the Oxford Sports Stadium, Sandy Lane, Cowley, tel: 778222.

Speedway racing: Also at the Stadium on Friday at 7.45 p.m.

Ice hockey: Oxford City's ice hocky team, Oxford City Stars, plays in the British Ice Hockey League. Home matches are from September to April, Sundays 6 p.m. at the Oxford Ice Rink, Oxpens Road.

PARTICIPANT

Golf: There are four 18-hole courses in the Oxford area and a driving range at Binsey.

Southfield Golf Club, Southfield, Hill Top Road, Oxford, tel: 242158.

North Oxford Golf Club, Banbury Road, Oxford, tel: 54415.

Frilford Heath Golf Club, Frilford Heath, near Abingdon, (7 miles/11 km from Oxford on A338), tel: Frilford Heath (0865) 390428.

Binsey Golf Range, Binsey Lane, Botley Road, Oxford, tel: 721592.

Burford Golf Club, Burford, Oxon, (19 miles/30 km from Oxford, 1 mile off A361), tel: Bicester (0869) 241204.

Chesterton Country Golf Club, Chesterton, near Bicester, Oxon, (10 miles from Oxford, off the A421), tel: Bicester (0869) 241204.

Haddon Hill Golf Course and **Range**, opened in 1990 at Didcot. Cost: from £10 per 18 holes weekdays; £12 at weekends, tel: Didcot (0235) 510410.

Swimming: The Temple Cowley Pools, Temple Road, Cowley, Oxford, tel: 716667 is a complex run by Oxford City Council. There are three pools: the Main Pool, 25 metres (82 ft) long and a depth from 1 to 1.8 metres; a Learner Pool for children; and a Diving Pool. Opening times vary and certain times are for women only, for the over-50s, for swimming clubs, lessons, or disabled swimmers—so it is advisable to telephone first or pick up a leaflet. Open: Weekdays: 6.10–8.30 a.m., 12 noon–10 p.m. (Wednesday 4 p.m.); Saturday 8 a.m.–4.30 p.m; Sunday 9 a.m.–6.30 p.m.

A sauna/solarium/steam suite is open most days from 10 a.m.–10 p.m. but some are mixed sessions, others women only or men only. All sessions can be booked 7 days in advance, tel: 716667. Charges are: Sauna £2.35 for 1 hour; Solarium, £1.60 for 20 minutes; Steam, £1.60 for 20 minutes.

A fitness room is open from 7 a.m.–10 p.m; Saturday 9 a.m.–5 p.m; Sunday 9 a.m.–6 p.m. (last booking an hour before). Cost: 90p for 50 minutes. All sessions can be booked in advance. For information about courses available, tel: 749449.

Ferry Sports Centre, Ferry Pools, Diamond Place, Summertown, tel: 510330. Admission charge. Swimming pool open: Monday–Friday 6.30–8 a.m., 1.30–4.30 p.m; Saturday 1–9.30 p.m; Sunday 10 a.m.–6 p.m.

Hinksey Pools, Lake Street or Abingdon Road. Open: end May–beginning September. Mixed swimming in a range of open-air pools. Admission: £1.40, children 70p, tel: 247737.

River bathing: Lifeguards are stationed at river bathing places weekends only in the summer and during summer school holidays. For information, tel: 716667.

Long Bridges, Thames towpath from Folly Bridge. Mixed swimming. Admission free.

Tumbling Bay, Thames Towpath from Botley Road. Mixed swimming. Admission free.

Wolvercote, Port Meadow, Wolvercote. Mixed swimming. Admission free.

Parson's Pleasure in the University Parks, South Parks Road is for men only. Admission charge.

Ice Skating: The Oxford Ice Rink, Oxpens Road, Oxford OX1 1RX, tel: 247676, is near the railway station, with a car and coach park next to the rink. Facilities include a 56 by 16-metre Ice Pad (185 by 52 ft); fully licensed bar and fast food cafeteria; professional instructors; ice shows and special events; fully stocked skate shop. Public Session Times are: Morning: Monday–Friday 10 a.m.–12 noon; Saturday 10 a.m.–12 noon (Under 16s only); Sunday 10 a.m.–12 noon. Afternoon: Monday–Friday 2–4 p.m; Monday–Friday 5.45–7.15 p.m. (Under 16s only)* (not Wednesday). Evening: Monday–Friday 8–10.30 p.m. (Wednesday–Friday Disco Session); Saturday 8–10.30 p.m. Disco Session; Sunday 9.30–10.30 p.m. (starts when matches finish). Prices: From £1.10 to £2.70. Hire of skates, 80p.
* Guardians/parents allowed on ice with their children on Monday and Tuesday only.

Squash: Ferry Sports Centre, Diamond Place, Summertown, tel: 510330. Open: Monday–Friday 7 a.m.–9 p.m; Saturday 7 a.m.–8.20 p.m; Sunday 9 a.m.–9.40 p.m.

Leisure Centres/Health Clubs: Blackbird Leys Leisure Centre, Oxford, tel: 771565.

Main Hall: badminton, short tennis: Open 7 a.m.–11 p.m. most days.

Fitness room: Open 7 a.m.–11 p.m. most days; women only Thursday 7–11 p.m.

Snooker room: Open 7 a.m.–11 p.m. most days; 9 a.m.–11 p.m. Saturday and Sunday.

Crèche: Open Monday 11 a.m.–2.15 p.m; Tuesday–Saturday 9.30 a.m.–2.15 p.m.

Cafeteria/bar: Open Monday 11 a.m.–8 p.m. Snacks available until 10.30 p.m; Tuesday–Friday 9.30 a.m.–8 p.m. Snacks available until 10.30 p.m; Sunday 12 noon–2 p.m., 7–10.30 p.m.

Inshape Health Studios, 6/7 High Street, Oxford, tel: 251261. For weight control and fitness. Exercise studio, dance studio, jacussi, sauna, sunbeds.

The Temple Club, 109 Oxford Road, Cowley, tel: 779115. Fully equipped gymnasium, computerised fitness assessment, saunas, aerobic classes. The place to see local sportsmen and women and to be seen.

Special Information

CHILDREN

Children are well catered for in Oxford, especially in recreation centres. During holiday periods, special programmes are designed by theatres, museums and sporting associations. Oxford City Council and the Information Centres have full details.

GAYS

Oxford has an active gay scene. For details contact: **The Oxford Friend** (Gays and Lesbians) 35–37 Cowley Road, tel: 726893. Meetings: Wednesday and Friday 7–9 p.m; **The Oxford Gay Society**, the secretary Dr Was, tel: 513737 or the chairman Mr S. Cooper, tel: 54813. **Lesbian Line**, tel: 242333.

DISABLED

A leaflet is available from the Information Centre giving details of access to public buildings for disabled people, tel: 714169 for details of the Young, Fit and Disabled Club.

FURTHER READING

GENERAL

Hugh Casson's Oxford—A College Companion (Phaidon).

John Betjeman's Oxford, illustrated by Osbert Lancaster and L Moholy-Nagy (OUP).

The Encyclopaedia of Oxford, edited by Christopher Hibbert (Macmillan).

Oxford Gardens—the University's influence on garden history, by Mavis Batey (Scolar Press).

Potter-Pourri—36 sketches of Oxford Life by Mary Potter (Daily Information, 10 Kingston Road, Oxford, OX2 6EF).

Oxford by Jan Morris—fully updated 1988; also her *Oxford Book of Oxford* (both OUP).

The Oxford Preservation Trust brings out Occasional Papers and No 4 is an entertaining *Brief History of Shopping in Oxford*.

OXFORD GUIDES

The Oxford guide; Student Guide to Oxford; What's On in Oxford: Three news sheets produced by Daily Information.

The Oxford Handbook: For a comprehensive guide to University life. Produced yearly by the Oxford University Students' Union.

Vade Mecum: Produced twice yearly by Lincoln College, a consumer guide aimed at students and townspeople. Excellent value at 50p for current information, though spelling could be improved—there is, apparently, a brassiere in the Turf Tavern garden.

USEFUL ADDRESSES

HELPLINES

Oxfordshire Young People's Helpline: Weekdays 3.30–4.30 p.m, tel: 310810.

Oxford Rape Crisis Line: Monday and Tuesday 7–9 p.m; Wednesday 2–8 p.m; Thursday and Friday 2–4 p.m. Answerphone at other times Tel: 726295.

Samaritans: 24 hours, tel: 722122.

TOURIST INFORMATION

Oxford Information Centre, St Aldate's, tel: 726871, has very helpful staff and is a mine of information on accommodation, guided walking tours and bus tours. Open: Monday–Saturday 9.30–5 p.m; Sunday (summer only), Bank Holidays 10.30 a.m.–4 p.m.

County Tourist Boards are:

Thames and Chilterns Tourist Board, 8 Market Place, Abingdon, Oxon OX14 3UD, tel: Abingdon (0235) 22711.

Burford Tourist Information Centre, The Old Brewery, Sheep Street, tel: Burford (099382) 3558.

Chipping Norton Tourist Information Centre, New St Car Park, New St, tel: Chipping Norton (0608) 44379.

Woodstock Tourist Information Centre, Hensington Road, tel: Woodstock (0993) 811038.

GENERAL

Police Station (and Bicycle Lost Property): St Aldate's, tel: 249881.

Post Office: 102–104 St Aldate's, tel: 814581 or 814785.

Telephone Manager: Paradise Street, tel: 244844.

Chamber of Commerce: 30 Cornmarket Street, tel: 292020.

Citizens' Advice Bureau: 7 St Aldate's,

tel: 247578. Open: Monday–Friday 10 a.m.–4 p.m. Closed: Thursday between 12.30–2 p.m.

College of Further Education: Oxpens Road, tel: 245871.

Oxford Polytechnic: Gipsy Lane, Headington, tel: 64777.

Magistrates' Court: The Courthouse, Speedwell Street, tel: 722422.

HM Customs and Excise (VAT) Peachcroft Centre: Abingdon, tel: 0235-35566.

CREDITS

3, 16/17, 82, 103, 107, 109, 114, 117, **Andrews, Chris**
120R, 122, 131R, 132, 135, 144L, 146,
148, 151, 159, 163, 167, 169, 172,
174, 175, 178, 181, 182, 184, 185,
186, 192, 196/197, 200, 204/205, 206,
207, 209, 211, 226, 228/229, 233,
235L, 237, 244, 247
24, 25, 26, 27, 37, 40/41 **Bodleian Library**
33, 35 **Bodliam Library**
119 **Brooke, Marcus**
70/71, 80L, 84/85, 121, 133, 140/141, **Davidson, Jon**
145, 149, 158, 170, 171, 189, 195,
199, 225
Cover, 22, 72/73, 74, 80R, 81, 92/93, **Donaghue, Chris**
94/95, 96/97, 98, 102, 104L, 105, 106,
111, 115, 118, 125, 126, 130, 136,
142, 147, 157, 162, 164/165,
166, 173, 179, 187, 193, 194, 248
46 **Henry Taunt Collection**
134, 154, 217, 235R, 243, 245, 246 **Höfer, Hans**
60/61, 63, 64, 67 **Hutton, Ray**
79, 180 **Jenkins, Sally**
18/19, 20/21, 68/69, 110, 112/113, **Lawson, Lyle**
124L, 124R, 127, 129, 137, 152/153,
160, 176/177, 183, 216
28, 36, 43, 44R, 108, 131L, 155, 201, **Le Garsmeur, Alain**
202, 203, 212, 213, 214, 215L, 215R,
218/219, 220, 221, 223, 224, 230, 231,
232, 234, 236, 238/239, 242L, 242R
14/15, 75, 76, 77, 83, 139R, 143, 188, **McBeath, Norman**
190, 191
9 **Mort, Robert**
56, 57, 58, 59, 66, 161 **Oxford & County Newspapers**
39, 42, 48/49, 50, 51, 52, 53, 54, 55, **Oxford County Libraries**
123
78, 120L **Topham Picture Source**

INDEX

U - V

W

B
C
D
E
F
G
H
I
J
a
b
c
d
e
f
g

i
j
k
l